THE UNITED STATES OF DIXIE

REDNECK COOK BOOK

Copyright © 2013 by David J. Pietras

All rights reserved. No part of this publication may be reproduced, distributed, or transmitted in any form or by any means, including photocopying, recording, or other electronic or mechanical methods, without the prior written permission of the publisher, except in the case of brief quotations embodied in critical reviews and certain other noncommercial uses permitted by copyright law. For permission requests, write to the publisher, addressed "Attention: Permissions Coordinator," at the web site below.

http://mrdavepp.wix.com/davidpietras

Cover design by David Pietras

ISBN-13: 978-1494937942

ISBN-10: 1494937948

1 2 3 4 5 6 7 8 9 10 13

Contents

Introduction

TIPS

Seasoning - Stock

Beverage Recipes

Bread and Biscuit Recipes

Breakfast Recipes

Main Courses

Southern Barbecue and Sauce Recipes

Vegetables

Salads/Soups/Side Dishes/Appetizers

Dessert Recipes

A Dozen Ways to Cook Gator

Index

Introduction
Welcome to the South

Welcome to the South!!! No matter where you live in this big ole world of ours. Good ole southern cooking is highly desired! I am almost sure that those little Pigmies down in the jungles would fancy themselves a good ole southern chicken dinner any day.

Well if you're from New York City or L.A. I am sure that we will have something here to tickle your fancy.

We have some good ole BBQ and some downright Cajun food on the menu here. And if you are feeling a bit frisky we even got ourselves some Gator recipes.

Now I don't recommend any of you city slicker kind of folks to pack up the SUV and head on down to Louisiana and try to catch yourselves a gator. Let's leave the hunting to the experts. I would recommend that you city folk start off easy with some good ole BBQ chicken and what not. And work your way up to the big stuff later.

Well most of these here recipes were given to my maw, and she got them from her maw and so on and so on.

Now seeing as I don't got me no sisters my maw decided to give them to me. Well ole Thelma Lou is in no situation to have any more children. Seeing we gots ourselves 6 youngins and they are all boys. So we decided to just go ahead and share these recipes with the rest of you guys out there.

I hope you enjoy them as much as we did.

Section 1
TIPS

Southern Cooking Techniques

Southern cooking has some characteristics that are unlike other styles of cooking. Additionally, some unique cooking techniques are employed. To become a good Southern cook, you should master these techniques. Don't worry; there is nothing difficult about Southern Cooking. It's just different.

CHARACTERISTICS

Southern dishes utilize a lot of vegetables, fried foods and crunchy food. And it is not, unfortunately, low fat. Southern food is not intended to be low fat. It is robust, stomach-filling, flavorful food. So I urge you to go for it and make it as it was intended to be.

TECHNIQUES

* **Cookware** *

One of the most important techniques in Southern Cooking is the use of cast iron cookware. Cast iron retains and transfers heat unlike other materials and is particularly suited for Southern dishes, especially cornbread. All that aside, it's simply the traditional way to cook Southern. See the article on Care and Use of Cast Iron

* **Cooking Time** *

Most recipes in Southern cooking require cooking longer than you may be accustomed to. For example Fried Okra is cooked until it is slightly burned around the edges. This gives it a tasty crunch. Also green beans are cooked until a dull, brownish, green color. They are not bright green (like canned beans...uuugh!) Southern fried chicken is also cooked until crunchy

* **Milk and Cornmeal** *

Milk and cornmeal are used a lot in Southern cooking. Of course cornmeal is the main ingredient in cornbread, but it is also used in breading (coating) fried foods such as chicken, okra, pork chops and fried green tomatoes.

Every cook has their own preference, but I recommend you use only white cornmeal, except for the Mexican cornbread and tamale pie recipes you will find in this book (and they are not really Southern dishes). There may be little difference, other than color, but the white cornmeal seems a finer grind and I prefer it.

When recipes call for milk, always use buttermilk (except in desserts). It simply adds more flavors. If you do not have buttermilk on hand, you can make a substitute by adding a tablespoon of white vinegar to a cup of regular milk, stir well and let sit for a minute before use.

* Made From Scratch *

Southerners pride themselves in making dishes from all original ingredients, as opposed to pre-packaged, frozen, boxed, store-bought, ready-made meals that you removed from the box and cook according to the box directions. My mom always referred to this as "made from scratch". Although the store-bought "boxed" foods are, perhaps, more fail-safe, they don't come close to "made from scratch" for flavor.

* Use of Butter and Bacon Grease *

Real butter is used in everything rather than low-fat substitutes. Yes, it is high calorie, but the flavor just can't be beat. Also, bacon grease is used in many dishes. Peas, beans, greens, cornbread are all enhanced with bacon grease.

* Cooking by sight and taste *

Finally, Southern cooks make their fabulous dishes by taste and sight. They will frequently taste their food as it is being prepared and cooked. And they have learned when a dish "looks right" through each stage of preparation. For example, when making biscuits, they know by sight when the dough looks right. The secret to good gravy knows when it looks right. And, cornbread batter is mixed until ...you got it...it looks right.

For this reason, it is very difficult to write a Southern recipe. Although you can easily write down the ingredients, it's hard to write when it "looks right". Therefore, I urge you not to take every Southern recipe too literally. It's a starting point to give you the ingredients. But, you will learn, through experience, when a little more or less of a certain ingredient is called for.

Cooking Tips

Basic Cooking Tips

Measurements
Many experienced home cooks seldom measure their ingredients. They use a pinch of this and a pinch of that, relying on look and feel to know what's right. The key word here is "experienced". For the beginner, it is best to always measure your ingredients. A vital part of your kitchen should be a set of measuring cups and measuring spoons.

When measuring you should comply with the recipe in using "heaping" or "level" measurements. A "heaping" spoonful is just what it says; you heap the ingredient on the spoon. However, a "level" spoonful should be leveled by raking a knife or your finger across the top edge of the spoon.

Seasoning
Proper use of seasoning is one of the secrets to cooking. Good cooks season "to taste". In other words, when possible use a little less seasoning than the recipe calls for and taste the dish when nearly finished cooking. Then add more seasoning to achieve the flavor you prefer.

Baking
Oven temperatures vary. Because the dial says 400 degrees does not necessarily mean your individual oven will be 400 degrees. The trick is to always use a timer when baking and check the dish a few minutes before the prescribed baking time expires. Then adjust the baking time as needed for your oven

Always pre-heat your oven to the required baking temperature. Never start your baking in a cold oven.

Tools of the Trade
A good set of pots and pans, while not essential, will certainly make the job easier and more pleasant. With some dishes the wrong cooking utensil may even ruin your dish. You should not use reactive pots and pans when cooking acidic foods. Reactive materials impart a metallic taste and can discolor your food. Two common acidic foods are tomato or vinegar based dishes. Reactive metals include aluminum, copper and cast iron. Non-reactive materials are enamel, glass and stainless steel.

Timing
A common problem beginners have is in timing their cooking so that everything gets to the table hot. This is not rocket science, just a matter of planning ahead. Here's how. Before putting anything on the stove, take a minute to think about the cooking time required for each food item. For example, you are preparing hamburgers and French fries. The French fries will take considerable longer to cook that the hamburgers, therefore, you want to start the fries first. Simple, huh?

You should also be aware of certain foods that are difficult to keep hot or do not lend themselves to re-heating, such as mashed potatoes. They should always be the last dish cooked since they do not stay hot long and are really not very good cold.

These are just a few basics to cooking like an expert. Additional basic tips are included in all the other articles on this site.

General Tips
* Lay out all your ingredients before you begin to cook. Measure out ingredients and complete all chopping and sizing. If baking, preheat oven.
* Buy a good timer and use it. They are fairly inexpensive. Also, invest in a meat thermometer.
* Place a damp paper towel under mixing bowls to prevent from sliding around while mixing.
* The secret to boiled corn on the cob that explodes in your mouth is to bring a pot of water to a boil first. Then put the corn in and wait to come back to a boil. Then cook for 3 minutes. No more!
* To make lighter and fluffier mashed potatoes, add a pinch or two of baking powder to the potatoes before whipping.

Baking Cooking Tips

* Always pre-heat your oven to the temperature specified in the recipe.

* Use an oven thermometer to determine the accuracy of the temperature control on your oven. You will only have to do this once. If you set the oven for 400 degrees F. and find that the thermometer shows the oven is actually 415 degrees F., you will know in the future to set the control just slightly below the 400 degree setting when you want 400 degrees.

* When making biscuits, do not overwork the dough. Just two or three folds is all that is needed. Overworking the dough results in heavy biscuits.

* Use the cookware specified in the recipe. If it says glass, use glass. If it says cookie sheet, use a cookie sheet. It makes a difference in the final product.

* When baking breads or any dish calling for baking soda, baking powder or yeast, use measuring cups and spoons to measure accurately. Breads to not take well to eye-ball measurements.

* Bleached and unbleached flours can be used interchangeably.

* Baking powder and baking soda are not interchangeable

* When baking pies or any dish with a crust on top, cover the outer edge of the crust with aluminum foil to prevent burning before the rest of the crust is brown.

* Invest in a biscuit cutter and rolling pin for smooth edged symmetrical biscuits.

Barbecue Cooking Tips

General BBQ Tips
When BBQ'ing, Try not to place the meat over an open flame. Instead, position over glowing coals or if using propane, to one side of the flame. A flame on the meat will tend to discolor it and impart off-flavors.

When using wooden skewers for shish kabob, soak the skewers in water for 30 minutes before placing on grill. This will help prevent the skewers from burning or smoking.

Wait for the charcoal to turn white (ash color) before beginning to cook. This will produce the hottest fire.

It is easy to overcook steaks on the BBQ since the heat is difficult to control. Over cooking is one of the largest causes for tough steaks. Check for doneness often and remove as soon as cooked to your preference.

A little non-stick cooking spray on the grill rack prior to cooking will prevent meat from sticking and ease the clean up afterwards.

The most flavorful cut of steak is the Sirloin and New York steak, but not always tender. The tenderest cut of steak is the Rib-Eye and Tenderloin (and the most expensive).

Marinating Meat
Marinating the meat before grilling will add flavor and tenderize it. Meat should always be marinated in the refrigerator. Any leftover marinade that has been in contact with raw meat should be disposed of. Do not save or re-use marinade.

Here's an easy recipe for marinade:
* 1 Small Onion (Minced)
* 4 tablespoon Olive Oil
* 5 tablespoon Soy Sauce
* 1 tablespoon brown sugar
* 1 tablespoon Worcestershire Sauce
* 2 tablespoon white Vinegar
* 2 teaspoons Liquid Smoke (in the BBQ section of your grocer)
* 1 teaspoon Black Pepper

Combine all ingredients in a saucepan and simmer on low heat for 5 minutes. Cool before using.

Marinating overnight is most effective, but if this is not practical, marinade at least 3 hours, turning the meat periodically.

How to Tell When Your Steak is Done
The surest method is to use an instant-read meat thermometer. For medium rare cook to 145 degrees F. For medium 160 degrees F and for well-done cook to 170 degrees F.

If you do not have a meat thermometer, you can get a fair idea using the following method: Hold your left hand in front of you with fingers closed together and thumb extended. Use the index finger of your right hand and push on the fleshy part of your left hand between your index finger and thumb. It will feel fairly soft. This is how a steak cooked rare will feel to the touch.

For medium to medium rare, extend the left hand but spread out your fingers and poke the same spot with your right index finger. It will feel a little firmer. This is how a steak cooked medium to medium rare will feel.

For well done, make a fist with your left hand and poke again. It should have very little give. This is how a well done steak will feel.

Final Thoughts
Always use thongs for turning your meat. Do not puncture the meat with a fork. Holes in your steak allow the juices to escape, resulting in a tough steak.

After removing meat from the grill, allow it to rest (sit) for 5 minutes before cutting. This allows the juices to settle and keeps the meat tender and flavorful.

Finally, stand up BBQs can tip over and cause serious burns. Keep children and pets at a safe distance.

Beef Cooking Tips

Grades of Beef
Although there are many grades of beef, as determined by the USDA, only 3 are generally used by grocery stores and restaurants: Prime, Choice and Select. These grades differ in texture, age and marbling, among other factors. Marbling is what gives the meat its flavor and tenderness. In order of tenderness and flavor (and price) Prime grade is the top grade, then Choice, then Select.

The label "lean" is used very loosely on beef and can apply to very different quality meat. It is probably better to ignore "lean" and look for "round" or "loin" on labels if you want what most people consider "lean".

Storage and Safety of Beef
Beef may be stored in the refrigerator set at 35 to 40 degrees F. or in the freezer at 0 degrees or colder. Steaks may be refrigerated for 3 to 4 days and in the freezer 6 to 12 months.
Ground beef may be kept in the refrigerator 1 to 2 days and in the freezer 3 to 4 months.
Cooked beef may be kept in the refrigerator 3 to 4 days and in the freezer 2 to 3 months.

If all the meat in a purchased package has turned gray or brown, it may be beginning to spoil. It is probably best to discard it.

Never leave ground beef or any perishable food out at room temperature for more than 2 hours.

You should fully defrost beef before cooking to prevent the exterior becoming overdone before the interior is cooked. It is best to thaw frozen beef in the refrigerator. You can also defrost in the microwave oven or in cold water. If using the microwave, cook the ground beef immediately because some areas may begin to cook during the defrosting. To defrost in cold water, put the meat in a watertight plastic bag and submerge. Change the water every 30 minutes. Cook immediately. Do not refreeze ground meat thawed in cold water or in the microwave oven.

Bacteria on food will rapidly multiply when left at a temperature between 45 and 140 degrees F. Beef should be cooked as soon as possible after it is defrosted.

It is advised to use a meat thermometer when cooking ground beef and cook to an internal temperature of at least 160 degrees F.

Tips on Cooking Beef
To slice meat thin, as in many Chinese dishes, place in the freezer for 10 or 15 minutes first and it will be much easier to slice.

When cooking over an open flame, as in barbecuing, do not place the meat directly over the flame. Place to one side, over glowing coals. An open flame will discolor the meat and impart undesirable flavors.

Be aware that meat with a bone in it will take longer to cook than without a bone.

When cooking hamburgers, handle the beef gently. Do not press down on the meat with a spatula while cooking. This makes tough hamburgers.

Cheaper cuts of meat can be very tough. However, meat may be tenderized by beating it thin with a mallet, marinating or cooking in liquid for extended times. One of the best ways to cook a tough cut of meat is to cook it in a crock pot (slow cooker). Five or six hours in a crock pot will make practically any meat tender.

Poultry Cooking Tips

Safety First
The most important tip in cooking poultry concerns safety. Raw (uncooked) poultry contains bacteria that can make you sick. The bacteria can be destroyed by cooking. The Food Safety and Inspection Service (FSIS) advises consumers to cook raw poultry to a minimum internal temperature of 165 degrees F. If roasting an entire chicken, the temperature should reach 180 degrees as measured in the thigh with a thermometer. Insert the meat thermometer into the thickest part of the chicken's thigh, without touching the bone. Poultry should be roasted at an oven temperature of 350 degrees. Never lower than 325 degrees.

It is extremely important to take care in handling and preparation of poultry. The juices of a chicken can contaminate anything it touches. This means cutting boards, utensils and your hands that touch the chicken should not touch other food or utensils before being washed. Additionally, care should be taken, when placing poultry in the refrigerator, which the juices do not drip onto other food.

Poultry should be refrigerated, frozen or on the stove being cooked at all times. Never leave poultry out on the counter while you attend to other matters. All frozen poultry (and other meat) should be defrosted in the refrigerator. Or you can defrost in **cold** water in a plastic bag, replacing the water every 30 minutes. Never defrost at room temperature.

Poultry should be consumed immediately after cooking. Leftovers should be refrigerated within two hours of cooking. Use refrigerated leftovers within 3 to 4 days. In the freezer you can keep cooked poultry 3 to 4 months.

Cooking Tips
* When buying turkey, allow one pound of turkey for each adult person (8 people = 8 pound turkey). This provides a little leftover for later meals.
* Look for a turkey that has a pop up timer. This eliminates all concern of determining when the bird is cooked.
* Rubbing the poultry with salt inside and out before cooking will enhance the flavor.
* For more flavor, season your poultry inside and out with herbs such as rosemary, thyme, sage or Tarragon.
* Place a small onion and 4 or 5 cloves of garlic into the body cavity.

Seafood Cooking Tips

Buying Seafood
When buying seafood, naturally, you want to get the freshest product possible. So, how do you tell if it's fresh? By using your eyes and nose. First pick a proper place to purchase seafood. If the location has a fishy or offensive odor, walk away. Find another place for your purchase. Also a store with a fast turnover will have fresher seafood. You may find a better price at a small, out of the way market, but you may be buying fish that has sat there for days. Ask store personnel when they receive fish shipments. Arrange to purchase the day the seafood arrives.

Inspect the proposed purchase. Look and smell (if possible). Fish should have clear eyes, firm (non-slimy) skin and bright red gills. There should not be any strong fishy smell. Live shellfish should be active, not sitting listlessly in a corner of the tank.

Clams and mussels should be tightly shut. Or if slightly open, they should close quickly when touched. Avoid clams and mussels that are open and do not close when touched.

Shrimp should look shiny and wet with no strong odor. Cleaning shrimp can take a little practice. Beginner cooks would be better off buying de-veined (pre-cleaned) shrimp.

Many foods seem to lose a degree of flavor when frozen, but seafood handles being frozen very well and loses little flavor.

Storing Seafood
All fresh seafood is best consumed the day it is purchased. It should be transported from the point of purchase directly to the refrigerator (40 degrees or lower) or the stove for cooking. If frozen, defrost in the refrigerator. Or you may place in a sealable plastic bag and submerge in cold water to defrost. Replace water every 30 minutes. Do not use warm or hot water.

Shrimp is especially prone to spoilage if handled improperly. If shrimp has a strong odor or if in doubt, dispose of it.

You should use fresh fish within 1 to 2 days of purchase. Live shellfish should be consumed the day it is purchased. Cooked seafood, in general, may be stored in an airtight container in the refrigerator for 2 to 3 days. Fresh shellfish (not live, not frozen) should be used within 2 to 3 days.

Cooking Seafood
Seafood is one of the most versatile of foods when it comes to cooking methods. Nearly all fish, shrimp and shellfish may be fried, boiled, steamed, grilled or baked. And in the case of sushi, raw! There are so many seafood recipes it is difficult to recommend a particular one. In general, cook fish until it is flaky but still firm. Cook shrimp until it changes to a pinkish color and crab or lobster according to size and cooking style. Follow recipe recommendations for cooking times. As a general rule cook fish 10 minutes per inch thickness, turning it halfway through the cooking process. Uncooked crab legs should be cooked 20-25 minutes in boiling water.

Avoid over cooking any seafood as it becomes tough and very bland.

To prevent lobster tail from curling, run a skewer through the tail lengthways prior to cooking.

Vegetable Cooking Tips

Probably the biggest mistake beginners make in cooking vegetables is in cooking time. Over cooking or under cooking seems to be a problem for many. And then, it has a lot to do with preference. Just like people prefer their steak rare, medium or well done, people also have a preference for their veggies. Some prefer crisp and crunchy, some prefer soft and tender. If you are cooking for someone that you do not know their preference, it is usually best to under cook vegetables. If needed you can always toss them back in the pan for a few more moments.

Vegetable Cooking Tips
* Start cooking larger cuts of vegetables first since they will take longer to cook.

* Cook dense veggies first (Carrots, broccoli and celery), then softer veggies (peppers, onions and garlic last).

* Remember garlic burns easily and imparts a bitter taste when burnt.

* Chop and mince all vegetables before you begin, and then you will be able to devote full attention to cooking.

* Invest in a quality vegetable peeler. It has many uses and is invaluable in the kitchen.

* For boiled corn on the cob that literally explodes in your mouth, bring a pot of water to a boil; put the corn in the pot and wait for the water to return to a boil. Boil 3 minutes. No longer. Remove and enjoy real corn flavor.

* Try the Southern style of cooking green beans. Cook until beans lose all green color and turn an olive drab color and are very tender.

* Did you know that tomatoes are technically a fruit, not a vegetable?

* Purchase a quality knife set for chopping all those vegetables and keep them sharp. More cuts are due to a dull knife than a sharp one.

* Use day old rice for making real Chinese style fried rice.

* Avoid cooking acidic foods (tomatoes, vinegar) in reactive cookware. This can discolor the food and impart an off-flavor. Reactive cookware is aluminum, copper and cast iron. Non-stick surfaces on this cookware help to eliminate the problem. Non-reactive cookware includes clay, enamel, glass, plastic, or stainless steel.

* Storage of fresh cucumbers may be prolonged by peeling, slicing and storing in the refrigerator in a sealed container filled with 1 cup water, 1/4 cup vinegar and 1 tablespoon salt. Sounds a little like pickles, huh?

An easy way to seed cucumbers is to slice the cucumber in half lengthways. Then use a knife to make a cut like a trench on each side of the seeds down the length of the cucumber. Finally, using a spoon rake out the seeds. They will come out clean and easy.

* While onions and garlic will keep quite a while without refrigeration they will lasts longer and you can prevent them from sprouting if you store them in the frig.

* To make lighter and fluffier mashed potatoes, add a pinch or two of baking powder to the potatoes before whipping.

Seasoning Tips

Salt
Salt is undoubtedly the world's all-time favorite seasoning. It was considered so valuable in some societies that it was used as money. Today we know that too much salt can lead to health problems in some people, but we still love our salt. As a beginner cook you should learn to use salt to enhance a bland tasting dish. Salt will liven up tasteless food. However, remember you can always add more salt, but you cannot remove it once cooked in. So, taste, taste, taste!

Salt Substitutes
If you are concerned about salt intake there are several natural foods you may use in place of salt. Lemon juice, lime juice, vinegar or dill weed satisfies the desire for salt for many people. Use dill weed and lemon juice on fish in place of salt.

Sweet and Sour
The Chinese learned long ago the secret of combining sweet and sour. It is used in many of their dishes. In dishes that are intended to be sweet, try adding a dash of salt. Likewise, in dishes intended to be sour try adding a dash of sugar. Examples: In any cooked greens (turnip, collard, spinach, mustard) add a touch of vinegar, salt and sugar. In chili, add a spoon of sugar or honey. In BBQ sauce and Italian or Ranch salad dressing, add a touch of sugar.

Experiment With the Unusual
Unsweetened cocoa powder, instant coffee, cola and beer/wine, in small amounts, impart flavors that are hard to identify but special. Don't be afraid to experiment with these ingredients in your recipes. Just use common sense (no beer in ice cream). Most of these ingredients add a subtle but distinctive taste to chili, soups, pasta and Mexican dishes.

Stock Your Kitchen
As a beginner cook you should stock your kitchen with the following spices and ingredients as a minimum:
* Salt
* Black pepper
* White sugar
* Baking powder
* Baking soda
* Cornstarch
* Basil
* Oregano
* Cayenne pepper
* Cinnamon
* Vanilla
* Garlic

Eventually, you should add the following:
* Yeast
* Thyme
* Rosemary
* Sage
* Nutmeg
* Lemon juice
* Mustard
* Olive oil
* Cooking wine
* Corn meal
* Soy sauce
* Brown sugar
* Tomato paste
* Chicken and beef stock
* Vinegar

Kitchen Gadget Tips

Today there is a gadget for practically every task in the kitchen. Most are very useful; a few are not. The beginner should start with the "must have" gadgets and over time add the extras.

Obviously, you should begin with dishes, silverware, pot and pans. It is not our goal here to discuss the necessities of the kitchen. Our purpose is to discuss gadgets. That is, items which you could cook without by improvising and/or extra work.

It is suggested that you begin by equipping your kitchen with the first four items in the "must have" list below.

Must Have Gadgets
* food timer
* food thermometer
* measuring cup (2 cup and 4 cup)
* measuring spoon set
* tongs (one with long handle)
* box grader
* colander
* cutting board
* whisk
* veggie peeler
* can opener
* coffee maker (even if you do not drink coffee, your guest may)
* pepper mill

The Extras
* Kitchen shears
* Strainer/sifter
* Biscuit cutter
* electric mixer
* pastry blender
* rolling pin
* egg slicer
* apple corer
* garlic press
* pizza wheel
* splatter screen
* cheese slicer
* ice cream scoop

Care of Cast Iron Skillets

Cast Iron is the traditional cookware used in Southern cooking. It retains and transfers heat like no other material. If you are unfamiliar with cast iron cooking, this page will help you get started.

Cast Iron Cookware - Pros and Cons

The Bad

1. Cast iron tends to stick and rust if not properly cured.
2. The entire skillet, including the handle, stays hot a long time. Burnt fingers are a concern.
3. It is heavy
4. Food continues to cook for a period after removed from heat

The Good

1. Cast iron is practically indestructible. It will last a lifetime with normal care.
2. It fries food and bakes cornbread better than any other cookware.
3. Cast iron is less expensive than other quality cookware.
4. It is the traditional way to cook Southern food.

Cast iron cookware comes in every style. Skillets, pots, pans, grills, deep fryers, whatever you need. Most Southern cooks have one special skillet for their cornbread and separate skillets for other food. The cornbread skillet is the pride of the kitchen and is never used for anything but cornbread.

There is much debate over using soap to clean cast iron as well as the method of curing. Our view is that properly cured cast iron can be cleaned with a dry paper towel in most instances. In stubborn cases, a damp cloth will do the job.

Some cast iron sold today advertises that it has been pre-cured by the manufacturer. We believe all new cast iron should be cured at home and periodically cured again according to the degree of usage.

Tips
1. Avoid putting water in cast iron anytime except during cooking.
2. Never put cold water in hot cast iron (it may crack)
3. Avoid using soap, abrasive cleaning utensils and vigorous scrubbing

CURING / SEASONING

Be aware that these instructions are not cast in stone, i.e., you may need to adjust time and temperature for your individual oven. Also, if you cure more than one item at the same time it will take longer to cure.

Method 1:
Step 1: Wash the skillet with hot soapy water (after curing, avoid use of soap if possible). Dry thoroughly.
Step 2: Rub a liberal coat of cooking oil over the entire skillet, inside and out, including the handle.
Note: Different types of oil will vary the time required in the following steps. We have used Crisco, peanut oil, safflower, bacon drippings and cheap vegetable cooking oil. We do not recommend bacon grease; we prefer melted Crisco.
Step 3: Place the skillet in the oven set on low temperature (about 250-300 degrees). Position the skillet upside down in the oven with aluminum foil under it to catch any dripping.
Step 4: Check the skillet in about 10 to 15 minutes. The oil should be tacky to the touch (use a spoon) over the entire inside surface. If you have wet spots, smooth them out with the back of a spoon. If you have spots that are not covered with a tacky surface, add oil to those spots. Place back in oven until you have the entire inner surface covered with a tacky oil coating. If you have trouble with this step, increase oven temperature slightly and allow more time.
Step 5: Once you have a tacky surface, turn up the oven setting to 500 degrees. Allow to cure for one hour in the oven.
Note: Your kitchen will be smoky from the oil so do this on a day when you can ventilate the kitchen.
Step 6: Check the skillet after one hour. When properly cured, your skillet will have an even, black, shiny sheen over the entire inner surface.
Step 7: If you have the shiny sheen, you are finished. If not, put back in oven and continue cooking as long as it takes to get the sheen. Since oven temperatures vary, the time required for this step will not be the same for all ovens.

CAUTION: Always use protection for your hands when handling hot cast iron. Remember it stays hot for a long time after being removed from heat. Touching with a bare hand will produce severe burns.

Method 2 (Easier but takes longer)
1. Rub a thin coat of cooking oil over entire surface of skillet.
2. Place skillet in oven set on 300 degrees F.
3. Leave in oven until a dry, dark, shiny sheen develops over entire inner surface of skillet. This may take 2-3 hours. Just keep checking every 30 minutes.

When storing your cured cast iron, make sure the cookware is dry and rub a light coating of vegetable oil on the skillet.

That's it. Follow these guidelines and you will have the perfect **cast iron cooking skillet** that you can pass down to your children.

Cooking Safety Tips

* Never allow chicken (or other raw meat) to contact other food, utensils, cutting boards or your hands before washing.

* Never use shrimp if in doubt of its freshness. Dispose of it.

* Take care in putting food in hot oil. Any moisture will cause the oil to splatter, possible causing burns.

* Always use a knife with cutting strokes away from you, not toward the hands.

* Keep knifes sharp. In general, dull knifes cause more accidents than sharp ones.

* Always keep pets and children at a safe distance from the stove or outdoor grills.

* Keep a fire extinguisher handy near the kitchen and know how to use it.

* Have a working smoke detector near the kitchen

* Do not leave food cooking on the stove unattended.

* Keep hot food hot and cold foods cold.

* Keep pot holders handy and use them.

* Wash down counters with a weak bleach solution periodically to sanitize them.

* Use a meat thermometer to determine the doneness of meat.

* Keep your freezer at 0 degrees.

* Keep pot handles turned away from the front of the stove.

* Uncover pots by lifting the side of the lid away from you.

* Wipe up spills on the floor immediately to prevent falls.

* Eat or freeze refrigerated leftovers within four days.

* Never pour water on a grease fire. Use a proper fire extinguisher.

Southern Meals (What Goes Together)

If you have not spent a lot of time in the South, you may find making a complete Southern meal a little confusing. What goes together? If you were cooking Chinese, you know Chow Mien and pizza do not go together. But what goes together for a Southern meal?

Well, we are going to tell you.

There are many combinations of dishes that work together, but we are going to present the most common, most popular here. They are listed by the dish's main ingredient, generally some form of meat.

With the following meat main courses, serve any combination of the listed dishes (i.e., not all the dishes):

Pork (Fried pork chops or oven baked)

Your Choice of:
Fried Potatoes
Green Beans
Boiled Corn on the cob
Greens (Collards, Mustard or Turnip Greens)
Cole Slaw
Fried Green Tomatoes
Fried Okra
Black Eyed Peas
Fresh Vegetable Plate (radishes, baby green onions, celery sticks, cucumber slices)
Required:
Southern Cornbread
Sweet Southern Iced Tea

Fish Fry (Fried Catfish or other fish)

Your Choice of:
Cole Slaw
Fried Potatoes
Boiled Corn on the Cob
Potato Salad
Required:
Hushpuppies
Sweet Southern Iced Tea

Southern Fried Chicken

Same as Pork

Barbecue (Beef, Pork or Chicken)

Your Choice of:
Sorghum Baked Beans
Boiled Corn on the Cob
Southern Cornbread
Hushpuppies
Mint Juleps
Required
Cole Slaw

These are just a few of the more popular Southern meals. Of course, you can serve anything you want with any of them, but we have tried to illustrate what is traditionally served together. Just to repeat, you should serve any combination of the listed dishes...not all of them, with the meat main

Section 2

Seasoning - Stock

Homemade Cajun Seasoning

Cajun seasoning may be purchased at your local market, but why buy when you can make your own? It cost less and, best of all, when you make your own, you can adjust it to your own taste. Here are a couple of recipes for Cajun Seasoning.

Cajun Seasoning Recipe #1

Ingredients:

- 2 tablespoons paprika
- 1 tablespoon salt
- 1 tablespoon black pepper
- 2 teaspoons garlic powder
- 2 teaspoons onion powder
- 2 teaspoons ground red pepper
- 1 teaspoon dried oregano
- 1 teaspoon dried thyme

Instructions:

Very simple! Combine all ingredients, mix well.

Makes about 1/3 cup. Store in an airtight container for up to 6 weeks.

Seasoning Recipe #2

Ingredients

- 1/4 cup salt
- 3 tablespoons granulated garlic or garlic powder
- 3 tablespoons ground black pepper
- 1/8 teaspoon ground cayenne pepper, or to taste

1 tablespoon paprika

Instructions:

Combine all seasonings and mix to blend thoroughly. Pour into a small jar with cover; seal tightly.

Blackened Seasoning for Fish, Steak or Chicken

Ingredients:

2 teaspoons ground paprika

4 teaspoons dried leaf thyme

2 teaspoons onion powder

2 teaspoons garlic powder

1 tablespoon granulated sugar

2 teaspoons salt

2 teaspoons black pepper

1 teaspoon ground cayenne pepper, or to your taste

1 teaspoon dried leaf oregano

3/4 teaspoon ground cumin

1/2 teaspoon ground nutmeg

Instructions:

Combine all ingredients, mix well. Store in a sealed contained in a cool dark place. Shake jar well before each use.

Beef Stock

Beef stock may be purchased but if you use it often it can be expensive. This recipe makes about a gallon of stock you can make ahead and keep available in the fridge when needed. And, it's more economical than buying it ready made.

Cajun food frequently uses stock in the recipe. Its purpose is to add a deeper flavor to food that plain water cannot provide. This recipe takes all day to make but we reduced the simmer time to half and thought the stock still came out great. Given the time required, we believe your goal should be a more flavorful stock (than store bought) rather than cost savings.

Prep time: 30 min
Cook time: 6 hours
Total time: 6 hours 30 min
Yield: 1 gallon

Ingredients:

  8 pounds beef bones, any kind, cut into 3-4 inch pieces

  Oil, as needed, to grease cookie sheet

  6-7 quarts water (or as needed)

  1 cup onions, coarsely chopped

  1 cup carrots, coarsely chopped

  1 cup celery, coarsely chopped

  2 cups tomatoes, quartered

  3/4 cup tomato paste, thinned with 2 tablespoons water

For the Spice Sachet:

The following ingredients are placed into a 4" square of cheesecloth and tied into a sack.

  1 tablespoon parsley

  1/2 teaspoon thyme leaves

1 bay leaf

1 whole clove

1/2 teaspoon black peppercorns

1 clove garlic, crushed

Instructions:

1. Heat the oven to 400F. Place the bones on a lightly oiled cookie sheet pan and roast for 30 minutes, turning occasionally. Brush the bones with a thin layer of the tomato paste, and roast for an additional 30 minutes, turning occasionally, until evenly browned.
2. Place the bones in the stockpot and cover with cold water. Bring to a boil, and then lower to a simmer. Periodically, skim any scum that forms on the surface.
3. Continue to simmer the stock for 4 hours, skimming periodically. Add more hot water, as needed, to keep the bones covered.
4. Add the vegetable mix and spice sachet to the stockpot. Simmer for another 1 hour. Add water as needed to maintain 1 gallon of liquid in the pot.
5. Strain the stock through cheesecloth, and allow to cool. Transfer to a container and refrigerate overnight.
6. The next day, skim off any fat that has risen to the surface.
7. Store in the refrigerator.

Chicken Stock

A good homemade Chicken Stock will be clear and thick (almost like Jell-O) when finished. And be prepared for some heavenly smells from your kitchen while cooking.

For Stock:

Ingredients

    6 quarts cold water

    1 whole cut up chicken (include everything - backs, necks, etc.)

    2 stalks celery with tops, chopped

    1 cup carrots, chopped

    1 medium onion, chopped

    2 small heads garlic, cut in half

For the Spices:

Ingredients:

The following ingredients are placed into a 4" square of cheesecloth and tied into a sack.

    1/2 tsp parsley

    1 bay leaf

    1/4 tsp. dried thyme leaves

    1/4 tsp. dried tarragon leaves

    1/4 tsp. dried oregano leaves

    1/4 tsp. dried basil leaves

    1 teaspoon black peppercorns

Instructions:

1. Remove the skin from the chicken and chop into 3-4 inch pieces, do not remove bones.

2. Put the chicken in the stockpot with the water and bring to a simmer. Periodically skim off the scum that forms on the surface.

3. Simmer 4 hours. DO NOT STIR while simmering.

4. Add the vegetable mix and spice sachet.

5. Simmer for one more hour.

6. Strain the stock through a strainer.

Notes:

* If you're using the stock immediately, skim off as much fat as you can with a paper towel
* If using later, cool the stock quickly by placing the container into another container of ice-water, stirring until cool.
* Do not put hot stock in the refrigerator; it must be cooled quickly first.
* After cooled, refrigerate overnight, then skim off solidified fat on the surface.

Makes 4 quarts of stock.

Fish Stock

Cajun food uses a lot of stock which can be expensive if bought. This recipe makes home made fish stock that is more flavorful, healthier and economical.

This stock may be made using, fish, shrimp, crawfish or other shellfish. Just substitute the fish ingredient in the recipe or you may use a combination of fish, shrimp, etc.

Ingredients:

Shells from 1 pound shrimp (if you use fish: 5-6 lbs fish bones, heads, etc)

5 quarts water

4 carrots, sliced

4 onions, quartered

1/2 bunch celery, sliced

2 bay leaves

3 cloves garlic, sliced

2 sprigs fresh parsley

5 whole cloves

1 teaspoon ground black pepper

1 tablespoon dried basil

2 teaspoons dried thyme

Instructions:

1. Bake shrimp shells at 375 degrees F (195 degrees C) until dried and starting to brown on edges.

2. In an 8-quart pot, combine all ingredients. Bring slowly to a boil.

3. Reduce heat, and simmer 5 to 7 hours. Replace water as needed, 2 or 3 times, by pouring more water down the inside of the pot.

4. Remove stock from heat, and strain. Press all liquid from the shells and vegetables, then discard them. Return liquid to heat, and simmer until liquid is reduced to 2 to 3 quarts.

Vegetable Stock

Cajun food uses stock (broth) in many dishes which can be expensive if store bought. With this recipe you can make your own and keep it available in the fridge till needed. Best of all it is cheaper, more flavorful and healthier than store bought with its chemicals and preservatives. Use with beef, pork or vegetable dishes.

Ingredients for Stock:

    10 pints cold water

    2 ounces vegetable oil

    1 medium onion, thinly sliced

    1 leek (white part only), washed and chopped

    2 stalks celery, sliced

    1 whole head garlic, sliced in half

    2 medium carrots, chopped

    1 large potato, thinly sliced

    1 cup white mushrooms, sliced

    2 small chopped tomatoes

For the Spice sachet:

The following ingredients are placed in a square of cheesecloth, tied into a sack

Ingredients:

    1/2 teaspoon black peppercorns

    1/4 teaspoon fennel seeds

    2 whole cloves

    1 tbs parsley

1 tbs thyme

1/2 tbs sage

2 bay leaves

Instructions:

1. Add the oil to a stockpot and place onion, leek, celery, garlic and carrots in the pot; cook the vegetables for about 5 minutes on medium heat.

2. Add the remaining ingredients (including the spice sachet). Bring to a boil, reduce heat and simmer uncovered for 1 hour.

3. Strain the stock, pressing the vegetables to extract as much liquid as possible.

4. Cool and store in refrigerator.

Yield: 1 gallon.

The stock will keep longer if you separate into one cup portions and freeze.

Seven Spice Dry Rub Recipes

Yes, we know...the 7 spice dry rub has 8 ingredients. That's because we decided to add Old Bay seasoning to the original recipe. But we just liked the name, 7 spice dry rub, so we kept it. The dry rub may be refrigerated or frozen up to 6 months.

This basic dry rub works well on chicken, fish, pork or beef. For beef you may want to increase the amount of chili powder to 1/2 cup and black pepper to 1 1/2 tablespoons.

Ingredients:

    1/2 cup dark brown sugar

    1/2 cup sweet paprika

    1/4 cup kosher salt

    1/4 cup chili powder

    1/4 cup dry mustard

    1 tablespoon freshly ground black pepper

    2 teaspoons Old Bay Seasoning (available in the spice section of most grocery stores)

    1/2 teaspoon ground ginger

Instructions:

1. In a small bowl, whisk together all ingredients. Store in an air tight container in a cool, dry location.

Cajun Rub Recipe

Some barbecue enthusiast cooks with BBQ sauce, some cook without sauce and only adds sauce at the table. And then there are those that prefer a "dry rub". This dry rub will produce a flavor-loaded crust on meat that will make it distinctive and have everyone asking for more.

Very good dry rub for use on beef, pork, seafood or poultry. We tripled the recipe to make enough to last the summer. You can keep up to a year in a sealed contained in the fridge.

Ingredients:

- 1/4 cup coarse salt (kosher or sea salt)
- 2 tablespoons garlic powder
- 2 tablespoons onion powder
- 3 tablespoons paprika
- 1 tablespoons ground thyme
- 2 tablespoons dried oregano
- 2 tablespoon black pepper
- 2 teaspoons ground sage leaves
- 2 teaspoons cayenne pepper

Instructions:

1. Combine all ingredients and mix well.
2. Place in an airtight, sealable container and store in a cool, dark location.

Section 3

Beverage Recipes

Refreshing Mint Julep

This old traditional Southern drink is ideal for your next party. Make a couple of batches and keep ready in the fridge.

This recipe makes a pretty good traditional mint julep. If you want a non-alcohol version just substitute bourbon with 2 1/2 ounces ginger ale.

Prep time: 10 min
Cook time: 5 min
Total time: 15 min plus overnight refrigeration of syrup
Yield: 8 servings

Ingredients:

- 2 cups sugar
- 2 cups water
- 16 Sprigs of fresh mint
- Crushed ice, as needed
- Bourbon Whisky (2 oz. per drink)

Instructions:

1. Make syrup by boiling sugar and water together for five minutes. Cool and place in a covered container with six or eight sprigs of fresh mint, then refrigerate overnight.
2. Make one julep at a time by filling a Collins glass with crushed ice, adding one tablespoon mint syrup and two ounces of Bourbon Whisky. Stir rapidly with a spoon to frost the outside of the glass. Garnish with a sprig of fresh mint.

Southern Iced Tea

Real Southern Ice Tea, like I grew up drinking, is sweet tea. Very sweet. Just like most Southerners I know never put sugar in cornbread, they also never make ice tea without it.

How you serve this tea is as important as how you make it. When serving, fill the glass with ice first, then pour in the tea. Never serve Southern tea with 2 cubes of ice like restaurants tend to do. After pouring the tea in the glass, the ice will settle down a little, add more ice to fill up glass.

Using an off-brand of tea we had to use 15 tea bags to obtain a dark colored tea. A name brand tea would have worked with 8-12 bags.

Prep time: 10 min
Cook time: 15 min
Total time: 25 min
Yield: 2 qt

Ingredients:

8-12 tea bags of black tea

2 cups sugar

1 qt. water plus additional as needed

Instructions:

1. Pour the sugar in a 2 quart pitcher. Sit aside.
2. Place 1 quart water in a large pot on the stove top burner set on medium-high heat.
3. Add tea bags to water.
4. Bring water just to the point where small bubbles begin to form around edge of pot (about 10-15 min). Do not bring to a hard boil. When cooked the tea should be a dark, dark amber (almost black) color. If it is pale red/amber, it is too weak; add more tea bags.
5. Remove from heat, stir well and then discard the tea bags.
6. Pour hot tea in pitcher containing sugar. Mix well until all sugar is dissolved.
7. Add one tray of ice. Stir.
8. Add water from tap to bring water level to within 4 inches of top of (2 qt.) pitcher.
9. Refrigerate for 30 minutes to an hour.

Syllabub (holiday grown up's drink)

This old English drink dates back to the middle ages. In years past it was popular in New England and the Southern states but is seldom seen today. It was often served at holidays, especially Christmas.

A surprisingly good sweet, yet tart, delectable drink. We used sherry and brandy and found that drinking more than one was tempting.

The recipe specifies using a glass or stainless steel bowls during refrigeration because they will not react with the acid in the lemon which could impart an off-flavor.
Difficulty: Easy

Prep time: 20 min
Total time: 20 min plus 4 hours cooling
Yield: 4 + servings

Ingredients:

3/4 cup superfine sugar (regular sugar may be used but be sure to stir until dissolved)

3/4 cup cream sherry

2 tablespoons brandy or Cognac

juice and grated rind of 1 lemon

1-1/2 cups lightly whipped cream

1-1/2 teaspoons ground nutmeg

Instructions:

1. In a 2 quart glass or stainless steel bowl, combine all ingredients EXCEPT whipped cream and nutmeg.
2. Cover and refrigerate at least 4 hours (up to 24 hours).
3. Remove from refrigerator and whisk briskly to blend ingredients thoroughly, and then strain.
4. Gently fold in whipped cream, folding until evenly blended.
5. Pour into glasses and dust tops with grated nutmeg.

Afton's Cold Peach Soup

This is an old recipe passed on to us from a friend in Idaho. It's sort of a cross between soup and a smoothie. And, it is really simple to make.

You will be delighted with how the Orange, pineapple and lemon juice come together to enhance the flavor of the peaches in this soup. If you love peaches, you must try this recipe.

Prep time: 20 min
Total time: 20 min
Yield: 4-6 servings

Ingredients:

    1 1/2 lbs. peaches (about 3 peaches)

    2 cups sour cream

    1 cup orange juice

    1 cup pineapple juice

    1 tablespoon lemon juice

    1 1/4 cups sugar

Instructions:

1. Peel and remove the pits from the peaches. Slice peaches to a size your blender can handle.
2. Combine peaches and all remaining ingredients in a blender and blend until smooth.
3. May be consumed immediately but is much better if chilled 30 minutes.

Watermelon Ice

This cool, refreshing treat is easy to make and ideal for a hot summer day. Or...anytime at all. Very nice, quick and tasty drink. We suggest tasting for sweetness after step 2 and adjust as necessary before step 3.

Prep time: 15 min
Total time: 15 min
Yield: 2 quarts

Ingredients:

Medium sized watermelon (about 4 lb.), cut from rind, seeds removed

3 tablespoons lemon juice

2 tablespoons sugar

1/2 tsp salt

Instructions:

1. Cut the melon into 1 inch chunks.
2. Puree in a food processor or blender with all the other ingredients.
3. Freeze.
4. To serve, pour into food processor and pulse until slush is formed. Serve immediately.

Southern Holiday Punch

1	Large Bottle of Ginger Ale
1	Large Can of Red Punch
1	Large Can of Pineapple Juice
1	Large Can of Orange Juice -- mixed as directed on can
1	Large Can of Frozen Lemonade -- Mixed as directed on can
1	Small Package of Cherry Jell-O -- Mixed as directed on box

Combine all ingredients.

Store in refrigerator.

Mix well before stirring.

Lime Sherbet Punch

1	Liter Ginger Ale

1	Quart Lime Sherbet

Chill Ginger Ale before using. Pour over Lime Sherbet. Stir.

Big Dave's Punch Recipe

3 Cups Sugar

1 Large Can Pineapple Chunks

1 Pint Bottle Cherries

2 Cups Lemon Juice

2 Quarts Club Soda

2 Quarts Champagne

Make sugar, pineapple juice and cherry juice into syrup day before. Chill. Add other ingredients.

Section 4

Bread and Biscuit Recipes

Help Fix My Biscuits

Hot, fluffy biscuits, right from the oven...are one of the real joys of life. But when your biscuits can be used as paper weights that joy fades.

Are your biscuits flat, heavy and tasteless? Well, you are probably making a few common mistakes that are simple to correct.

Biscuits are generally thought of as a breakfast food, but they are very popular in many restaurants served any time of day (Kentucky Fried Chicken for one) So biscuits are not just for breakfast any more. However, good biscuits are not that easy to make at home, unless you know a few tips.

Here's How:

You should start with a good recipe.
Then you need to follow these few simple tips:

1. Do not overwork the dough. Biscuits do not need to be kneaded. That will make heavy, tough biscuits. After you roll the dough out on your board, simply fold the dough over on itself about three times. Then Stop! Next, gently form a round shape and roll it out to about a 1 inch thickness with your rolling pin.

2. When you cut out the biscuits from the dough, push the biscuit cutter straight down, then straight up. Do not push down and twist. This compacts the edges of the dough and causes uneven cooking and tough biscuits.

3. Always pre-heat your oven completely (generally 400-425 degrees). Different ovens vary in the time required to get up to temperature. I recommend you always allow at least 10-15 minutes after turning the oven on before putting the biscuits in. A cold (or not fully pre-heated) oven is the leading cause for failure of the dough to rise (flat biscuits).
Note: If you do not know how long it takes your oven to reach a specific temperature, I suggest you do a test to find out. Simply turn on the oven set for 400 degrees, places an oven safe thermometer in the oven and start a timer. Monitor the thermometer until it reaches 400 degrees and note the expired time. Once you know this time for your particular oven, you will always know how long to pre-heat.

4. When you mix the ingredients and form dough, your mixture should be tacky when you turn it out on the board. It should not be sticky wet or crumbly dry. Make sure your board is well floured and flour the dough as you fold it over on itself to keep from sticking to your hands.

5. This should be obvious, but it's a common mistake. If you want higher, fatter biscuits, you have to start with thicker dough. (duh!) If you roll out the dough to 1/4 inch thickness, you are going to have thin biscuits even if you do everything else right. We recommend rolling out the dough to a thickness about 1 inch. You can make them even bigger but when you roll out the

dough much over 1 inch thick the biscuits tend to tilt to one side when baking, resulting in lop-sided biscuits...still good but makes the kids laugh.

6. Place the cut out dough on the cookie sheet with the sides just barely touching. This give a better rise than if the dough is separated.

7. You can use a biscuit cutter of any size but the 2 inch cutter (actually measures about 2 1/4 inch) seems to make biscuits that rise more than larger cutters.

8. After placing the cut out dough on the cookie sheet, use your thumb to make a small indentation (dimple) on the top of each biscuit. This promotes a good rise and helps prevent lop-sided biscuits.

9. Here's perhaps the most important tip to avoiding flat biscuits: use fresh baking powder! If your baking powder can have been opened much over a month, do not use it. You don't have to throw it away; just don't use it for your biscuits.

I recommend you use buttermilk instead of regular milk for your biscuits. It provides better flavor and seems to make lighter biscuits. If you do not keep buttermilk on hand (I don't), you can make a substitute by adding a tablespoon of white vinegar in a cup of regular milk. Stir and allow sitting for a minute before use.

Biscuits for Dummies

If you cannot make good biscuits with this easy recipe...maybe you should think about staying out of the kitchen (kidding).

This is simply the instructions from a box of Bisquick Biscuit Mix. So why present it here? Because there are a few tips included to help you make good biscuits that are NOT on the Bisquick box.

Prep time: 10 min
Cook time: 12 min
Total time: 22 min
Yield: 8 biscuits

Ingredients

* 2 1/2 cups baking mix (Bisquick is popular but you can use your favorite)

* 1 cup milk, more or less (you can substitute a 50/50 mix of milk and heavy cream for very moist biscuits)

Instructions:

1. Pre-heat oven to 400 degrees F.
2. Place baking mix in a large bowl and slowly add milk while stirring.
3. When the mix forms a tacky dough that pulls away from the sides of the bowl, roll out dough on a flat, floured surface. The dough should be shiny and "stick to your fingers" tacky. It should not be crumbly dry or have liquid milk in bottom of the bowl. You may need more or less than the 1 cup of milk.
4. Roll out dough to about 1 inch thickness and cut our biscuits with a 2 inch biscuit cutter.
5. If you have parchment paper, line a cookie sheet with the paper. If not, just use an ungreased cookie sheet.
6. Place the cut out biscuits on the cookie sheet with sides just barely touching. Use a finger to make a slight dimple in the center of the top of each biscuit. Place the biscuits in the pre-heated oven.
7. Bake until the tops turn brown (8-12 minutes). See note below.

Note: Check the bottom of the biscuits after about 8-10 minutes. If the bottoms are starting to burn before the tops is brown, turn the oven setting to broil but leave the oven door open. Watch the biscuits until the tops are brown then remove from oven. DO NOT WALK AWAY with broiler on. The biscuits will burn very quickly if not watched.

Southern Biscuits

Some experienced cooks never learn to make good homemade biscuits from scratch. But with a little effort and this recipe you can make real Southern biscuits that will get compliments aplenty.

These are soft, country biscuits meant to be smothered with strawberry preserves or sausage gravy. If you like layered bread that is full of air, get store bought frozen biscuits. But if you like a "stick-to-your-ribs" biscuit loaded with flavor, this recipe is for you.

Prep time: 20 min
Cook time: 15 min
Total time: 35 min
Yield: 6 biscuits

Ingredients

* 2 cups all-purpose flour

* 4 teaspoons baking powder

* 1/4 teaspoon baking soda

* 1/2 teaspoon salt

* 1/2 cup Crisco shortening

* 3/4 cup buttermilk (more or less - see directions)

Instructions:

1. Preheat oven to 400 degrees F.
2. Combine the dry ingredients in a medium size bowl.
3. Using a pastry cutter or fork (or your fingers), gently cut in the shortening until the mixture looks like "meal" (a very course powder)
4. Add the buttermilk a little at a time, stirring *GENTLY* until dough starts to form. You may need more or less than the 3/4 cup milk (type flour and your mixing technique may vary amount of liquid required).
5. When you get a "sticky" dough ball, turn out on a floured surface and form a flat mass with your hands. Turn the dough over on itself and flatten again with your hands, repeat a second time. DO NOT KNEED!
6. Roll out the dough to a 1 to 2 inch thickness according to how thick a biscuit you want.. Cut out the biscuits with a biscuit cutter (see tip 7 below).

7. Place the biscuits on a cookie sheet lined with parchment paper. If you do not have parchment paper just use an ungreased cookie sheet. Use your thumb to make a small indentation on the top center of each biscuit.
8. Place biscuits into the preheated oven. Bake until tops are a golden brown (about 15 minutes). Note: Closely watch the bottom of the biscuits by lifting one biscuit and observing. Some cookie sheet materials tend to burn the bottoms quickly. If bottoms are getting too brown, turn oven to broiler setting, leave oven door open and watch until tops are brown. Do not walk away with broiler on, they will burn quickly. Make sure the inside of the biscuits are cooked through before removing from oven.

Serve with Sausage Gravy

TIPS

Tip 1: If you like big (circumference)) or small biscuits, fine...but we have found that using a 2 inch biscuit cutter makes biscuits that seem to rise better. Actually my cutter measures a little less than 2 1/2 inches.

Tip 2: If you like thin biscuits roll out the dough to 1 inch thickness. If you like big, fat biscuits roll out the dough to 1 to 1 1/2 inches.

Tip 3: Obtaining the correct consistency of the dough takes a little practice. Just add the buttermilk a little at a time and watch for the dough to form a ball as you stir. You may need more or less milk than called for in the recipe.

Tip 4: Do NOT handle the dough any more than necessary. Over handling will make tough biscuits. When you turn the dough out on your board, try to double the dough over on itself only two or three times while flattening it out. Do not kneed.

Tip 5: If you do not have buttermilk, you can make a substitute by adding 1 tsp. white vinegar in 1 cup regular milk. Stir and allow sitting for 1 minute before use.

Tip 6: Make sure to preheat the oven. Never start your biscuits in a cold oven.

Tip 7: When cutting out the biscuits do not push down and "twist" or turn the biscuit cutter. Push straight down and slide hand sideways to free the dough. Twisting the biscuit cutter compacts the edges of the dough causing uneven cooking.

Tip 8: Place the cut out dough on the cookie sheet with their sides just barely touching. The dough will not rise as much if there is space between the biscuits.

Tip 9: After placing the dough on the cookie sheet, use your thumb to make a small indentation (dimple) on the top of each biscuit. This promotes even rising to prevent lop-sided biscuits.

Tip 10: The cookie sheet you use can affect the browning of the biscuits. Dark material like non-stick tends to burn the bottoms before the tops are brown. Light material like aluminum or steel (without non-stick) tends to brown more evenly.

Tip 11: Here is probably the most important tip to avoiding flat biscuits: USE FRESH BAKING POWDER! Check the expiration date on the container, if your baking powder has been opened over a couple of months, don't use it. It is relatively inexpensive so why risk a batch of flat biscuits. You don't have to throw away the old baking powder; just don't use it for your biscuits

Perfect Biscuits

If you like super soft, creamy biscuits then you will agree that these are the perfect biscuits.

These light, fluffy biscuits just may be the perfect biscuits. Our only caution is that you should break open one biscuit when finished cooking to make sure the inside is done. They tend to be very moist inside even when the tops are golden brown.

Prep time: 20 min
Cook time: 15 min
Total time: 35 min
Yield: 8 biscuits

Ingredients

* 2 cups all-purpose flour

* 1 teaspoon sugar

* 2 teaspoons fresh baking powder

* 1/2 teaspoon salt

* 1 1/2 cups heavy cream (whipping cream), more or less

Instructions

1. Preheat oven to 400 degrees F.
2. Line a baking sheet with parchment paper (if unavailable, omit this step. It just helps to keep the bottoms from browning too fast. Do not grease or spray the baking sheet.)
3. Combine all dry ingredients in a medium bowl and mix well.
4. Add heavy cream slowly while stirring with a wooden spoon.
5. Continue adding cream and stirring until dough forms a ball and pulls away from sides of bowl. You may need more or less cream than listed in the ingredients. The dough should be tacky to the touch but not shiny and sticky. If too dry, add more cream. It too wet add more flour.
6. Turn out the dough on a flat, floured surface.
7. Gently, press the dough flat and fold it over on itself. Do these 3 or 4 times then form into a smooth ball. Do not knead. Roll the dough out to 1 to 1 1/2 inch thickness.
8. Cut out biscuits with a 2 inch biscuit cutter. Dip the cutter in flour to prevent sticking and push straight down and back up. Do not twist the biscuit cutter (after pushing down, slide your hand sideways to free the dough).
9. Place biscuits on the baking sheet with sides just barely touching.
10. Use your thumb to make a small depression (dimple) in the top of each biscuit.
11. Bake in preheated oven 12-15 minutes or until tops are golden brown.

12. Note: Because these biscuits are so moist inside, they may require extended baking time. Just watch closely and bake until they are firm and brown on top.

Garlic Biscuits

Many old time Southern cooks frown on using packaged mixes...especially for biscuits. But there are times when a mix just makes things easier, particularly for new cooks. This recipe uses a packaged mix and...It makes pretty good biscuits.

This recipe makes a good garlic biscuit and is simplified by using a baking mix. Bisquick is a popular mix but we have used a store brand with identical results. Garlic biscuits go well with any meat but are especially good with fish and chicken.

Prep time: 10 min
Cook time: 12 min
Total time: 22 min
Yield: 8 biscuits

Ingredients

* 2 cups Biscuit Baking Mix (Bisquick)

* 2/3 cup milk

* 1/2 cup cheddar cheese, shredded

* 1/4 cup margarine, melted

* 1/4 teaspoon garlic powder

Instructions:

1. Preheat oven to 425 degrees F.
2. In a bowl, combine baking mix, cheese and milk then stir into a soft dough. Mix thoroughly for 30 seconds.
3. Drop dough by spoon fulls on an ungreased baking sheet. If you want flat, round biscuits, mash tops of dough with the back of a spoon to about 1/2 inch thickness.
4. Bake until golden brown (8-12 minutes).
5. While biscuits bake, melt the margarine, and then blend garlic powder into margarine.
6. When biscuits are done, remove from oven and immediately brush tops with the margarine/garlic mix.

Red Lobster Biscuits (copycat)

If you like the garlic biscuits served at the popular Red Lobster restaurants, you will find this copycat recipe to be very similar.
Very close to the original and easy to make using a packaged mix. New cooks should have no trouble with this recipe.

Prep time: 20 min
Cook time: 12 min
Total time: 32 min
Yield: 8 biscuits

Ingredients

* 2 1/4 cups baking mix (Bisquick)

* cold milk as needed per Bisquick package instructions (about 2/3 cup)

* 3 tablespoons confectioner's sugar

* 1/4 cup minced fresh parsley (use dried parsley if you have to)

* 8 ounces (about 1 cup) shredded cheddar cheese

* 1 stick (8 tablespoons) butter or margarine

* 1 teaspoon minced garlic

Instructions

1. Pre heat the oven to 400 degrees F.
2. Make the biscuit dough per baking mix package instructions. Or you can make the dough from scratch using our recipe.
3. Add the confectioner's sugar, parsley and shredded cheese to the dough and mix well.
4. Place the butter (or margarine) and garlic in a baking dish and melt the butter in the oven (if using sticks butter, cut into 4 or 5 chunks). Watch closely. You want the butter to be just melted, not cooked.
5. Place the melted butter/garlic mix on counter next to biscuit dough and using two spoons (or your hands) form balls of biscuit dough about 2-3 inches in diameter. Place the dough balls in the melted butter mix and roll to cover all sides.
6. 6. Line a cookie sheet with parchment paper if you have it. If not, place biscuit dough balls on a dry cookie sheet (no oil or spray).
7. Place biscuits in pre heated oven. Bake until golden brown (about 10-12 minutes).
8. Remove from oven and drizzle any remaining butter/garlic mix over top of hot biscuits. Serve immediately.

Southern Cornbread

No sugar in this recipe...this is real Southern cornbread

This authentic Southern cornbread is straight from Alabama. It contains no sugar, no eggs and very little flour. The resulting bread is crumbly with soft insides and a crunchy crust. As mom says its bread to accompany a meal. It's not dessert. It's not cake. Of course, if you like sweet cornbread...put sugar in it.

Prep time: 15 min
Cook time: 25 min
Total time: 40 min
Yield: 6 servings

Ingredients:

* 2 cups white cornmeal (use yellow if that's what you have on hand)

* 2/3 cup flour

* 1-1/2 tablespoons baking powder

* 1/2 teaspoon baking soda (omit if you use regular milk rather than buttermilk)

* 1/2 teaspoon salt

* Dash of black pepper

* 1 and 1/2 cups buttermilk (more or less)

* 3 to 4 tablespoons of bacon drippings (you can substitute cooking oil)

Instructions:

1. Preheat the oven to 400 degrees
2. Prepare the skillet by placing the bacon drippings in the skillet and roll the skillet or use a paper towel to coat the interior sides of the skillet with the bacon grease. Place the skillet in the oven while preparing the following batter.
3. In a medium size bowl, combine all the dry ingredients and mix well.
4. Add about 1/2 cup of the buttermilk and stir.
5. Remove skillet from oven and slowly add about 1 or 2 tablespoon of the hot oil (bacon grease) from the skillet into the batter, stirring well. (Use a pot holder to pick up the skillet!!) The skillet and bacon grease should be very hot but not smoking.
6. Sprinkle the inside of the skillet with (dry) cornmeal and return to oven.

7. Watching the consistency of the batter, carefully add remainder of buttermilk while stirring. The consistency of the cornbread batter should look like a thick pancake mix. This may require a little more or less of the remaining buttermilk. If the mix is too thick, add more buttermilk. If the mixture is too thin, add more cornmeal.
8. Remove the skillet from oven and pour the batter in the skillet. Return the skillet to the pre-heated oven and start timing.
9. Bake at 400 degrees approximately 25 minutes. Time will vary according to the consistency of the batter you end up with and your oven. Watch the cornbread after about 20 minutes and cook until the top begins to brown.
10. Remove the cornbread from the oven and flip the cornbread over in the skillet (see tip below), then continue baking another 5 minutes (this will add a little more browning to the top...which is now on the bottom).

Tip: If you are using a skillet that is not well seasoned the cornbread may stick when you attempted to flip it over (step 10). Run a table knife completely around the inside wall of the skillet while gently shaking. This will usually free the bread for you to flip it over. Protect your hand...its hot! If the bread does not come out easily, do not try to turn it over; just skip step 10. When you are satisfied with the color of the top of the bread, remove from the oven, allow to cool 10-15 minutes. Then try again running a knife around the edge, while shaking, and the bread should come out easily.

Jalapeno Cornbread

Also called "Mexican" Cornbread this spicy treat may not be a traditional Southern dish but it is so good we had to include it.

This tasty treatment of traditional Southern cornbread is slightly spicy while the cream corn produces a delicate, moist, soft inside. For a change from regular cornbread we recommend this recipe.

Prep time: 20 min
Cook time: 25 min
Total time: 45 min
Yield: 6-8 servings

Ingredients:

- 2 cups white cornmeal
- 6 tablespoons flour
- 1 and 1/2 tablespoons baking powder
- 1/8 tablespoon baking soda (omit if you use regular milk rather than buttermilk)
- 1/4 tablespoon salt
- Dash of black pepper
- 1 cup buttermilk
- 8 tablespoons of cooking oil (or bacon grease)
- 1/2 cup grated medium cheddar cheese
- 1 cup cream style corn - DRAINED WELL
- 1 medium jalapeno pepper, diced (Adjust the amount to your taste; one whole pepper will be just a little tangy. Use more if you want "hot").
- 1/3 cup onion - diced

Instructions:

1. Preheat the oven to 400 degrees
2. Prepare the skillet by placing the oil in the skillet and roll the skillet or use a paper towel to coat the sides of the skillet with oil. Place the skillet on the stove top on medium heat.
3. In a medium size bowl, combine all the dry ingredients and mix well. Add corn, cheese and jalapeno pepper and mix.
4. Add 1/2 of the buttermilk and stir.
5. Slowly, add the hot oil from the skillet, leaving about 1 tablespoon in skillet. Stir well.
6. Place skillet back on the stove top.
7. Watching the consistency of the corn meal batter carefully, add additional buttermilk while stirring. The consistency of the batter should look like a thick pancake batter. This may require a little more or less of the remaining buttermilk. If the mix is too thick, add more buttermilk. If the mixture is too thin, add more cornmeal.
8. Lightly sprinkle the skillet bottom with dry corn meal and pour in the batter. Immediately, place skillet in pre-heated oven.
9. Bake at 400 degrees approximately 25 minutes. Watch the cornbread after about 20 minutes and cook until the top is golden brown. This may take more than 25 minutes according to the consistency of batter you finished with.

Cracklin Cornbread

A soul food favorite, this Cracklin Cornbread is crumbly with a crunchy crust embedded with pork Cracklins.

What's better than Southern cornbread? Southern Cracklin cornbread. With few ingredients this crunchy crusted bread is easy to make. The cracklings add additional body and a ton of flavor.

Prep time: 20 min
Cook time: 25 min
Total time: 45 min
Yield: 6 servings

Ingredients:

1 1/2 cups white cornmeal

1/4 cup bacon drippings

1/2 cup flour

1 tablespoon baking powder

3/4 teaspoon baking soda

1/2 teaspoon salt

dash black pepper

1 cup Cracklins

1 cup buttermilk

Instructions:

1. Preheat oven to 425 degrees.
2. Pour bacon drippings (you can substitute cooking oil) in cast iron skillet and heat until hot, but not smoking.
3. Combine dry ingredients and Cracklins in a mixing bowl. Add milk and mix well (see note below).
4. Add heated bacon drippings, leaving about 1 or 2 tablespoons in the skillet. Mix well.
5. Pour mixture into hot skillet and bake 20 to 25 minutes until golden brown or wooden toothpick inserted into center comes out clean.

Note: When adding the milk in step 3, you are looking for a batter that looks like a thick pancake batter. You may need more or less than the 1 cup buttermilk.

Cornbread, Dressing (Stuffing)

Call it stuffing or dressing, they are the same thing. It just depends on where you cook it. Stuffed in poultry it is called "stuffing". Cooked on the side, it is called "dressing".

This recipe makes a slightly moist dressing. We prefer a dry dressing and found if we reduce the 1/2 cup milk in the dressing ingredients to 1/4 cup it produced what we liked. If you like an extra moist dressing try adding extra 1/4 cup milk to the dressing ingredients.
Difficulty: Medium

Prep time: 30 min
Cook time: 1 hour
Total time: 1 hour 30 min
Yield: 8 servings

For The Cornbread:

Ingredients:

* 2 cups cornmeal

* 1/2 cup flour

* 1 tablespoon baking powder

* 1/4 teaspoon salt

* 1/4 teaspoon baking soda

* 2 eggs beaten

* 1-2 cups buttermilk

* 2 tablespoons bacon drippings (substitute vegetable oil if bacon drippings are unavailable)

For The Dressing:

Ingredients:

* 3 stalks celery, chopped

* 1 medium onion, chopped

* 1/3 cup butter or margarine, melted

* 12 slices day old bread, crumbled

* 2 cups turkey or chicken broth

* 1/2 cup milk

* 2 eggs, beaten

* 1/4 teaspoon salt

* 1 teaspoon poultry seasoning

* 1/2 teaspoon sage

* 1/4 teaspoon pepper

Instructions:

1. First, make the cornbread. Combine cornmeal, flour, baking powder, salt, and baking soda. Mix well. Add eggs, buttermilk, and bacon drippings and stir into a batter.
2. Heat a well-greased 10-inch cast iron skillet in a 450 degree oven for 4 minutes or until hot. Remove skillet from oven and pour batter into skillet. Bake at 450 for 20-35 minutes or until cornbread is lightly browned.
3. Cool cornbread, then crumble into a large bowl.
4. Place celery and onion in a large frying pan with one tablespoon of cooking oil and cook until tender (about 4-5 min.).
5. Transfer cooked celery and onion, with all remaining ingredients, to crumbled cornbread, stirring well.
6. Spoon dressing into a lightly greased 13 x 9 x 2-inch pan or casserole dish.
7. Bake at 350 degrees F. for 25 to 30 minutes.

Southern Hushpuppies

How Southern can you get? Hushpuppies are traditional with a fish fry but also go well with turnip greens and black eyed peas.

Very easy recipe for this Southern favorite. Very crunchy with a soft crumbly insides. Be sure to serve them hot while they have that good crunchy crust.
Difficulty: Easy

Prep time: 15 min
Cook time: 3 min
Total time: 18 min
Yield: 7-8 hushpuppies

Ingredients:

- 1 cup white cornmeal
- 4 tablespoons flour
- 1 tablespoon baking powder
- 1/3 cup onion - diced
- 1/8 tablespoon baking soda
- 1/2 cup buttermilk (more or less)
- 1/8 tablespoon salt
- 1/8 tablespoon black pepper
- Cooking oil (see instructions for amount)

Instructions:

1. In a medium sauce pot place enough cooking oil to provide at least a 4 inch depth of oil.
2. Place the pot on medium high heat. The oil temperature is very important. It must be hot but not smoking hot. Here's a tip. Place the end of a wooden spoon or any wooden utensil you have in the hot oil. If bubbles swirl up around the wood immediately, you have the correct temperature. If no bubbles, it's not hot enough.
3. In a medium size bowl, combine all the dry ingredients (including the onions) and stir well. Add the buttermilk slowly while closely observing the consistency. Stir to a consistency of wet sand. The mix should stick together without crumbling when rolled in your hands. If too dry, add milk. If too mushy, add cornmeal.
4. Using your hands, roll the cornmeal mixture in balls, slightly larger than golf balls.
5. Place balls on a large wooden spoon and submerge in the preheated oil.
6. Cook until golden brown (only about 2-3 minutes).
7. Place the hushpuppies on paper towels as they are removed from the pot to absorb some of the oil (but DO NOT cover the hushpuppies).
8. Serve hot.

Hoecakes Recipe

Hoecakes, sometime called Johnny Cakes, are an old Southern favorite that can be made many different ways. Some serve hoecakes as bread, some serve with various sweets as a dessert or snack. .

Some cooks do not use milk or eggs to make hoecakes but this recipe does and we like it prepared this way. It adds body and a firmer structure to the hoecakes for spreading on butter or other condiments.

Some people like small hoecakes, some like large; the size is up to you but we prefer small 3 to 4 inch diameter hoecakes.

Prep time: 10 min
Cook time: 6 min
Total time: 16 min
Yield: 6 plus according to size of hoecakes made

Ingredients:

3/4 cup flour

1 1/2 cups corn meal

4 teaspoons baking powder

1 teaspoon salt

2 beaten eggs

1 1/2 cups milk

1/4 cup oil

extra oil, as needed for frying

Instructions:

1. In a medium bowl, combine all ingredients except the extra oil. Mix well.
2. The batter should resemble a thick pancake batter. You may need more or less milk than called for. Just add milk slowly while watching the batter consistency.
3. In a heavy skillet, heat enough oil to coat the bottom of the pan.
4. Place several spoonful of batter in the skillet, according to the size hoecakes you want, and smooth into a pancake-like shape.

5. Cook on one side until brown (about 2-3 minutes), turn and brown other side. Add additional oil to skillet as needed to prevent sticking.

Dinner Rolls

Making bread at home from scratch can be a challenge. It generally requires an experienced cook. And this recipe is no different. We have had good and not so good results.

Several factors can affect your outcome when working with dough. The temperature, humidity, the elevation at your location, your kneading technique, your skill in using the right amount of flour. If you are a novice cook and do not get the results you want, don't be discouraged, and keep trying...that's how you learn.

We agree that working with dough can be a challenge but we had good results with this recipe. However, the texture of the bread was not what we hoped for and would not recommend this for those looking for store bought-type rolls.

Prep time: 30 min
Cook time: 15 min
Total time: 45 min plus 1 hour 30 min dough rise time
Yield: 8 + rolls

Ingredients:

  1 cup water

  1 cup milk

  1/4 cup margarine

  4-5 cups all-purpose flour

  3 tablespoons sugar

  1 teaspoon salt

  2 packages active dry yeast

Instructions:

1. Combine water, milk and margarine in a small saucepan and heat until very warm to the touch. For best results use a candy thermometer and heat to 120 degrees F. (the margarine does not have to be completely melted). DO NOT BOIL.
2. In a stand up mixer bowl, place 3 cups of the flour along with the other dry ingredients.
3. Mix on low speed using dough hook attachment until well blended.

4. Gradually add the warm milk mixture and mix on low speed until well blended.
5. Slowly add the remaining 1-2 cups of flour, 1/2 cup at a time, until the dough pulls away from the sides of the bowl and clings to the dough hook of the mixer. You may need more or less than the 1-2 cups flour.
6. Turn out on a floured counter top and kneed 5 or 6 times by hand. (Note: fold the dough over on itself and press with the heels of hands. Do not squeeze.)
7. Place dough in a large greased bowl, cover with a dish towel and let rise in a warm location away from drafts for 30 minutes.
8. Turn out on counter top and divide into rolls. Using hands, mold into any shape you desire or you can make loafs if you prefer.
9. Place dough on a cookie sheet lined with parchment paper and allow to rise for 45 minutes (dough should be about doubled in size).
10. Pre heat oven to 425 degrees F.
11. Bake in oven for 10-12 minutes or until golden brown. Remove from oven and brush tops with room temperature butter while rolls are still hot.

Corn Fritters

I think of corn fritters as a cross between cornbread and pancakes infused with whole kernel corn. This is a very simple, easy recipe that may be served in place of cornbread.
Difficulty: Easy

Prep time: 10 min
Cook time: 20 min
Total time: 30 min
Yield: 6 servings

Ingredients:

* 1 and 1/2 cups all-purpose flour

* 1/4 cup cornmeal

* 3 teaspoons baking powder

* 1/2 teaspoons salt

* 1 egg, slightly beaten

* 1 cup milk

* 1 tablespoon melted shortening

* 2 cups whole kernel corn (drain liquid if using canned)

* oil for frying (enough for about a 3/4 inch depth in your frying pan)

Instructions:

1. In a medium size bowl, combine all of the ingredients except the corn and frying oil. Mix until smooth.
2. Add the corn and mix well. The batter should look like a thick cornbread or pancake batter. You may need more or less than the 1 cup milk. You should be able to compress a small handful and have it hold its shape without crumbling or running through your fingers.
3. In a large skillet, heat the frying oil until very hot (365 degrees F.). If you do not have a thermometer, place the handle of a wooden spoon or other wooden utensil into the oil. You should see bubbles rise around the wooden handle immediately. If not, wait for oil to get hotter.
4. Drop the batter by the tablespoon into the hot grease and fry until browned on both sides, Serve Hot!

Sweet Walnut Zucchini Bread

This Zucchini Bread may be made plain or with walnuts or with walnuts and raisins. Although it is called "bread" it is sweet and can be served as a dessert. Very good as a coffee cake.

If you shy away from baking because you have not had much luck at it, this is the recipe for you. This very moist, sweet zucchini bread is almost fail proof. We love this recipe.

Prep time: 20 min
Cook time: 1 hour 10 min
Total time: 1 hour 30 min
Yield: 2 loafs

Ingredients:

   3 eggs

   1 cup vegetable oil

   2 cups sugar

   2 cups grated zucchini

   2 tsp vanilla

   3 cups all-purpose flour

   3 tsp ground cinnamon

   1 tsp baking soda

   1/4 tsp baking powder

   1 tsp salt

   1/2 cup chopped walnuts

   1/3 cup raisins (optional)

   2 - 8x4 inch loaf pans

Instructions:

1. Preheat oven to 325 degrees F. Grease and flour two 8x4 inch loaf pans. Set aside.

2. In a large bowl, beat eggs until light and frothy. Mix in oil and sugar. Stir in zucchini and vanilla.
3. In a separate bowl, combine remaining ingredients. Raisins are optional.
4. Stir flour mixture into the egg mixture. Mix well into a smooth batter.
5. Divide batter into prepared pans.
6. Bake 60-70 minutes (when done a toothpick stuck into top of loaf should come out clean with little or no moisture).

No Zucchini...Zucchini Bread

This recipe was created as a result of having left over Thanksgiving dinner ingredients. We found that substituting pumpkin pie filling and berries makes a very zucchini bread-like dessert that is pretty good.

Prep time: 20 min
Cook time: 1 hour
Total time: 1 hour 20 min
Yield: 8-12 servings

Ingredients:

   3 eggs

   1 cup vegetable oil

   2 cups sugar

   2 teaspoons vanilla extract

   3 cups all-purpose flour

   1 cup pumpkin pie filling

   1/2 cup blueberries

   1/2 cup cranberries (pre-cooked) or canned whole berry cranberry sauce.

   3 teaspoons cinnamon

   1 teaspoon baking soda

   1/4 teaspoon baking powder

   1/2 teaspoon salt

   1/2 cup chopped walnuts

   water, as needed

Instructions:

1. If you are using fresh cranberries, cook according to package instructions.
2. Pre-heat oven to 325 degrees F.
3. Grease and flour two 8x4 inch loaf pans.
4. In a medium size bowl, beat eggs until light and frothy. Add oil and vanilla and mix well.
5. In a separate large bowl, combine all remaining ingredients and mix well.
6. Add egg mixture to flour mix and stir until well blended.
7. At this point, you may need to add enough water to obtain a batter. Should look like pancake batter.
8. Pour mixture equally into prepared loaf pans.
9. Bake about 60 minutes or until a knife inserted into top of loaf comes out dry.

Walnut Zucchini Bread

This Zucchini Bread may be made plain or with walnuts or with walnuts and raisins. Although it is called "bread" it is sweet and can be served as a dessert. Very good as a coffee cake.

If you shy away from baking because you have not had much luck at it, this is the recipe for you. This very moist, sweet zucchini bread is almost fail proof. We love this recipe.

Prep time: 20 min
Cook time: 1 hour 10 min
Total time: 1 hour 30 min
Yield: 2 loafs

Ingredients:

   3 eggs

   1 cup vegetable oil

   2 cups sugar

   2 cups grated zucchini

   2 tsp vanilla

   3 cups all-purpose flour

   3 tsp ground cinnamon

   1 tsp baking soda

   1/4 tsp baking powder

   1 tsp salt

   1/2 cup chopped walnuts

   1/3 cup raisins (optional)

   2 - 8x4 inch loaf pans

Instructions:

1. Preheat oven to 325 degrees F. Grease and flour two 8x4 inch loaf pans. Set aside.
2. In a large bowl, beat eggs until light and frothy. Mix in oil and sugar. Stir in zucchini and vanilla.
3. In a separate bowl, combine remaining ingredients. Raisins are optional.
4. Stir flour mixture into the egg mixture. Mix well into a smooth batter.
5. Divide batter into prepared pans.
6. Bake 60-70 minutes (when done a toothpick stuck into top of loaf should come out clean with little or no moisture).

Section 5

Breakfast Recipes

Breakfast Grits

Grits are a traditional Southern favorite generally served with breakfast. They may also serve as a side dish for any meal.

Grits are made by coarsely grinding dried corn. If it is ground further you have cornmeal. It is usually cooked by boiling but can be fried and enhanced with many additives as noted in this recipe.

Grits are so simple to make...you hardly need a recipe. And there appears to be no right or wrong way to cook them. They seem to come out the same. Assuming you start with the proper amount of water, about the only way to go wrong is to burn them.

Today you can buy instant and "quick cook" grits. They are convenient, fast and pretty good, but I prefer the old fashioned, traditional "regular" grits. Since grits can be bland alone, try some of the suggested variations following the recipe.

Prep time: 5 min
Cook time: 40 min
Total time: 45 min
Yield: 4 servings

Ingredients:

    4 1/2 cups water

    1 teaspoon salt

    1 cup grits (regular not "quick cook")

    4 tablespoons butter

Instructions:

1. In a large saucepan, bring 4 1/2 cups water, seasoned with 1 teaspoon salt, to a boil.
2. Stir in 1 cup regular grits.
3. Reduce heat to low and continue stirring.
4. Cook 30 to 40 minutes, stirring frequently. (They will burn if you do not stir!)
5. Remove from heat and stir in 4 tablespoons of butter. Serve hot

Variations:

1. Add bacon grease (2 tablespoons) when the grits start boiling. Adds a lot of flavor.
2. Stir in one slightly beaten egg while cooking.
3. Add 2 tablespoons chopped onion when starting to boil.
4. Add one slice of (uncooked) bacon when adding the grits to the water
5. Cook grits per regular recipe above, allow cooling slightly, beating in one egg. Refrigerate until firm, then slice and fry in bacon fat or butter. Good idea for left-over grits.

Spicy Grits

A common complaint from those that do not like grits is, "they are tasteless". Well, it's true that grits have little flavor on their own but they tend to take on the flavor of anything they are cooked with.

One way to give grits their own flavor is to turn up the heat. This recipe adds a little spiciness to traditional Southern grits. You may like them or not...but you will not say they are tasteless!

The recipe has instructions on toning down the heat if you like but we loved the spicy full heat version. We served with fried chicken and it was a wonderful compliment to the chicken.

Prep time: 15 min
Cook time: 20 min
Total time: 35 min
Yield: 4 + servings

Ingredients

- 4 cups instant grits, cooked

- 2 tablespoons soy sauce

- 1/3 cup sour cream

- 1 clove garlic, minced

- 1 egg

- 1/2 cup cheddar cheese, shredded

- 1/3 cup jalapeno peppers, minced

- Optional Topping: bacon bits and/or dry roasted tomatoes may be scattered over the top before baking.

Instructions:

1. Pre-heat oven to 350 degrees
2. Cook grits according to package instructions
3. Combine cooked grits and all remaining ingredients (except topping ingredients, if used) in a bowl. Mix well.
4. Pour into a casserole dish, add topping if desired and bake for 20 minutes.
5. You may substitute small can (4 oz.) green chilies for the jalapeno peppers if you want the flavor without the heat. Canned chili's come in mild, medium and hot. Use the appropriate can for the degree of heat you want in your final dish. You can also substitute fresh Anaheim peppers for a milder flavor.

Sausage Gravy

Although this recipe makes sausage gravy you can substitute bacon, chopped ham or leave the meat out. We found making the roux the only difficult part but we got the hang of it quickly. The secret is, as the recipe says, to make the roux so there is no visible oil or lumps of flour showing.

Prep time: 5 min
Cook time: 15 min
Total time: 20 min
Yield: 4-6 servings

Ingredients:

12 ounces ground pork sausage

1/4 cup bacon grease or cooking oil, as needed

1/4 cup diced onion

2-4 tablespoons all-purpose flour

1-2 cups milk (see instructions)

salt and pepper to taste

parsley for garnish (optional)

Instructions:

1. In a skillet over medium heat, add the sausage and onion to the bacon grease. Cook while stirring until sausage is brown and onion tender. Remove sausage and onion and set aside (or if using a large pan, push to one side).
2. To make roux: Add one tablespoon of flour to the bacon grease while stirring constantly. Watch the consistency of the roux and add more flour as necessary to obtain a thick, dull colored paste. There should be no visible liquid grease or lumps of flour in the roux. You must get the roux consistency correct now. You can NOT add flour or grease after this point
3. If you want white gravy, go to the next step (adding milk) just as the roux begins to show color. If you want brown gravy cook the roux until it turns a rich brown color (just before burning). You must constantly stir the roux.
4. Add 1/2 cup milk while stirring. As the roux dissolves and the milk begins to boil, add more milk a little at a time while watching the thickness of the gravy. The thickness will be determined by how much milk you add and how long you cook it. When the gravy is removed from the heat and cools, it will become a little thicker.

5. As you approach the thickness you want, add the sausage/onion mix back into the gravy if they were removed. Add salt and pepper to taste and cook one minute.
6. If you want the gravy spicy, add a dash of crushed red pepper flakes in the previous step.
7. Pour the steaming hot gravy over biscuits and garnish with chopped parsley

Potato Pancakes

A great way to use leftover mashed potatoes or you can cook up a new batch of boiled potatoes. These patties are a great side dish for any entree.

With soft insides and a fried potato-like crust we really liked these patties as a little something different to do with potatoes.

Prep time: 20 min
Cook time: 6 min
Total time: 26 min
Yield: 4 + servings

Ingredients:

   3 pounds potatoes, peeled (about 6-8 medium potatoes)

   1/2 onion, peeled

   1 egg, beaten

   1 cup pancake mix (or 6 tablespoons all-purpose flour)

   1 teaspoon salt

   1/2 teaspoon ground black pepper

   1 tablespoon vegetable oil or as needed

Instructions:

1. Chop potatoes and onion into small chunks.
2. In a food processor grate potatoes and onion medium fine.
3. Combine all ingredients except vegetable oil in a bowl and mix well.
4. Heat vegetable oil in a non-stick skillet over medium high heat.
5. Drop large spoonful of potato mix into hot oil and flatten slightly with back of spoon. Fry until golden brown, about 2-3 minutes on each side. Serve hot.
6. You can substitute 2 cups left over mashed potatoes for the fresh potatoes, grate the onions alone in step 2 and continue with step 3 using the mashed potatoes.

Best Waffle Recipes

Most all waffle recipes contain the same basic ingredients. Flour, sugar, salt, milk, eggs, vanilla. The many varieties of waffles come from the additives to the batter, or toppings added when served. Other than that, they are basically the same.

So what makes some waffles good...and others the best? Technique and a few little secrets. And...that's what we are going to discuss here. There are only a few tips you need to know, but they will make a difference in your waffles.

The Batter

Tip 1:
The batter should have a consistency similar to gravy. Thick but easy to pour. This may call for more or less of the milk called for in the recipe. Only experience will tell you when it looks right. Don't worry though; you will still get good waffles. They just may be a little thin if your batter is too thin. And if too thick, they will be a little chewy, but still pretty good.

Many recipes call for a little oil in the batter. Some do not. You should always put about 1/2 tablespoon of oil (cooking oil/vegetable oil) in your batter. It helps develop the outer crust. It does not matter if you make your waffles crisp and crunchy or if you cook them soft like pancakes, the oil is needed.

Tip 2:
DO NOT BEAT THE BATTER VIGOROUSLY! This makes tough, chewy waffles. Gently stir the batter only long enough to thoroughly moisten the dry ingredients. Do not worry about the small lumps in the batter. You will never know they were there after the waffles are cooked.

You're Waffle Iron (Griddle):

Tip 1:
This may seem to be a "no brainer", but I have seen so many people pour their batter in a waffle iron that they turned on 1 minute earlier. The batter will not rise properly in an iron that is not fully up to temperature. You will get heavy, flat waffles. Most waffle irons today have lights that tell you when the iron has reached cooking temperature. If you do not have such lights on your waffle iron, be sure to allow it to heat up at least 5 minutes.

Tip 2:
Manufacturers of waffle irons advise you not to use cooking spray on your iron. Yes, I know, it is convenient and it seems to work well to prevent sticking, but the manufacturer state that, over time, spray will damage the non-stick surface of your griddle.

Instead, you should use a vegetable oil (Crisco works good). Just take a basting brush or a paper towel and cover the surface lightly with oil. Your waffle iron will last much longer and Crisco seems to make a better crust on the waffles.

Vanilla and Sugar:

Unless you are making some exotic jalapeno waffle, always add a touch of sugar and a little vanilla to your batter. Many recipes do not list sugar or vanilla in their ingredients. But it will add that little extra "something"...and it is so good.

Eggs

No matter what kind of waffles you are making, always add beaten egg whites. You can add the yolks or leave them out, but beaten egg whites are essential to light waffles. The egg whites should be beaten until stiff (like whipped cream) and then gently folded into the batter as the last step.

Check our recipes at the top of the left column on this page and use these few simple tips and your next waffles will be the "best" waffles.

Biscuits, Southern

Some experienced cooks never learn to make good homemade biscuits from scratch. But with a little effort and this recipe you can make real Southern biscuits that will get compliments aplenty. These are soft, country biscuits meant to be smothered with strawberry preserves or sausage gravy. If you like layered bread that is full of air, get store bought frozen biscuits. But if you like "stick-to-your-ribs" biscuits loaded with flavor, this recipe are for you.

Prep time: 20 min
Cook time: 15 min
Total time: 35 min
Yield: 6 biscuits

Ingredients

* 2 cups all-purpose flour

* 4 teaspoons baking powder

* 1/4 teaspoon baking soda

* 1/2 teaspoon salt

* 1/2 cup Crisco shortening

* 3/4 cup buttermilk (more or less - see directions)

Instructions:

1. Preheat oven to 400 degrees F.
2. Combine the dry ingredients in a medium size bowl.
3. Using a pastry cutter or fork (or your fingers), gently cut in the shortening until the mixture looks like "meal" (a very course powder)
4. Add the buttermilk a little at a time, stirring *GENTLY* until dough starts to form. You may need more or less than the 3/4 cup milk (type flour and your mixing technique may vary amount of liquid required).
5. When you get a "sticky" dough ball, turn out on a floured surface and form a flat mass with your hands. Turn the dough over on itself and flatten again with your hands, repeat a second time. DO NOT KNEED!
6. Roll out the dough to a 1 to 2 inch thickness according to how thick a biscuit you want.. Cut out the biscuits with a biscuit cutter (see tip 7 below).

7. Place the biscuits on a cookie sheet lined with parchment paper. If you do not have parchment paper just use an ungreased cookie sheet. Use your thumb to make a small indentation on the top center of each biscuit.
8. Place biscuits into the preheated oven. Bake until tops are a golden brown (about 15 minutes). Note: Closely watch the bottom of the biscuits by lifting one biscuit and observing. Some cookie sheet materials tend to burn the bottoms quickly. If bottoms are getting too brown, turn oven to broiler setting, leave oven door open and watch until tops are brown. Do not walk away with broiler on, they will burn quickly. Make sure the inside of the biscuits are cooked through before removing from oven.

Serve with Sausage Gravy

TIPS

Tip 1: If you like big (circumference)) or small biscuits, fine...but we have found that using a 2 inch biscuit cutter makes biscuits that seem to rise better. Actually my cutter measures a little less than 2 1/2 inches.

Tip 2: If you like thin biscuits roll out the dough to 1 inch thickness. If you like big, fat biscuits roll out the dough to 1 to 1 1/2 inches.

Tip 3: Obtaining the correct consistency of the dough takes a little practice. Just add the buttermilk a little at a time and watch for the dough to form a ball as you stir. You may need more or less milk than called for in the recipe.

Tip 4: Do NOT handle the dough any more than necessary. Over handling will make tough biscuits. When you turn the dough out on your board, try to double the dough over on itself only two or three times while flattening it out. Do not kneed.

Tip 5: If you do not have buttermilk, you can make a substitute by adding 1 tsp white vinegar in 1 cup regular milk. Stir and allow sitting for 1 minute before use.

Tip 6: Make sure to preheat the oven. Never start your biscuits in a cold oven.

Tip 7: When cutting out the biscuits do not push down and "twist" or turn the biscuit cutter. Push straight down and slide hand sideways to free the dough. Twisting the biscuit cutter compacts the edges of the dough causing uneven cooking.

Tip 8: Place the cut out dough on the cookie sheet with their sides just barely touching. The dough will not rise as much if there is space between the biscuits.

Tip 9: After placing the dough on the cookie sheet, use your thumb to make a small indentation (dimple) on the top of each biscuit. This promotes even rising to prevent lop-sided biscuits.

Tip 10: The cookie sheet you use can affect the browning of the biscuits. Dark material like non-stick tends to burn the bottoms before the tops are brown. Light material like aluminum or steel (without non-stick) tends to brown more evenly.

Tip 11: Here is probably the most important tip to avoiding flat biscuits: USE FRESH BAKING POWDER! Check the expiration date on the container, if your baking powder has been opened over a couple of months, don't use it. It is relatively inexpensive so why risk a batch of flat biscuits. You don't have to throw away the old baking powder, just don't use it for your biscuits.

Grillades (gree-YHADS),
Brunch or breakfast Beef dish

Grillades (gree-YHADS), a traditional Louisiana brunch or breakfast dish, served over grits. For those that are not fond of grits, it may be served over rice.

This recipe serves 6-8 so if you have left over's you can keep in a covered container in the fridge for 3 days. Just reheat to serve again.

Ingredients:

1 to 1 1/2 pounds lean beef or veal steaks, about 1/2-inch thick

1/4 cup all-purpose flour (for dredging meat)

1/2 teaspoon salt (for dredging meat)

1/2 teaspoon freshly ground black pepper (for dredging meat)

2 tablespoons bacon drippings or vegetable oil (for browning meat)

1 large onion, chopped

1/2 cup chopped celery

1 cup chopped green pepper

1 cup mushrooms, sliced

2 garlic cloves, minced

2 tablespoons bacon drippings or oil (for sauce)

2 tablespoons flour (for sauce)

1 1/4 cups beef broth

1 can (14.5 ounces) diced tomatoes

1/2 teaspoon dried thyme

1/2 teaspoon dried leaf basil

1/2 teaspoon crushed red pepper

salt and freshly ground black pepper, to taste

2 tablespoons chopped fresh parsley

4 to 5 cups hot cooked grits (or rice if you prefer)

Tabasco or pepper sauce to taste

Instructions:

1. Cut the steaks into 2-inch pieces.

2. Combine 1/4 cup flour, 1/2 teaspoon salt, and 1/2 teaspoon pepper; dredge steak pieces in the mix.

3. Heat the bacon drippings in a heavy skillet over medium-high heat; sauté the meat, turning pieces to brown both sides. Remove the meat to a plate and set aside.

4. Sauté the onion, celery, and pepper in the same pan until tender. Add garlic and stir well. Push the vegetables to one side of the pan. Add the additional bacon drippings or oil and stir in the 2 tablespoons of flour. Stir the mixture well and cook, stirring constantly, until mixture is medium brown in color.

5. Add the beef broth; stir until smooth.

6. Return the meat to the pan and pour tomatoes over meat. Sprinkle with the thyme, basil, red pepper, and a little Tabasco or pepper sauce. Reduce heat to a simmer and cook until tender, about 40 to 60 minutes.

7. Taste and add salt, pepper and/or Tabasco as needed; stir in the fresh chopped parsley.

Serve Grillades with hot buttered grits (or rice).

Serves 6 to 8.

Omelet Recipe Tips

Do your omelets end up as scrambled eggs? Are they like rubber? Well, that's easy to fix. All you need is a few simple tips and some good recipes. And we have them here.

Omelets used to be thought of as a breakfast dish (because of the eggs, I suppose) but today many people serve omelets at any time of the day. An omelet can be made with everything from sausage to fish to strawberry jelly. And, of course, what's an omelet without an assortment of fresh vegetables?

So, let's get started getting you on the road to "The Perfect Omelet".

Tip #1 - The Skillet
Here is the most important tip of all. You must use a non-stick skillet. Cast iron also works well if it is seasoned (cured) properly. An 8 inch skillet is recommended even if you are cooking for ten people. Do not attempt to make a giant omelet...make several individual omelets. Oh, a giant omelet is possible but it takes a lot of skill so we don't recommend it. Use about 2 tablespoons of cooking oil in the skillet (see next tip).

Tip #2 - The Oil
Most any type cooking oil may be used but select one with a high smoking point. Some cooks like to use butter, but it generally has a low smoking point and it makes the omelet a shade of brown that is undesirable to many. Olive oil also will smoke at a low temperature. We recommend corn oil, canola oil or peanut oil.

Tip #3 - The Cooking Temperature
Place the skillet on the stove set at medium high. Add cooking oil and allow to get very hot (a drop of water in the skillet should immediately sizzle). Reduce heat to medium and add eggs. Reduce heat to medium low when the eggs show no more liquid on top.

Tip #4 - Cooking Technique
After placing the eggs in the skillet, don't touch it for about 20 seconds. As the eggs set (dry and firm around the edges) start lifting the edges with a spatula and tilting the skillet to allow the liquid eggs on top to pour onto the skillet. Continue this procedure until there is no liquid showing. As the eggs set, you should be able to get the entire omelet to slide freely back and forth in the skillet by running the spatula around the edges. When the eggs are firmly set (solid, with no liquid egg) lift one side with the spatula and fold the omelet in half. Remove to a plate immediately. **The entire cooking time should be about one to two minutes for a plain omelet.** Avoid over-cooking or your omelet will be tough and rubbery. You are looking for a slight brown coloring on the bottom side as it cooks.

Tip #5 - Adding ingredients

You can put practically anything in an omelet. Here's the rule: use ingredients that complement each other. For example, sausage with onion and bell pepper, shrimp with parsley and cocktail sauce, ground beef with chili powder, onions, tomatoes and jalapeno pepper. Get the idea? Don't combine ingredients that you would not normally put together in any other dish. **Important:** any meat and firm vegetables (celery, onions, broccoli, carrots, etc.) should be cooked separately in advance to soften before adding to the omelet.

You should add the ingredients as soon as the eggs are almost completely set (the last 10 seconds of cooking).

Finally

The final tip is to serve the omelet hot. Cold eggs are not very appetizing. You can hold an omelet hot by placing in a glass baking dish and covering loosely with aluminum foil, then place in the oven set on low (150-200 degrees F.). But don't leave in the oven too long or your omelet will dry out and become rubbery. Since it only takes about a minute to cook an omelet, you should be able to make four in less than 10 minutes if you have all the ingredients prepared in advance.

Cheater Omelet

(for those that just can't make an omelet)

Do your omelets always end up looking like scrambled eggs? Are you one of those people that just can't make an omelet? Well, here's a simple method that will produce a pretty decent looking omelet every time. It's very simple. We call it the "Cheater's Omelet" because it is not fried in a skillet like the traditional omelet. Give it a try and see if your family can guess how you cooked it.

We were amazed at how easy this was and the omelet came out looking and tasting like...an omelet.

Prep time: 10 min
Cook time: 20 min
Total time: 30 min
Yield: 1 omelet

Ingredients:

　　2 eggs (use 3 eggs for hearty appetites)

　　2 tablespoons water or milk

　　1/2 teaspoon salt

　　1/2 teaspoon white pepper (black pepper may be substituted but you will see the black specks in your omelet)

　　You can add any of the following for a filling (meat and hard vegetables should be pre-cooked)

　　1/2 cup chopped ham, crumbled sausage or bacon

　　2 tablespoons onion, minced

　　bell pepper, spinach, zucchini, broccoli

Instructions:

1. If you intend to add a filling (meat, vegetables) cook them first. Just sauté onions, peppers, etc. in a frying pan until tender. If adding meat, cook until lightly browned. Set the cooked vegetables and meat aside for now.
2. Combine eggs and water (or milk) in a small mixing bowl and beat the eggs with a fork or whisk until light and frothy. Add salt and pepper.
3. Pour egg mixture into a zip lock plastic bag. For a one to three egg omelet, use a quart size bag. If cooking more than 3 eggs, use a gallon size bag.
4. Add any other ingredients (pre-cooked vegetables/meat and/or shredded cheese/salsa) to the plastic bag. Seal the bag and shake to mix.
5. Add 4-6 inches water to a pot that is large enough to hold the plastic bag without having to fold it.
6. Bring water to a boil.
7. Place the plastic bag containing the omelet egg mixture in the boiling water and cook 10-15 minutes or until egg is firm with no liquid egg showing in the bag.
8. Remove the omelet from water using a spatula under the bottom of the bag. Note: While the plastic bag is in the boiling water it will be very delicate and can not be handled without the risk of bursting. If the bag burst the egg mix will be dumped into the water and you will have to start over. Do not attempt to lift or rearrange the bag by lifting the top of the plastic bag. Always use a spatula under the bottom of the bag if you need to rearrange or to remove the plastic bag.
9. Open or cut open the plastic bag and fold omelet out on a serving plate.

Classic Plain Omelet Recipe

This recipe makes a classic plain egg omelet for those that just like their eggs without any embellishment.

Nothing fancy here, just a plain egg omelet that is very simple and easy. Sometimes you just want your eggs with a side of sausage and coffee. This recipe makes a good, quick omelet with no frills.

Prep time: 10 min
Cook time: 5 min
Total time: 15 min
Yield: 1 omelet

Ingredients:

- 2 eggs (use 3 eggs for hearty appetites)
- 2 tablespoon water or milk
- 1/2 teaspoon salt
- 1/2 teaspoon white pepper (black pepper may be substituted)
- 2 teaspoons of cooking oil (canola, corn or peanut)

Instructions:

1. Combine eggs and water (or milk) and beat the eggs with a fork or whisk until light and frothy. Add salt and pepper and mix.
2. Heat the oil in a non-stick frying pan on medium-high heat.
3. Pour in the eggs.
4. Don't touch until eggs begin to set (solid and firm around edges). Reduce heat to medium.
5. Carefully lift the edges of the omelet with a spatula and tilt pan to allow the uncooked portion to run underneath.
6. Continue until omelet is set with no more liquid eggs in the center.
7. When the eggs are set, lift one side with a spatula and fold over.
8. Plate omelet and serve hot.

Asparagus Omelet Recipe

Many people have never heard of an asparagus omelet, but for you asparagus lovers you are in for a treat. If you love asparagus and you love omelets, here's your asparagus omelet recipe.

Simply a combination of a good omelet with asparagus. Very tasty and easy recipe.

Prep time: 10 min
Cook time: 8 min
Total time: 18 min
Yield: 1 large omelet

Ingredients:

   3 eggs

   2 tablespoon water or milk (cream may be substituted)

   1 tablespoon cooking oil (peanut, canola or corn)

   1/4 teaspoon salt

   A dash of white pepper (black pepper may be substituted)

   1/2 cup young asparagus tips

Instructions:

1. Cook the asparagus tips in boiling water until tender (about 5 min). Season with salt and pepper. Set aside.
2. Combine the eggs, water (or milk), salt and pepper and beat with a whisk or fork until light and frothy.
3. Add the cooking oil to a non-stick frying pan (10 inch) and heat on medium-high.
4. When oil is very hot, pour in the egg mixture.
5. Do not touch until eggs begin to set (firm and dry around the edges).
6. As soon as eggs begin to set, reduce heat to medium and lift the edges away from the pan while tilting the pan to allow the uncooked egg to reach the pan.
7. When the omelet is completely set (no liquid, uncooked egg in the center) place the cooked asparagus tips on one side of the omelet.
8. Use a spatula to lift the other side and fold over the top of the asparagus.
9. Serve immediately.

Basic Cheese Omelet Recipe

This is the classic simple cheese omelet that nearly everyone loves. You can start with this basic recipe and add whatever comes to mind and make a different creation all your own. Try adding onions, mushrooms, bell pepper, jalapeno pepper, sausage, ham or whatever.

Very easy recipe for the old standby cheese omelet. If you skip adding any filling and just go with this basic cheese omelet it is hard to fail with this recipe.

Prep time: 20 min
Cook time: 30 min
Total time: 5 min
Yield: 1 omelet

Ingredients:

3 large eggs

1 tsp. water

1/4 teaspoon salt

1/4 teaspoon white pepper (black pepper may be substituted)

1/2 cup shredded cheddar cheese

Instructions:

1. Spray a 10 or 12-inch non-stick skillet with a thin coating of cooking spray and heat over medium heat.
2. Beat eggs, water, salt and pepper together until light and fluffy.
3. When skillet is hot, pour the egg mixture in.
4. As the omelet starts to set, lift an edge of the omelet with a spatula and tilt the pan so that the liquid, unset portion of the omelet can run underneath and start to set. Repeat on the opposite side.
5. When the omelet is just about completely set (no liquid egg showing), sprinkle the cheese over half of the omelet. Fold the other half over the cheese half. Slide onto a plate, and serve.

Cajun Omelet Recipe

If you like omelets and Cajun food, well, we have combined them for you in this recipe. To complete the Cajun "Holy Trinity" (onions, celery and bell pepper) you can add 1/2 cup chopped celery if you want.

If you have a low tolerance for spicy food you can tone down the spiciness a touch by replacing the spicy sausage with a mild sausage and omit the jalapeno pepper. But you will miss a whole lot of flavor if you eliminate the "kick"

Prep time: 15 min
Cook time: 23 min
Total time: 38 min
Yield: 4 servings

Ingredients:

   8 eggs

   1/2 pound spicy sausage (Andouille or Italian)

   1/3 cup sliced mushrooms

   1/2 medium onion - diced

   1/2 medium bell pepper - diced

   1/4 cup green onions - chopped

   1 jalapeno pepper - chopped

   2 Tablespoon water or milk

   1 Tablespoon Dijon mustard

   1 pinch salt

   1 pinch cayenne pepper

   olive oil as needed

Instructions:

Fry and crumble the sausage in a large non-stick frying pan over medium heat (10 min). Transfer to a paper towel.

In the same frying pan, sauté the mushrooms, onions and peppers with a little olive oil until mushrooms are browned and peppers are tender (5 min).

Combine eggs, water (or milk), salt and pepper in a small bowl and beat with a fork or whisk until light and frothy.

Pour egg mixture over cooked vegetables (still in frying pan). Sprinkle crumbled sausage over egg mixture.

Don't touch until eggs begin to set (solid and firm around edges).

Carefully lift the edges of the omelet with a spatula and tilt pan to allow the uncooked eggs to run underneath.

Continue until omelet is set with no more liquid eggs in the center (about 5-8 min).

When the eggs are set, lift one side of omelet with a spatula and fold over.

French Omelet Recipe

To make a classic plain omelet into a French omelet we simply add extra egg yolks to a basic omelet resulting in a fluffy, rich breakfast treat.

Prep time: 10 min
Cook time: 7 min
Total time: 17 min
Yield: 1 omelet

Ingredients

    2 whole eggs

    2 egg yolks

    3 tablespoons water or milk

    1/4 teaspoon salt

    Dash of white pepper (black pepper may be substituted)

    1 tablespoon cooking oil (corn, canola or peanut)

Instructions:

1. Beat two whole eggs and the yolks of two additional eggs until thick and frothy.
2. Add salt, water (or milk), and a dash of pepper. Mix thoroughly, then strain into a bowl.
3. Heat cooking oil in a non-stick 10 inch skillet on medium-high heat.
4. When oil is hot, add the egg mixture.
5. Let the eggs sit undisturbed until they begin to set (dry and firm around the edges).
6. Reduce heat to medium. Using a spatula, lift one edge of the omelet and tilt the skillet so that the uncooked egg runs down on to the hot pan.
7. Continue this procedure until the omelet is completely set (no liquid egg showing).
8. Lift one side of the omelet with a spatula and fold over other half (or roll into a log shape).
9. Remove from skillet and serve hot.

Peach Omelet

Never heard of a peach omelet? Neither had we until a friend made this yummy treat and here is the recipe for you to try. It takes a little extra time to pre-cook the peaches but well worth it. We tried this recipe with fresh and canned peaches. Of course the fresh peaches had that "fresh" flavor but we were pleased with the canned peaches as well.

Prep time: 20 min
Cook time: 10 min
Total time: 30 min
Yield: 1 omelet

Ingredients:

    1 or 2 fresh ripe peaches

    2 tablespoons sugar

    Water as needed for cooking peaches

    2 eggs (use 3 eggs for hearty appetites)

    2 tablespoon water or milk

    1/2 teaspoon salt

    1/2 teaspoon white pepper (black pepper may be substituted)

    2 teaspoons of cooking oil (canola, corn or peanut)

Instructions:

1. Peel and slice peaches in quarters.
2. Place peaches in a saucepan with sugar and just enough water to keep them from burning.
3. Simmer slowly, stirring often and watching to prevent burning. When peaches are tender, set aside.
4. Combine eggs and water (or milk) and beat the eggs with a fork or whisk until light and frothy. Add salt and pepper and mix.
5. Heat the oil in a non-stick frying pan on medium-high heat.
6. Pour in the eggs.
7. Don't touch until eggs begin to set (solid and firm around edges). Reduce heat to medium.

8. Carefully lift the edges of the omelet with a spatula and tilt pan to allow the uncooked portion to run underneath.
9. Continue until omelet is set with no more liquid eggs in the center.
10. Spread the cooked peaches on one side of the omelet.
11. Use a spatula to fold other half of omelet over peaches. Serve immediately.

Ham Omelet Recipe

This classic ham omelet is ideal for breakfast, lunch, brunch or even as a night time snack. Many hams purchased today are already cooked but if yours is not, be sure to pre-cook before adding to the omelet.

Recipe makes a very quick and simple omelet for ham lovers. We added a little shredded cheese for extra flavor and the kids loved it.

Prep time: 10 min
Cook time: 8 min
Total time: 18 min
Yield: 2 servings

Ingredients:

- 3 eggs
- 1/4 teaspoon salt
- A dash of white pepper (black pepper may be substituted)
- 2 tablespoon water or milk
- 1-2 tablespoons cooking oil (canola, corn or peanut)
- 2 tablespoons of finely minced **cooked** ham
- 1 teaspoon minced parsley.

Instructions:

1. Combine the eggs, salt, pepper and water (or milk). Beat until light and frothy.
2. Place cooking oil in a non-stick pan on medium-high heat.
3. When the oil is hot, pour in the egg mixture.
4. Don't touch until eggs begin to set (solid and firm around edges). Reduce heat to medium.
5. Carefully lift the edges of the omelet with a spatula and tilt pan to allow the uncooked liquid eggs to run underneath.
6. Continue until omelet is set with no more liquid eggs in the center.
7. Spread cooked ham and parsley over one side of the omelet.
8. Lift the other side of the omelet with a spatula and fold over the ham.
9. Remove from heat and serve hot.

Spanish omelet

This recipe makes the very popular Spanish omelet. Be sure to use a good 12 inch non-stick skillet and to cook only one omelet at a time (unless you use more than one skillet).
Very straight forward recipe for the classic Spanish omelet. Even if you do not like spicy food we suggest you add at least a touch of jalapeno pepper. It adds so much to this omelet.

We like the idea of pre-cooking the vegetables so they are softened a little. There's nothing worse than having a fluffy, soft omelet with hard, raw vegetables inside.

Prep time: 15 min
Cook time: 8 min
Total time: 23 min
Yield: 1 large omelet

Ingredients:

- 2 tablespoons cooking oil (for vegetables)
- 2 tablespoons finely chopped green pepper
- 2 tablespoons finely chopped red pepper
- 2 tablespoons finely chopped onion
- 2 tablespoons coarsely chopped mushrooms
- 1 tablespoon finely chopped jalapeno pepper (omit if you don't like spicy)
- 3 eggs
- 2 tablespoons water or milk
- Salt and pepper to taste
- 2 tablespoons cooking oil (for omelet)
- 1/2 cup salsa, heated (any brand you like or homemade)

Instructions:

1. Heat 2 tablespoons cooking oil (canola, corn or peanut) in a saucepan.
2. Sauté peppers, onion and mushroom until tender (5-10 min). Set aside.

3. Combine eggs, water (or milk), salt and pepper in a small bowl and beat with a fork or whisk until light and frothy.
4. Heat 2 tablespoons cooking oil in a non-stick frying pan on medium-high heat.
5. Pour in the egg mixture.
6. Don't touch until eggs begin to set (solid and firm around edges). Reduce heat to medium.
7. Carefully lift the edges of the omelet with a spatula and tilt pan to allow the uncooked portion to run underneath.
8. Continue this procedure until omelet is set with no more liquid eggs in the center (about 2-5 min).
9. Spread the cooked vegetable mix over one side of the omelet.
10. Lift the other side of the omelet with a spatula and fold over the vegetable mix.
11. Transfer omelet to a serving dish.
12. Cover generously with heated salsa.

Section 6

Main Courses

Drunken (Beer Butt) Chicken

While this may be a novel way to cook chicken and you may think it is just for fun...this cooking method actually makes a very tender, juicy chicken.

This recipe can be a challenge. But only if you have a problem keeping the chicken standing upright. That is the challenge. The weight of the chicken tends to tip the can over. The easy solution is to use a "Beer Can Chicken Rack" made for this purpose. Amazon has several models ranging from about $5 to $24. Target and many other large stores also sell chicken racks.

But if you do not have a chicken rack you must improvise. I used 3 small pots, filled with water, positioned around the chicken to keep it propped up. On the outdoor grill you can use bricks or?

Prep time: 30 min
Cook time: 1 hour 30 min
Total time: 2 hours
Yield: 4 servings

Ingredients

- 1 (4 pound) Fryer Chicken
- 1/2 Can of Beer (16 oz can)
- 1 tbsp salt
- 1/2 tbsp ground black pepper
- 4 tbsp Cajun Seasoning
- Vegetable Oil
- Non-stick Cooking Spray
- Olive oil
- clove of garlic

Instructions

1. Open the can of beer and drink half of it.

2. Cut the clove of garlic in half and put it in the beer can. Add the salt and pepper and 2 tablespoons Cajun seasoning to the beer can. Spray the outside of the beer can with cooking spray so the chicken doesn't stick to it.
3. Rinse the chicken with cold water, and pat dry.
4. Place the chicken down on the beer can so it is standing on its rear and legs, with the can in the cavity.
5. Brush the chicken with olive oil, and rub 2 tbsp Cajun seasoning on the skin.
6. Place the chicken, with the can upright, in a roasting pan in a 350 degree F oven, or standing up on a low-to-medium-heat grill. Use a chicken rack or other method to keep chicken upright. If cooking on an outdoor grill, do not place chicken directly over the flame or coals. Place to one side of the heat.
7. Cook until internal temperature of chicken is 180 degrees F. Cooking time will vary, but about an hour and a half.

Turkey, Roasted

Roasted turkey is traditional for holidays but can be enjoyed any time of year. If using a frozen turkey be sure to buy your turkey far enough in advances to defrost in the refrigerator. Time required depends on the size of the turkey. Use the following as a guide:

* 8 to 12 pounds..........1 to 2 days
* 12 to 16 pounds.........2 to 3 days
* 16 to 20 pounds.........3 to 4 days
* 20 to 24 pounds.........4 to 5 days

Use the following as a guide for cooking times, you should always use a thermometer to verify the turkey is done.

weight 6-8 lb.   2 1/2 - 3 hr unstuffed   3 - 3 1/2 hr stuffed
weight 8-12 lb.   3 - 4 hr unstuffed   3 1/2 - 4 1/2 hr stuffed
weight 12-16 lb.   4 - 5 hr unstuffed   4 1/2 - 5 1/2 hr stuffed
weight 16-20 lb.   5 - 5 1/2 hr unstuffed   5 1/2 - 6 hr stuffed
weight 20-24 lb.   5 1/2 - 6 hr unstuffed   6 - 6 1/2 hr stuffed

Our only failure cooking turkey was when we tried to do too much with it. Keep it simple is the key to success. We strongly suggest buying a turkey with a pop-up thermometer already inserted. It takes all the guess work out of cooking the proper time. Also, we find that placing stuffing inside the turkey makes it difficult to control the moisture of the stuffing. So we cook the stuffing/dressing separate in its own pan.

Prep time: 30 min
Cook time: 5 hours (16 lb turkey)
Total time: 5 hours 30 min
Yield: 12 + servings

Ingredients

1 fresh or frozen turkey (size according to number of servings desired)

1/2 cup melted butter

cooking oil, as needed

salt, as needed

Instructions:

1. Remove turkey parts from the neck and tail cavities.
2. Wash the turkey and pat dry.
3. Rub melted butter over entire turkey.
4. Lightly salt the turkey inside and out.
5. Place turkey in a lightly oiled roasting pan, breast side up.
6. Lightly oil a piece of aluminum foil and make a tent over the top of the turkey breast with the oiled side facing the turkey.
7. Cook at 350 degrees F. until the "pop-up" thermometer (if provided) pops up or an instant read thermometer inserted deep in the thigh registers 180 degrees F. (do not allow thermometer to touch bone) (refer to cooking time chart above as a guide).
8. Remove the aluminum tent the last half hour of cooking to brown top of turkey.
9. After removing from oven, allow turkey to sit for 20 minutes before carving to seal in juices.

Southern Meatloaf Recipe

Served as a main course, this meat loaf only needs a salad and iced tea to be a complete meal.

Very good straight forward recipe like mom use to make.

Prep time: 20 min
Cook time: 1 hour
Total time: 1 hour 20 min
Yield: 6-8 servings

Ingredients:

    2 lbs ground beef

    1/2 cup breakfast sausage, crumbled

    2 eggs

    2 slices crumbled up bread

    1/2 to 1 cup crumbled up saltine crackers

    1/2 cup finely chopped onions

    1/3 cup finely chopped bell pepper

    1/3 cup finely chopped celery

    1 teaspoon salt

    1 teaspoon black pepper

    1 and 1/4 cups ketchup

    1/2 cup milk

    1 tablespoon Worcestershire Sauce

    1 tablespoon garlic powder

For the Glaze:

1. Mix 1 cup ketchup with 1/4 cup honey. Heat in microwave long enough to be able to mix well (about 20-30 seconds).

Instructions:

1. Combine all meatloaf ingredients (without glaze). Form into a loaf and place in a loaf pan.
2. When combining ingredients, add liquids slowly while watching the consistency. You want to end up with a moist, firm consistency that holds it's shape. It should not be crumbly-dry or runny-wet. This may require adding more or less liquid. If too wet, add crackers and bread. If too dry, add milk.
3. Make glaze
4. Covers top of meatloaf with 1/2 the glaze. Save remaining half of glaze.
5. Bake meatloaf in a 350 degree, pre-heated oven for 1 hour.
6. Heat remaining glaze and spread over individual slices of meatloaf at the table when served.

Stuffed Bell Peppers

These hearty stuffed bell peppers are nearly a complete meal in themselves. They combine meat, vegetables and cheese all in one dish. Add a side salad or Cole slaw and you have a filling, nourishing meal.

These stuffed peppers take a little time to make but are quite easy. Try to buy the largest bell peppers you can find when you shop. They are easier to work with and are more filling.

The sauce made from tomato juice and ketchup was a little thinner than we wanted but adding a touch more ketchup thickened it nicely.

Prep time: 30 min
Cook time: 1 hour
Total time: 1 hour 30 min
Yield: 6 servings

Ingredients:

    6 large bell peppers (green, orange, red or yellow)

    1 pound ground beef

    1 small onion, finely chopped

    2 garlic cloves, minced

    1 eight ounce can corn kernels, drained

    1/2 teaspoon salt

    1/2 teaspoon pepper

    1/2 teaspoon thyme

    2 cups tomato sauce mix (combine 1 cup tomato juice and 1 cup ketchup)

    3 cups cooked rice<

    shredded cheese, as needed

Instructions:

1. Preheat oven to 350 degrees F.
2. Make tomato sauce mix by combining 1 cup tomato juice and 1 cup ketchup. Set aside.
3. Cut off tops of bell peppers and remove the spines and seeds.
4. In a large pot, cover the bell peppers with water and boil for 3 minutes. Set bell peppers aside.
5. In a large skillet over medium-high heat, stir and cook ground beef until it is browned (about 10 min). Crumble beef into small pieces while stirring.
6. Add onions and garlic, stir and cook for an additional 2-3 minutes.
7. Remove skillet from heat. Stir in corn, salt, pepper, thyme, cooked rice and 1 cup tomato sauce mix. Mix all ingredients well, and then stuff mixture into peppers.
8. Place stuffed bell peppers upright in a shallow baking dish and cover with the remaining 1 cup tomato sauce mix. Cover with aluminum foil and bake stuffed bell peppers for 35 minutes.
9. Remove foil, add shredded cheese topping and bake an additional 5 to 10 minutes or until cheese melts.
10. Spoon any remaining tomato mix from the bottom of the baking dish over the stuffed bell peppers and serve hot.

Texas Style Chili Recipe

Most Texans say "Texas Chili" should never have beans in it. But...some people just like it with beans. So, we provide both methods here.

Everyone seems to have their version of Texas chili, and they all seem to be different. This one has a lot of ingredients but is easy to make.

Having tried both ways, we prefer with beans but certainly respect the opinions of those that opt without (it's pretty darn good too).

Prep time: 30 min
Cook time: 1 hour 15 min
Total time: 2 hours 15 min
Yield: 4 + servings

Ingredients:

* 2 tbs olive oil

* 5 cloves garlic, minced

* 2 onions, diced

* 1 and 1/2 lb lean ground beef

* 1/2 tsp salt

* 1 tsp ground black pepper

* 2 tbs red chili powder

* 4 Roma tomatoes (8 oz) blanched, peeled and diced (omit for Texas style)

* 1/2 cup tomato paste (omit for Texas style)

* 1/2 cup beef stock (for Texas style add 1 full cup)

* 1 cup dark beer

* 2 tbs cider vinegar

* 3/4 tsp cumin

* 2 tsp oregano

* 1/4 cup parsley

* 1 can 15 oz red kidney beans, drained (or 2 cups fresh cooked beans) (omit for Texas style)

* 4 oz cheese, for garnish

Instructions:

1. Heat olive oil in large pot. Add garlic and onions and cook over med-high heat for 5 min. or until onion is tender.
2. Add beef and cook for 7-8 min longer. Stir frequently, until beef is well browned.
3. Season with salt and pepper, stir in the chili powder and cook for 2 min more.
4. Add the tomatoes, tomato paste, beef stock, beer, vinegar, cumin, and oregano, and parsley, stirs well. Bring to a simmer, reduce heat to low and cook for 45 min.
5. Add beans and cook for 15 min longer, stirring occasionally. Ladle into serving bowls and top with shredded cheese.

Beefy Cornbread Pie Recipe

This slightly spicy beef and cornbread pie is a complete meal alone. All you need add is a big glass of sweet Southern ice tea.

If you like hamburger and cornbread with a Mexican touch, you will love this simple casserole. The tomato based filling is full of corn and hamburger that is spiced mildly and topped with crunchy cornbread. A very filling dish.

Prep time: 25 min
Cook time: 45 min
Total time: 1 hour 10 min
Yield: 6 servings

For The Filling

Ingredients:

* 1 pound lean ground beef

* 1 large onion, coarsely chopped

* 1 can tomato soup

* 2 cups water

* 1 teaspoon salt (or to taste)

* 1 teaspoon black pepper (or to taste)

* 3 tablespoons chili powder

* 1/2 cup green pepper, chopped

* 1 can whole kernel corn, drained

Instructions:

1. Brown beef and onion in skillet. Drain fat.
2. Add remaining ingredients, mix well. Simmer 15 minutes.
3. Transfer beef mixture to a 10 inch square baking dish and set aside.

For The Cornbread Topping

Ingredients:

- * 3/4 cup cornmeal
- * 1 tablespoon flour
- * 1/2 tablespoon salt
- * 1 1/2 tablespoons baking powder
- * 1 egg
- * 1/2 cup milk
- * 1 tablespoon oil

Instructions:

1. In a medium bowl, beat egg, oil and milk together until well blended.
2. Slowly add remaining dry ingredients and mix well.

Cooking Instructions

1. Pre heat oven to 350 degrees F.
2. Pour cornbread topping mix over top of beef mix in baking dish.
3. Bake in pre heated oven for 20-25 minutes or until top of cornbread has browned.
4. Serve steaming hot.

Southern Fried Chicken

This classic Southern favorite is universally popular but seldom duplicated outside Southern kitchens. Authentic Southern Fried Chicken is not difficult to make but it helps to know the techniques presented here.

If I had to choose one dish that best represents real Southern cuisine I would select either cornbread or this Southern Fried Chicken. The flavor and tenderness of the meat with its unique crunchy crust just isn't duplicated in any other dish.

Best of all, it is not difficult to make.

Prep time: 20 min
Cook time: 24 min
Total time: 44 min
Yield: 4 servings

Ingredients:

* Fresh, cut-up chicken

* 2 cups flour

* 2 tablespoons salt

* 1/2 tablespoon black pepper

* 1 whole egg

* 3/4 cup buttermilk

* Cooking oil as required (see directions)

Instructions:

1. Using a large frying pan (cast iron works best), fill with enough cooking oil to cover at least half the thickness of the chicken (about 2-3 inches oil depth in the pan).
2. Place frying pan on medium-high heat
3. In a medium size mixing bowl, combine egg and buttermilk, mix well
4. On a large plate, combine flour, salt and pepper, mix well
5. Wash chicken parts, pat dry.
6. Dip each chicken part in the egg-milk wash, then roll in the flour mix to coat on all sides

7. Place coated chicken parts on a cake cooling rack and allow to dry for 3-5 minutes.
8. Place chicken parts back in the egg wash again and then in the flour mix again to coat a second time.
9. Allow chicken to dry on the cooling rack another 3-5 minutes.
10. Check oil temperature in the frying pan (place handle of wooden spoon in oil. You should get bubbles rising around the handle immediately.)
11. Place chicken parts in frying pan (should not be touching each other)
12. Fry chicken on first side 2 minutes then turn to other side
13. REDUCE HEAT TO MEDIUM
14. Continue to fry on each side until golden brown (total cook time about 12 min each side)

Tips

* Do not use skinless chicken. Although the skin adds fat it also provides the crispy crust essential for Southern fried chicken. You will not get a good crust without the skin. Also, the double dip (step 7) is important to achieve that special crust.

* Use a cast iron skillet if possible.

* Use an oil that handles high heat. We recommend refined peanut, canola or safflower oil. (Must be "Refined").

* Be sure the skillet and oil are hot before placing chicken in the pan. The first few minutes of frying is what seals in the flavor and gives a good crust.

* Use thongs to turn chicken. Do not use a fork or other utensil that will puncture the chicken skin.

* After removing cooked chicken from skillet, do not cover chicken. Covering will affect the crispness of the crust. If you need to keep chicken warm to serve later, put it in an oven set on low.

* To tenderize chicken, cover with buttermilk in a deep bowl and refrigerate overnight before cooking.

Buttermilk Baked Chicken

This simple buttermilk baked chicken recipe has a little spicy kick with a crunchy crust. It is easy to make even for the inexperienced cook.

The 2 teaspoons of hot sauce in this recipe will make a medium spiciness. Add more or less sauce according to your taste for spicy food. Use 1 teaspoon sauce if you just barely want to taste the spice and 3 (or more) teaspoons for a fiery chicken.

Prep time: 25 min
Cook time: 35 min
Total time: 1 hour plus 1 hour chill
Yield: 4 servings

Ingredients:

* 1 1/2 lbs. boneless, skinless chicken
* 1/2 cup low-fat buttermilk
* 2 teaspoons hot pepper sauce (Tabasco)
* 1/2 teaspoon salt
* 1 1/2 cups corn flakes, finely crushed
* 1/3 cup unflavored dry bread crumbs
* cooking spray (as needed)

Instructions:

1. Combine buttermilk, hot sauce and salt in a large zip lock plastic bag. Add chicken, seal and toss to coat chicken well. Chill in refrigerator for one hour.
2. Heat oven to 425 degrees F.
3. In another large plastic bag, combine cornflakes and bread crumbs.
4. Add chicken pieces, one at a time, and toss to coat with bread crumb mixture.
5. Line a baking sheet with foil and spray lightly with cooking spray
6. Arrange chicken on the baking sheet and coat chicken lightly with cooking spray.
7. Bake 30-35 minutes, turning after 20 minutes.

Chicken with Potatoes and Peppers

This complete meal in one dish is easy to make. Be sure to serve with French or Italian bread.

Very straight forward recipe for a chicken casserole. No special skill needed here. The rosemary, thyme and garlic add a nice flavor to the chicken along with the onions and peppers.

Prep time: 20 min
Cook time: 1 hour
Total time: 1 hour 20 min
Yield: 4 servings

Ingredients:

* 1/4 cup Italian Dressing

* 1 whole chicken, cut into serving pieces

* 1 can (28 oz) peeled tomatoes with juice, chopped

* 1 pound potatoes, cut into chunks

* 2 medium onions, cut into quarters

* 2 medium peppers (red, green or yellow) cut into strips

* 1 tablespoon fresh or dried rosemary

* 1 teaspoon fresh or dried thyme

* 1 teaspoon garlic powder

* 1 teaspoon salt

* 1/4 teaspoon ground black pepper

Instructions:

1. Preheat oven to 375 degrees F.
2. In a large skillet, heat Italian Dressing and brown chicken over medium high heat. Set aside.
3. In a 13x19 inch baking pan, combine remaining ingredients, add chicken and turn to coat all sides.
4. Bake, uncovered, stirring occasionally, 50 minutes or until chicken is done and vegetables are tender.

Crockpot Chicken and Sweet Potato Stew

This hearty stew will warm your tummy on those cold winter days. Actually, it's good any time at all. Just place the ingredients in a crock pot in the morning and forget it until dinner time. Serves 6.

Ingredients:

    6 bone-in chicken thighs, skin removed

    2 pounds sweet potatoes, peeled and cut into spears

    1/2 pound white button mushrooms, thinly sliced

    6 large shallots, peeled and halved

    4 cloves garlic, peeled

    1 cup dry white wine

    1/2 teaspoon dried rosemary, crushed

    1 teaspoon salt

    1/2 teaspoon black pepper

    1 teaspoon lemon juice

    1 1/2 tablespoons white wine vinegar (optional)

Instructions:

1. Place all ingredients **except white wine vinegar** in a 6 quart or larger crockpot (slow cooker) and stir well.
2. Place the lid on the crockpot and cook on low until potatoes are tender (about 5 hours).
3. Remove bones from chicken, stir in vinegar if desired and serve steaming hot.

Jalapeno Lime Chicken

A little spicy, a little lime tang and a crunchy crust, this delightful chicken will have everyone asking for more. The recipe may be cooked in the oven or on the outdoor grill.

A very different treatment for roasted or grilled chicken. The marinade imparts a sweet, mildly spicy flavor which we liked. You can grill or roast the chicken but we prefer the oven roasted version.
Difficulty: Easy

Prep time: 15 min
Cook time: 30 min
Total time: 45 min plus 2 hours marinade
Yield: 6 servings

Ingredients:

1/2 cup lime juice

2 teaspoons grated lime peel

2/3 cup chopped onion

1 cup orange juice (frozen O.K.)

1/2 cup honey

1 or 2 jalapeno peppers, seeded and diced (leave seeds in for more spicy)

2 teaspoons ground cumin

2 cloves garlic, minced

1/2 teaspoon salt

6 skinless, boneless chicken breast

Instructions:

1. Make the basting mix by combine all the ingredients except the chicken in a bowl.
2. Pour half of the mix in a 1 gallon size freezer bag, then place the chicken in the bag. Seal and place in the refrigerator for 2 hours.
3. Cover the remainder of the basting mix and place in refrigerator.
4. If using a grill: place the chicken on the grill on medium heat. Cook both sides until golden brown, basting often with the reserved marinade (about 6 minutes per side). Do not use the marinade that was in the plastic bag with the chicken, discard it.
5. If cooking in the oven: place chicken in a roasting pan lightly sprayed with non-stick spray.
6. Cook in pre-heated 350 degree F. oven for 30 minutes, basting often, or until chicken is cooked through.

Corned Ham

If you are unfamiliar with corned ham, you may be surprised to know that corn has nothing to do with it. Corning means curing with salt.

This is a simple recipe for Corned Ham, a Southern holiday favorite. Please note that you must use a fresh ham, not a pre-cooked ham, which may be difficult to find. Most markets today sell ready to eat (pre-cooked) hams, so you might have to shop around.

The recipe states to use a non-reactive pan to refrigerate the ham. Reactive pans are aluminum, cast iron, copper and a few others. Non-reactive pans are made of clay, enamel, glass, plastic, or stainless steel. Reactive means that the metal reacts with acidic foods such as vinegar or tomatoes and imparts an off-flavor to the food. We suggest using a stainless steel pan.

Prep time: 30 min
Cook time: 6 hours
Total time: 6 hours 30 min plus 11 days refrigeration
Yield: 20 plus servings

Ingredients:

1 (16- to 20-pound) fresh ham (not pre-cooked)

2 pounds kosher salt

Instructions:

1. Rinse and dry the ham.
2. There are three places where the bones protrude: at each end and on one side near the hip end. Use a sharp knife to make incisions of about 3 inches deep along all three. Fill these incisions with salt. Then rub the outside of the ham all over with more salt. Just cover the ham lightly; you don't want a paste of salt.
3. Place the ham in a non-reactive pan, cover with plastic wrap and then aluminum foil and refrigerate. Let it cure for 11 days, turning the ham from time to time, rubbing it with salt again and pouring off any juice that the ham has produced.
4. The day before you plan to cook the ham, wash it under cold running water. Be sure to flush out the salt pockets. Then submerge under clean cold water and refrigerate overnight.
5. Preheat the oven to 325 degrees. Put the ham on a rack in a covered roasting pan and bake for 20 minutes a pound. The internal temperature should reach 150 degrees for safety reasons. The meat should be ready to fall off the bone.
6. About 30 minutes before the ham is done, uncover and increase the temperature to 375 degrees so the ham will brown.
7. Store in the refrigerator

Cajun Soup

This soup with a Cajun touch has everything but the kitchens sink in it. A great way to clean out the fridge. And...It's pretty good too.

As long as you start with onion, celery and bell pepper you can add whatever you want in this soup. Don't worry about following the ingredients list precisely. Just add whatever strikes your fancy, within reason. Pretty hard to fail with this "clean out the fridge soup if you taste as you go.

Prep time: 25 min
Cook time: 30 min
Total time: 55 min
Yield: 6 servings

Ingredients:

* 3 cups water

* 1 (10 oz) can diced tomatoes with chili's

* 1 (14.5 oz.) can diced tomatoes

* 1 (26 oz.) can spaghetti sauce (garlic and onion works good)

* 2 tomatillo (diced)

* 1 tablespoon basil

* 1 tablespoon oregano

* 1 tablespoon Old Bay Seasoning

* 1 medium onion, diced

* 1 medium bell pepper, diced

* 2 stalks celery, diced

* 3 Hot Sausages, cut into bite size chunks

* 4 cloves garlic, minced

* 1 teaspoon seasoning salt

* 3 dried bay leaves

* 1/2 cup ketchup

* 2 tablespoons honey

* 1/2 can Pepsi (or any cola)

* 1 teaspoon unsweetened cocoa

* Salt and pepper to taste

Instructions

1. Put everything in a large soup pot and bring to a boil. Reduce heat and simmer until all vegetables are tender (about 10 min), then simmer another 20 minutes. When you think it is done, taste, and then taste again. Add any additional ingredients to suit your taste.

Tips:

1. If too watery, add ketchup and/or tomato sauce (or tomato paste).
2. If too thick, add water
3. If bland, add salt and more spices.
4. Freeze left over's for up to 6 months

Cioppino - San Francisco Style

If you like seafood...if you like Italian...and if you have never had cioppino...you are in for a treat. You will love this delectable dish.

I cannot say enough about this dish. This may be my all-time favorite recipe. It has a lot of ingredients and takes a while to make but it is worth the effort. It would almost be sinful to serve cioppino without San Francisco crusty, sourdough bread to soak up the magical sauce.

Prep time: 30 min
Cook time: 1 hour
Total time: 1 hour 30 min
Yield: 6-10 servings

Ingredients:

* 1/2 cup butter (or olive oil)

* 1 large onion, chopped

* 4 cloves garlic, minced or pressed

* 1 large green bell pepper, stemmed, seeded and chopped

* 1 can (15 ounces) tomato sauce

* 1 can (28 ounces) diced tomatoes with juice

* 1 cup dry red or white wine

* 1 tablespoon sugar

* 2 bay leaves

* 1/3 cup dry Italian seasoning

* salt and black pepper to taste

* 12 clams in shell, suitable for steaming, scrubbed (optional)

* 1 pound large scallops

* 1 pound large shrimp, shelled and deveined

* 2 cooked large Dungeness crab (about 2 pounds each), cleaned and cracked

* 1 pound any firm white fish such as Snapper, Grouper, Orange roughy or Mahi-Mahi (optional)

Instructions:

1. In 6-8 quart soup pot, over medium heat, melt the butter. Add onion, garlic and bell pepper. Cook, stirring often, until onion is soft.
2. Stir in tomato sauce, chopped tomatoes and their liquid, wine, sugar, bay leaf and Italian seasoning. Cover and simmer on low heat until slightly thickened, about 30-40 minutes.
3. Taste and add salt and pepper as needed.
4. Add clams, shrimp, crab and any other seafood you have chosen (see note #2 below concerning shrimp). Cover and simmer gently until clams pop open and shrimp turns pink, about 20 minutes.
5. Remove bay leaves and discard.
6. Serve in soup bowls with generous portions of sourdough bread on the side.

Notes: This dish requires you to taste and adjust as necessary. There should be a good quantity of soupy liquid in the cioppino. If too dry, add water or wine, but if the water/wine thins the cioppino too much, add more tomato sauce and seasoning. The cioppino should be robust and flavorful with a strong oregano presence. If too bland, add salt and Italian seasoning. Taste, taste, taste!

Note #2: For a party you may need to keep the cioppino hot for long periods of time. Be aware that the shrimp will get rubbery and tasteless when over cooked. Therefore, you should reserve some fresh shrimp and add more periodically. You might even want to discard any over cooked shrimp from the pot.

Note #3: If you need to keep the cioppino hot for an extended period, keep it at a slow simmer. Do not allow to continue at a full boil.

Note #4: For larger quantities just continue doubling the recipe.

Note #5: You may freeze left over Cioppino for up to six months.

Crawfish Feast

Also known as crayfish and crawdad this little crustacean may be the po' man's lobster. Crawfish can be found in many streams of North America but about 90 per cent of commercial crawfish comes from Louisiana

If you buy crawfish from the store they should be cleaned and ready to cook. If you have live crawfish they should have the sand vein removed. Grasp behind pincers and turn stomach side up. The tail has 3 sections; twist the center section, snapping the shell, then gently pull out the sand vein and discard.

We serve our crawfish hot with pots of melted butter and mayonnaise. You should plan on about 1 pound of crawfish per person.

Prep time: 20 min
Cook time: 25 min
Total time: 45 min
Yield: 4 servings

Ingredients:

* 2 cups dry white wine

* 2 medium sized onions, sliced

* 2 medium sized carrots, sliced

* 1 lemon, sliced

* 8-10 whole black peppercorns

* 2 teaspoons salt

* 2 bay leaves

* melted butter and mayonnaise for dip, as needed

* 4 pounds crawfish (allow 1 lb. per serving)

Instructions:

1. Fill a 6-8 quart soup pot 2/3 full of water. Add wine, onion, carrots, lemon, peppercorns, salt and bay leaves.
2. Cover and bring to a boil, reduce heat and simmer 15 minutes.
3. Uncover and bring to a vigorous boil over high heat.
4. Drop up to 30 crawfish into the pan at once, pushing them to the bottom (if they are live).
5. Cook until crawfish turn a bright red (about 5-8 minutes) and the meat in tail is opaque (break one off and test).
6. Remove with a slotted spoon and repeat until all crawfish are cooked. Add water as needed and maintain a boil.
7. Serve hot with melted butter.

Eggplant Casserole

Tomatoes and cheese compliment this eggplant dish with loads of flavor. If you think eggplant is tasteless you should give this recipe a try. Instructions are provided to prepare with or without meat.

Prep time: 20 min
Cook time: 1 hour
Total time: 1 hour 20 min
Yield: 8 servings

Ingredients:

* 1 large eggplant, peeled and sliced

* 3 tablespoons bacon grease or butter, divided

* 1 medium onion, chopped

* 1 cup diced tomatoes

* 2 teaspoons salt

* black pepper to taste

* 1 tablespoon powdered garlic

* 1 cup Cheddar cheese, grated

* 1 cup bread crumbs, divided

* 1/2 teaspoon baking powder

Instructions:

For Casserole without Meat

1. Boil eggplant in water until tender, about 15 to 20 minutes; drain and mash.
2. Put 2 tablespoons of bacon grease or butter into a large skillet; add chopped onion and cook until tender
3. Add tomatoes, salt, garlic and pepper; simmer for 5 minutes.
4. In a large bowl, combine tomato mixture with eggplant, cheese, 3/4 cup bread crumbs. Add baking powder and mix well.

5. Spoon mixture into greased casserole dish. Sprinkle with remaining tablespoon of bacon grease or butter and remaining bread crumbs.
6. Optional - If you have eggplant left over; cover the top of the casserole with eggplant slices.
7. Bake in pre-heated 325 degree oven for 25 to 30 minutes.

For Casserole with Meat

1. Prior to step 2 above, brown 1/2 lb. ground beef in separate skillet. Pour off grease. Add cooked meat in step 3 above.

Fried Pork Chops

The most popular meat dish in the South is probably fried chicken or perhaps BBQ, but a close second has got to be fried pork chops. We suggest using Panko bread crumbs made by Kikkoman for the breading mix. It is available in the baking/cake or oriental section of most supermarkets.

We used boneless thin cut chops for this dish and they were so tender. This recipe is very simple, no special skills required here.

We served with black eyed peas and collard greens with fresh radish and green onions for a real Southern meal.

Prep time: 20 min
Cook time: 10 min
Total time: 30 min
Yield: 4 servings

Ingredients:

- 4 thick cut or 8 thin cut Pork Chops (Allow one large or two small chops per person)
- Cooking oil (enough to submerge half the thickness of chops in oil)
- 1 egg
- 1 cup milk
- 2 cups cornmeal
- 1/2 cup dried bread crumbs ("Panko")
- 1/2 teaspoon salt
- 1/2 teaspoon black pepper

Instructions:

1. In a medium mixing bowl, combine egg and milk. Beat lightly to mix well.
2. Combine cornmeal, bread crumbs, salt and pepper on a flat plate.
3. Heat cooking oil in large frying pan over medium heat
4. While oil heats, dip chops in egg/milk bath, drain excess then dredge in the cornmeal mix, turning over several times to coat both sides.
5. Place breaded chops in hot oil and fry until golden brown on both sides (about 10 minutes).

Hog's Breath Chili

It's called Hog's Breath, but actually it smells pretty good. We call it chili with an attitude.

This is one of the best chili recipes we have tried. We like the fact that it is very forgiving, in that you can substitute most of the ingredients you do not have on hand (except for the spices) and it still comes out good.

Some chili purest insist that real chili should not contain beans but we like this recipe with beans. Your choice.

Prep time: 20 min
Cook time: 30 min
Total time: 50 min
Yield: 6 + servings

Ingredients:

1 onion, diced

2 tbsp vegetable oil

3/4 pound lean ground beef

1 (14.5 oz.) can re-fried beans

1/2 cup cooked pinto beans (optional)

1 (14.5 oz.) can diced tomatoes (or 1 1/2 cups fresh diced tomatoes)

1 (10 oz.) can enchilada sauce

1/2 cup tomato sauce

2 tbsp cumin

2 tbsp honey or maple syrup (you can substitute plain sugar)

1 tbsp cider vinegar

1 tbsp garlic powder (or 2 cloves fresh, minced)

3 tbsp chili powder

2 to 4 jalapeno peppers, minced (adjust as needed to suit your taste for spiciness)

salt and black pepper to taste

2-3 cups water, as needed

Instructions:

1. Place 2 tbsp of vegetable oil in a large soup pot over medium heat.
2. Add ground beef and cook until browned. Remove beef and set aside.
3. Add diced onion to pot and cook until onion is tender but not browned.
4. Replace browned beef to pot. Add 2 cups water and all remaining ingredients and bring to a boil. Stir well to incorporate re-fried beans completely.
5. Reduce heat and cook until all ingredients are tender and combined (about 20 minutes)
6. Add salt and black pepper to taste.
7. The chili should be slightly thick at this point. If too thin, continue cooking to reduce liquid. If too thick, add water, mix well and cook another 5 minutes.
8. Serve hot with your favorite toppings. Shredded cheese and diced onions are traditional toppings.

Macaroni and Cheese

Pretty straight forward recipe for this all-time kid's favorite. Nothing fancy or difficult here, just good mac and cheese..

To kick it up a notch, try adding chopped ham, a teaspoon garlic powder and 1/2 teaspoon honey in step 6.

Prep time: 20 min
Cook time: 20 min
Total time: 40 min
Yield: 6-8 servings

Ingredients:

1 (8 oz) box elbow macaroni

3 tablespoons butter

2 tablespoons flour

1/2 cup milk

salt and black pepper to taste

1 cup grated cheddar cheese

grated Parmesan cheese as needed (optional)

Instructions:

1. Cook one box (8 oz.) elbow macaroni according to box instructions. Set aside.
2. In a saucepan, melt 3 tablespoons butter over medium heat.
3. Add 2 tablespoons flour and stir until dissolved and all lumps removed.
4. Pour in 1/2 cup milk and cook until thickened.
5. Season with salt and pepper. Add 1 cup grated cheese and stir until melted.
6. Add **cooked** macaroni and stir.
7. Pour mixture into 2 qt. casserole dish. Bake for 20 minutes at 350 degrees.
8. Remove from oven and sprinkle top with grated Parmesan cheese (optional)

Hamburger Steak

This is an old favorite that can be served as a hamburger snack on a bun or as an entire meal with brown gravy and vegetables on the side. The kids love these yummy burgers.

Prep time: 20 min
Cook time: 18 min
Total time: 38 min
Yield: 4 servings

Ingredients

1 cup bread crumbs

1 pound ground round

1 egg, lightly beaten

2 garlic cloves, minced

1/2 teaspoon salt

1/2 teaspoon black pepper

1 tablespoon vegetable oil

1 cup fresh mushrooms, sliced

1 medium sweet onion, thinly sliced

A-1 steak sauce (optional)

package brown gravy mix prepared per package instructions (optional)

Directions

1. Place bread crumbs in a mixing bowl; add ground round, beaten egg, garlic, salt and pepper. Gently combine until blended, using your hands. Shape mixture into 4 patties.
2. Cook patties in hot oil in a large skillet over medium-high heat on each side until browned (about 2 minutes). Remove patties from skillet. Add mushrooms and onion to skillet, and sauté until tender (about 5-6 minutes).
3. Return patties to skillet, reduce heat to low and cook another 8-10 minutes or until cooked through.
4. If using gravy: In a separate pan, prepare packaged brown gravy according to package instructions. In step 3 above, add the gravy with the patties and continue with step 3 instructions.
5. Serve topped with A-1 steak sauce.

Marinated Steak

We all like those tender, juicy, expensive steaks but who can afford them regularly? Here's how to buy cheaper cuts and still have them as tender as expensive steaks.

The solution is a simple technique that has been around for years...marinade!

Marinating meat not only tenderizes it, it also adds a lot of flavor. We had best results by marinating overnight in the refrigerator as the recipe suggest. We cooked to medium well and the steaks were very tender and juicy despite being a cheap cut of meat.
Difficulty: Medium

Prep time: 20 min
Cook time: 10 min
Total time: 30 min plus marinade time 2 + hours
Yield: 2 8oz. servings

Ingredients:

1 pound of flank, London Broil or chuck steak

1/2 cup cooking sherry

1/2 cup soy sauce

2 tablespoons vegetable oil

1 large clove garlic, minced

1/4 teaspoon ground ginger

Instructions:

1. Score steak in a crisscross pattern on both sides.
2. Combine remaining ingredients in a shallow dish and mix well. Pour mix into a sealable plastic bag.
3. Place steak in the bag with marinade mix and toss to cover steak on all sides with marinade.
4. Place in the refrigerator for a minimum of 2 hours, turning occasionally (overnight is better).
5. Grill or broil steak to your choice of rare, medium or well done. Cooking time will vary by the thickness of the steak but, in general, cook about 5 minutes per side for medium. Internal temperature should register 140 to 150 degrees F. on a meat thermometer.

Ketchup Glazed Meat Loaf

This yummy, easy meat loaf is made in eight individual servings that may be frozen or refrigerated, reheated and served as needed.

We like the idea of individual servings that may be frozen and re-heated as needed. Ideal for single people living alone that need small portions. And this is good tasting meatloaf.

Prep time: 20 min
Cook time: 20 min
Total time: 40 min
Yield: 8 servings

Ingredients:

2 eggs

1 cup ketchup, divided (use hot and spicy ketchup to kick it up a notch)

1 cup fine dry bread crumbs

1/2 envelope onion soup mix (about 1 ounce)

1/4 teaspoon ground black pepper

1 tablespoon minced garlic (about 6 cloves)

2 pounds lean ground beef

Instructions:

1. Preheat oven to 350 degrees F.
2. In a large bowl, beat eggs, whisk in 1/2 cup ketchup. Stir in bread crumbs, soup mix, pepper and garlic. Add meat and mix well.
3. Form mixture into eight 4-inch loaves. Arrange loaves in a foil-lined 15x10x1-inch baking pan.
4. Bake about 20 minutes or as needed until internal temperature reaches 160 degrees F.
5. Remove from oven and let stand 10 minutes.
6. Spoon remaining 1/2 cup ketchup over meat loaves.
7. To Store: Wrap individual loaves in foil and freeze for up to 3 months. To serve: thaw overnight in refrigerator. Unwrap, place in a shallow baking pan and reheat in a 350 degrees F. oven for 15 minutes. Or you may store in a covered container in the refrigerator for up to 3 days.

Po Man's Ribs

This simple and economical recipe makes tender, flavorful ribs using few ingredients and practically no effort. Put 'em on the stove and take a 2 hour nap. Dinner will be ready when you awake.

You can use this simple recipe for beef, pork or even chicken but we like pork ribs the best. The meat almost falls off the bone when cooked this simple way.

If you want to make a complete meal in one step, add whole, peeled potatoes and carrots the last half hour of cooking. Just check that they and the ribs are tender before removing from the stove.

Prep time: 10 min
Cook time: 2 hours 30 min
Total time: 2 hours 40 min
Yield: 4 servings

Ingredients:

- 2 tablespoon cooking oil
- 2 lbs. short ribs
- 1/2 cup water
- 1 (10 oz) can onion soup
- 1 (4 oz) can mushrooms
- 1 cup beef bullion
- 1/2 tsp. salt
- 1 tablespoon Tabasco Sauce

Instructions:

1. Place cooking oil in large soup pot (cast iron if available) over medium heat.
2. Add ribs and brown on both sides.
3. Add all remaining ingredients and simmer 2 1/2 hours or until ribs are falling off the bone tender.
4. Check ribs periodically to make sure all the liquid does not boil off. Add water or bullion if needed.

Tenderizing Grilled Pork Chops

This is simply an old technique to tenderize pork chops before grilling. Recommended especially for cheaper cuts of pork or beef.

You can use any pork chops for this recipe but we like the boneless, center cut. They are smaller than regular chops so allow two per person if you use them. The salt bath does tenderize the chops and while we like tender meat we found this process unnecessary for quality chops. Recommended for cheaper cuts of meat.

Prep time: 10 min
Cook time: 10 min
Total time: 20 min plus 2 hour salt soak
Yield: 1 pork chop per serving

Ingredients:

1 large center cut pork chop per person

1/2 cup sea salt (or kosher)

1 qt. water

pepper, to taste

barbecue sauce, buy or make your own

Instructions:

1. Stir sea salt into 1 qt. water. Place chops in a large bowl and completely cover with the salt water. Place in refrigerator for 2 hours.
2. Remove pork chops from salt water, pepper both sides of chops and brush barbecue sauce on both sides.
3. Grill on hot grill 5 minutes on each side. Cut into one pork chop and check if done to your taste. Continue cooking if necessary.

Slow Cook Orange Sesame Ribs

Put these ribs in the crock pot in the morning and come home to a dinner of "falling off the bone" tender ribs.

Like most slow cooker recipes these ribs take hours to cook but the tenderness of the ribs is worth the wait. This is a delightful Oriental treatment of an old Southern favorite.

Prep time: 20 min
Cook time: 8 hours
Total time: 8 hours 20 min
Yield: 4 servings

Ingredients:

    2-3 pounds boneless country-style pork ribs

    non-stick cooking spray (as needed)

    1 ten oz. jar orange marmalade

    one 7 oz. jar hoisin sauce (available in the oriental section of markets)

    3 cloves garlic, minced

    1 teaspoon toasted sesame oil (also in oriental section)

Instructions:

1. Trim fat from ribs.
2. Lightly spray a large skillet with non-stick spray and heat over medium heat. Brown ribs on all sides in skillet. Pour off fat.
3. Place ribs in a 3 1/2 or 4 quart slow cooker (crock pot).
4. In a medium bowl, stir together marmalade, hoisin sauce, and garlic and sesame oil.
5. Pour sauce mixture over ribs in the slow cooker. Stir to coat ribs on all sides with sauce.
6. Cover and cook on low heat setting for 8 hours (or cook on high setting for 4-5 hours). Ribs are done when cooked through and super tender.
7. Transfer ribs to a serving platter. Skim any fat from surface of sauce and serve sauce over ribs and on the side for those that want to add more.

Shrimp, Baked, Spicy

This Cajun, spicy, baked shrimp recipe is quick and easy to make. Excellent as an appetizer but can be a main dish using large or jumbo shrimp.

There are about 30-35 medium size shrimp in a pound so adjust the number of shrimp for the number of people you are serving. In general, you should plan on about 1/3 pound per person.

Be aware that shrimp is highly perishable and should not be used if the aroma of ammonia is present. In general, it is safer to buy frozen shrimp and keep it frozen. Defrost in the bottom of the refrigerator prior to cooking.

This recipe is adjustable to the number of servings you require. We found it simple to adjust for 12 people. You can remove the shells of the shrimp before cooking or cook with the shells intact. We prefer to cook with shells and remove them at the table because there is fewer tendencies to overcook.

Over cooked shrimp is tough and tasteless so we cook just until the shrimp turn pink and curl into a "C" shape. If they curl beyond a "C" shape, they are over cooked.

Prep time: 15 min
Cook time: 12 min
Total time: 27 min
Yield: 6 servings

Ingredients:

   2 lb fresh shrimp, with tails intact (adjust as needed for number of servings)

   olive oil, as needed

   1/4 cup Worcestershire sauce, or as needed

   2 teaspoons sea salt, or as needed (regular salt may be substituted)

   pinch of powdered cayenne pepper, to taste

   juice of one medium lime

Instructions:

1. Preheat oven to 350 degrees F.
2. Place shrimp in an oven safe baking dish
3. Cover shrimp generously with Worcestershire sauce. Adjust amount according to how much shrimp you are cooking. Mix well to cover all sides of shrimp.
4. Add olive oil (about 3 or 4 tablespoons) and mix well.
5. Add lime juice and mix well.
6. Sprinkle salt and cayenne pepper over top of shrimp. Be careful with the cayenne pepper, it is very hot.
7. Bake in preheated oven about 10-12 minutes

Tamale Pie

While we focus on Southern recipes here, you will note that this recipe is not a traditional Southern dish. But it is so good we just had to include it. .

This tamale pie is made in two stages: the filling and the crust. It looks like a little more work than it really is.

The corn kernels and enchilada sauce really give this a Mexican touch. If you are fond of spicy food load up on the jalapeno peppers for a garnish.

Prep time: 20 min
Cook time: 52 min
Total time: 1 hour12 min
Yield: 8 or more servings

For the Filling:

Ingredients:

- one and one half pounds ground beef
- 1 cup whole kernel corn
- 1/2 cup chopped onions
- 1/2 cup chopped bell pepper
- 1 tsp chili powder
- 1 tsp salt
- 2 cloves garlic (minced)
- 2 cups (16 oz can) enchilada sauce
- 1 tsp sugar

Instructions:

1. Cook beef until browned (about 10 min), adding onion, bell pepper and garlic the last 1 minute of cooking. Drain off oil.
2. Stir in enchilada sauce, corn and salt. Cook another 5 min or just until sauce begins to boil. Remove from heat. Set aside.

For the Crust

Ingredients:

2 1/2 cups cornmeal (you may want to try the "blue" cornmeal)

2 cups water

12 oz (can) evaporated milk

1/2 cup shredded cheddar cheese

1 tsp salt

1/3 cup sliced jalapeno peppers (optional)

Instructions:

1. Combine corn meal, water, milk and salt in saucepan and cook over medium heat until mixture thickens (about 5-7 minutes) Stir constantly and watch carefully. You should watch for a paste-like consistency.
2. Set aside 2 cups of the crust mixture and spread the remainder on the bottom and up sides of a well-greased skillet (or oven proof casserole dish).

Cooking Instructions:

1. Preheat oven to 425 degrees.
2. Place skillet (with bottom crust) in preheated oven for 10 minutes, Remove and allow to cool 5 minutes.
3. Place beef filling mix into the skillet on top of the bottom crust. Spread the remainder of the crust mix on top of the beef filling.
4. Bake for 15 to 20 minutes. Center of crust should be cooked and the top golden brown. If not, continue cooking and watch closely for brown crust. Sprinkle shredded cheese on top of crust the last 5 or 10 minutes to melt.
5. Garnish top with sliced jalapeno, if desired, and serve hot.

Fish Fry - Fried Catfish

Southerners love a good fish fry and the usual fish of choice is catfish. However, this recipes works for any firm fish. Of course, Cole slaw and hushpuppies are an absolute "must" to accompany a Southern fish fry.
This simple and traditional method of Southern frying always produces a flavorful, crunchy crust. The catfish crust is a little spicy and certainly crunchy, while the fish meat is tender and well cooked.

Prep time: 20 min
Cook time: 15 min
Total time: 35 min
Yield: 4 servings

Ingredients:

8 Catfish fillets (2 or 3 medium size pieces per person) any firm fish may be used.

1 cup White Corn Meal (or yellow)

1/3 cup all-purpose flour

2 teaspoons salt

1 teaspoon black pepper

1/2 teaspoon cayenne pepper

1/4 teaspoon garlic powder

2 medium eggs

1/4 cup buttermilk

Enough cooking oil to cover the fish (I use peanut or canola oil)

Instructions:

1. Heat oil in a large, heavy frying pan over medium heat.

2. Combine all dry ingredients on a plate, mix well

3. Beat eggs and buttermilk together in a separate medium size bowl

4. Wash catfish fillets and pat dry.

5. Dip fillets in the egg wash, shake off excess then roll in the cornmeal mix to coat thoroughly on all sides.

6. Make sure oil is hot, (place handle of a wooden spoon in the oil. Bubbles should rise around the handle immediately. If not, the oil is not hot enough.)

7. Place the fish in the hot oil and fry until golden brown on both sides. Do not crowd the fish in the pan.

8. Drain on paper towels and serve hot

TIP: If you bought fillets from the store they should be already de-boned and skinned. If not de-bone by simply pulling out all the bones with a pair of pliers. It's quick and easy. You can also use the pliers to skin the fish. Just hold one end with a towel or stick a fork in it and pull the skin off with the pliers. It should come off in one piece.

Cajun Casserole

This recipe was one of the first Cajun dishes I ever made. I was trying to impress a friend from work, who was an excellent cook. I thought my friend was not very familiar with Cajun food and that this casserole would be different and exotic.

Well, it was different. I forgot to put the onions in it.

As it turned out my friend was very familiar with Cajun cuisine. His first remark was, "it's good...but I've seldom eaten Cajun food that did not include onions".

I was embarrassed and admitted that the dish was supposed to contain onions. However, my embarrassment was subdued, somewhat, by the fact that the casserole was actually very good, sans onions.

Note: You can use your favorite sausage in the recipe. Several good spicy Cajun sausages are available at most markets. I have even made this using spicy breakfast sausage and loved it. Some types of sausage contain enough fat that you will not need the 1 tablespoon of vegetable oil in step 1. It depends on what type sausage you use. Regular spicy breakfast sausage will not need any added oil. Other types of sausage may.

Note 2: Some types of sausage have a casing that must be removed (skinned) before cooking. The package cooking instructions will tell you if you need to remove the casing.

Note 3: You can substitute seafood (shrimp, crawfish, etc) for the sausage and keep everything else the same to make a totally different dish.

Ingredients:

　　1 tablespoon of vegetable oil

　　1 lb. fresh (hot and spicy) sausage skinned and cut

　　2 cans whole tomatoes, drained and chopped

　　1 peeled eggplant, chopped

　　1 large onion, chopped

　　1 large bell pepper, chopped

　　1 cup of celery, chopped

　　3 medium zucchini, sliced in rings.

Parmesan cheese, as needed

Instructions:

1. Heat 1 tablespoon of vegetable oil (if needed - see note above) in a large frying pan.

2. Brown the sausage first then add all the remaining ingredients EXCEPT THE PARMESAN CHEESE.

3. Heat and stir just until well mixed and vegetables are starting to soften, then transfer to a greased casserole dish.

4. Sprinkle the top generously with Parmesan cheese. Bake in a pre-heated oven set at 350 degrees F for 30 minutes.

Add salt and pepper to taste.

Seafood Casserole

An easy, quick Cajun dish for a main course. If you do not favor food that is a little spicy, reduce the Tabasco sauce to 3 or 4 drops and omit the crushed red pepper flakes.

Ingredients:

    1 package (8 oz) cream cheese

    1 1/2 stick butter or margarine

    2 large onions, chopped

    1 bell pepper chopped

    2 celery ribs chopped

    1/2 pound fresh sliced mushrooms

    1 pound shrimp, peeled and de-veined

    1 tbsp garlic salt

    1 tsp Tabasco sauce

    1/2 tsp crushed red pepper

    1 can cream of mushroom soup,(no water added)

    1 1/2 cup cooked rice

    1 pound fresh crabmeat (canned if fresh unavailable)

    grated cheddar cheese

    Ritz cracker crumbs

Instructions:

1. In a small sauce pan, melt cream cheese and 1 stick of butter together on low heat.

2. In a separate pan, melt remaining 1/2 stick butter, add onions, bell pepper, celery, and mushrooms. Simmer until vegetables are tender.

3. Add shrimp and continue cooking until shrimp turns pink. Remove from heat.

4. Transfer to a large mixing bowl and add garlic salt, Tabasco, red pepper, soup, rice, and cream cheese mixture; mix well.

5. Gently fold in crabmeat.

6. Pour into 2-3 quart casserole dish, top with cracker crumbs and cheese. Bake at 350 degrees for 30 minutes

Serves 8

Cajun Tomato Casserole

This recipe is sort of like meat loaf but in a Cajun style with a little "kick". This yummy casserole is a complete meal alone. Left over's may be frozen and re-heated later. Or you can make it ahead and refrigerate for a tasty, filling meal when you do not have time to cook. You can quickly reheat in the microwave or oven.

Ingredients:

   3 tablespoons vegetable oil

   2 cups onion, chopped

   1 bunch green onions, chopped

   1 cup bell peppers, chopped

   1 cup celery, chopped

   2 cloves garlic, minced

   1 pound ground beef

   6 Roma tomatoes, peeled, seeded and chopped

   1 teaspoon salt

   1/4 teaspoon dried Cayenne powder

   1 teaspoon dried oregano

   1/2 teaspoon dried sweet basil

   1 cup bread crumbs

   6 tablespoons butter, melted

   1/4 cup grated Parmesan cheese

Instructions:

1. In a large heavy pot, heat the oil over medium heat.

2. Add the onions, green onions, bell pepper, celery and garlic. Saute for about five minutes, or until the vegetables are soft.

3. Add the ground beef and cook, stirring often, until brown.

4. Add the tomatoes, salt, cayenne, oregano and basil. Cook, uncovered, over medium-low heat, stirring occasionally, for one hour.

5. Preheat the oven to 350 degrees F.

6. Pour the mixture into a baking dish. Sprinkle the top with the bread crumbs, then drizzle with melted butter. Sprinkle the top with Parmesan cheese.

7. Bake for 15 minutes or until the cheese melts.

Makes 6 servings.

The Perfect Oven Roast Beef

Considering the price of a beef roast now days we would all like our roast to be perfectly cooked every time. It is very disappointing to have it come out over cooked, under cooked, dry, tasteless or perfect on the outside and raw on the inside. Follow these procedures and you can cook a perfect oven roast every time.

The secret to this recipe is slow cooking and use of a meat thermometer to cook to perfection. The meat comes out very tender and juicy. You can accomplish the same with a slow cooker but the oven provides a crisp outer skin that slow cookers do not duplicate.

Use the following guide to determine how long to cook your roast (as read on the meat thermometer).
120 to 125 degrees F. for rare (120 is very rare)
130 to 140 degrees F. for medium rare
145 to 150 degrees F. for medium
155 to 165 degrees F. for well-done

Prep time: 10 min
Cook time: 3 hours 40 min
Total time: 3 hours 50 min
Yield: 12 + servings

Ingredients:

    1 beef roast (about 7 lbs.)

    2 tablespoons vegetable oil

    salt and pepper to taste

    meat thermometer

    roast pan with wire rack

Instructions:

1. Adjust oven rack to lowest position and heat oven to 200 degrees F.
2. On stove top, heat vegetable oil in roast pan with wire rack removed (place over 2 burners if necessary).
3. Place roast in pan and cook, turning frequently, until all sides are brown (about 10 min.).
4. Remove roast from pan. Pour off all oil from pan. Place wire rack in pan. Set roast on wire rank.
5. Season roast with salt and pepper.
6. Place meat thermometer in roast in the thickest part of the roast. If your roast contains any bone, make sure the thermometer is not touching bone.
7. Place roast in oven and cook until meat thermometer reads 125 degrees F. for medium rare (about 3 and 1/2 hours or 30 minutes per pound).
8. When done, remove from oven and allow to rest for 20 minutes before carving.

Classic Grilled Burgers

Who doesn't love a classic burger? They are fast and easy to make and this recipe adds a flavor boost with a touch of ginger and cumin. In addition to the burger's you will need fresh buns and all the usual condiments such as mustard, ketchup, mayonnaise, relish, sliced tomatoes, pickles and lettuce.

This recipe makes the best grilled burger's we have ever cooked. Pay attention to the cooking instructions about not using a spatula and not flipping the burger's more than once and you will make some fantastic burgers.

Prep time: 20 min
Cook time: 11 min
Total time: 31 min
Yield: 8 servings

Ingredients:

    2 pounds ground beef

    1 small onion, finely chopped

    1/2 inch fresh ginger, shredded (or 1/2 teaspoon ginger powder)

    1 Tablespoon finely chopped garlic

    1 teaspoon ground cumin

    2 teaspoons salt, or to taste, freshly ground black pepper, to taste

Instructions:

1. Mix all ingredients together. Shape into patties gently with hands. Do not squeeze/pack the patties tight. Squeeze just enough for the patty to hold together. Using your thumb, make a small indentation (dimple) in the center, top of each patty.
2. Heat the grill very hot. You want to cook the burger's fast.
3. Place patties on grill, dimple side up. DO NOT FLATTEN BURGER'S WITH A SPATULA!
4. Cook burgers until you see juices forming on top of burger's (about 5-6 min). Turn burgers and brown other side (about 4-5 min). Only flip burger's one time! Resist the temptation to continually turn burger's over.
5. Remove from grill and serve hot.
6. If weather is bad you can cook burgers under the broiler indoors. Just watch closely to prevent burning.

Chicken Fried Steak

Many people use the terms "country fried steak" and "chicken fried steak" interchangeably. Well, they are similar but cooked a little different. Country fried steak is dredged in a flour coating, and then fried in either white or brown gravy. Chicken fried steak is deep fried similar to fried chicken and served with white gravy on the side. It is not cooked in the gravy.

This was my mom's favorite recipe but she always insisted on the gravy being on the side. This recipe is one of the best for turning an inexpensive cut of meat into a tender, flavorful dish.

Prep time: 20 min
Cook time: 20 min
Total time: 40 min
Yield: 4 servings

Ingredients:

1 pound round steak, cut into 4 portions, pounded to tenderize

1/2 cup all-purpose flour

1/8 teaspoon black pepper

salt, to taste

2/3 cup buttermilk

1 cup cracker meal or crushed saltine crackers

3 tablespoons cooking (vegetable) oil

1 can (10 3/4 ounces) condensed cream of mushroom soup

1 cup milk

Instructions:

1. Combine flour and pepper in a shallow bowl or pie plate.
2. Pour buttermilk into a second shallow bowl
3. Put cracker meal into a third shallow bowl.
4. Sprinkle steaks with salt; dredge in the flour, dip into the buttermilk, then coat well with the cracker crumbs, pressing with hands if necessary to help crumbs adhere.
5. Place cooking oil in a large skillet over medium-high heat.
6. Cook steaks for about 3 minutes on each side, or until nicely browned and cooked through. Drain off most of the excess fat, leaving the dregs, or browned bits.

7. To make gravy, add soup and milk to the skillet drippings with the steaks; stirring and scraping up browned bits from the bottom of the skillet. Continue cooking, stirring constantly, until mixture comes to a boil. Serve steaks with the hot, creamy gravy.

As mentioned above, to make chicken fried steak, first fry the steaks until done then remove steaks from pan and make the gravy. Serve gravy on the side.

Chicken and Dumplings

Growing up this was Sunday dinner at grandma's house. Fried chicken was a favorite but this savory dish was a close second.

This classic Southern dish is generally reserved for after church or special occasions but it is good enough to serve any time.
Difficulty: Medium

Prep time: 20 min
Cook time: 55 min
Total time: 1 hour 15 min
Yield: 6-8 servings

For Chicken, Vegetables and Broth

Ingredients

* 4 cups chicken broth (low salt recommended)

* 4 cups water

* 2-3 boneless, skinless chicken breasts

* 1 1/2 tablespoons olive oil

* 2 carrots, chopped

* 1 stalk celery, chopped

* 1 onion, chopped

* 1 1/2 teaspoons salt (or to taste)

* 1 teaspoon dried thyme

* 1/4 teaspoon black pepper (or to taste)

* 1/2 cup frozen peas

* 1/2 cup cold water

* 1/4 cup all-purpose flour

Instructions:

1. Place the chicken broth, water, and chicken breasts in a large pot and bring to a boil. Boil until the chicken is cooked through (about 15 minutes). Remove the chicken from the broth and shred using 2 forks. Set the chicken aside. Keep the broth warm on the stove.
2. Heat the olive oil in a large skillet over medium heat. Add the celery, carrots, and onion and cook until the vegetables are softened (about 6 to 7 minutes).
3. Add the cooked vegetables to the broth, along with the salt, thyme, and black pepper. Stir to combine, and bring the broth to a simmer.
4. In a small bowl, stir together the cold water and the flour. Slowly pour the flour mixture into the hot broth and vegetables, whisking constantly until well combined. Add peas and chicken to broth.

For the Dumplings:

Ingredients:

* 1 cup all-purpose flour

* 2 tsp. baking powder

* 1/2 tsp. table salt

* 1/4 tsp. dried thyme

* 1/2 cup sour cream

* 1/2 cup milk

* 1 Tablespoon vegetable oil (we prefer canola oil)

Instructions

1. Combine the flour, baking powder, salt, and thyme in a medium bowl.
2. In another bowl, stir together the sour cream, milk, and vegetable oil.
3. Add the wet ingredients to the dry ingredients and stir until just combined (do not over mix).
4. Bring the broth (with chicken) back to a boil.
5. Drop teaspoons of the dumpling dough into the broth in a single layer. Reduce the heat to medium-low, cover the pot, and let the dumplings cook undisturbed for 15 minutes. (Do not lift the lid during the cooking time.)
6. Serve hot.

Sage Roasted Chicken Recipe

This simple sage chicken recipe makes people think you spend hours preparing a complicated dish...when you actually did not. It's hard to fail with this recipe so it is ideal for the novice cook.

This recipe actually is easy and it is hard to fail if you use a meat thermometer. It only requires experience if you attempt to cook without a thermometer. You can achieve a beautiful golden brown skin and still have the inside under cooked. So...use a thermometer.

Prep time: 20 min
Cook time: 2 hours 10 min
Total time: 2 hour 30 min
Yield: 4 servings

Ingredients:

- 1 roasting chicken, about 5 1/2 pounds
- Fresh sage, about 6 to 8 large leaves (or 2-3 tablespoons dried sage).
- Dash pepper
- clove garlic, coarsely chopped
- Salt and pepper
- 1 apple, cored and cut in wedges (leave skin on, do not peel)

Instructions:

1. Heat oven to 450 degrees F.
2. Wash chicken and pat dry.
3. Place chicken on a wire rack in a roasting pan.
4. In a food processor, process the sage, pepper, and garlic until finely minced or pasty consistency.
5. Using your fingers spread the spice mixture over the entire chicken until all sides are well coated. (Make additional spice mix if needed).
6. Place apple wedges in the cavity of the chicken. Sprinkle the chicken lightly with salt and pepper.
7. Cover chicken loosely with aluminum foil.
8. Roast the chicken for 10 minutes at 450 degrees F. Reduce heat to 350 degrees F. and roast until an instant-read thermometer reads 165 degrees when inserted into the thickest part of the thigh (without touching bone) or about 20 minutes per pound.
9. Remove foil the last 10 minutes of cooking and brown top of chicken.
10. Allow chicken to stand for 10 minutes before slicing.

Crockpot Chicken and Sweet Potato Stew

This hearty stew will warm your tummy on those cold winter days. Actually, it's good any time at all. Just place the ingredients in a crock pot in the morning and forget it until dinner time. Serves 6.

Ingredients:

   6 bone-in chicken thighs, skin removed

   2 pounds sweet potatoes, peeled and cut into spears

   1/2 pound white button mushrooms, thinly sliced

   6 large shallots, peeled and halved

   4 cloves garlic, peeled

   1 cup dry white wine

   1/2 teaspoon dried rosemary, crushed

   1 teaspoon salt

   1/2 teaspoon black pepper

   1 teaspoon lemon juice

   1 1/2 tablespoons white wine vinegar (optional)

Instructions:

4. Place all ingredients **except white wine vinegar** in a 6 quart or larger crockpot (slow cooker) and stir well.
5. Place the lid on the crockpot and cook on low until potatoes are tender (about 5 hours).
6. Remove bones from chicken, stir in vinegar if desired and serve steaming hot.

Cajun Chicken over Rice

Want a complete Cajun meal in just a few minutes? This simple dish takes a few minutes to prepare the ingredients but is cooked in a matter of minutes. Just add rice for a quick, complete and filling dinner.

Ingredients:

1-1/2 lb Boneless chicken breast, cut into 1" pieces

1/8 teaspoons Garlic powder

5 Tomatoes, peeled and chopped

2 large Onions, chopped

1 Green pepper, chopped

1/4 cup Worcestershire sauce

1/4 cup Soy sauce

1 teaspoon basil

1 teaspoon marjoram

1 teaspoon oregano

2 teaspoons Black Pepper

Rice, cooked

Instructions:

1. Sprinkle chicken with garlic powder.

2. Combine all ingredients, EXCEPT RICE and CHICKEN, in a large pot. Bring to a boil; reduce heat, and simmer 15 minutes.

3. Add chicken and return to a boil. Cover, reduce heat, and simmer 30 minutes or until tender. If needed, add a small amount of water if mixture begins to dry out.

Serve over rice.

Cajun Pork Chops

This is a simple pork chop recipe with mushrooms. The mushroom steak sauce may be found with other sauces and gravy at most major super markets.

The longer you marinate the chops the more flavorful they will be. Marinate overnight if possible but at least 2 hours.

Ingredients

- 1/4 cup vegetable oil
- 6 center cut pork chops (boneless thin cut works best)
- Salt and pepper to taste
- 1/2 cup onions, minced
- 1 cup Italian salad dressing
- Two 6 oz cans mushroom steak sauce
- One 4 oz can mushroom stems and pieces
- 1 cup water or more if needed
- Parsley for garnish (optional)

Instructions:

1. Season pork chops with salt and pepper. Put chops in a plastic bowl and pour Italian Dressing over the chops. Cover and refrigerate for at least 2 hours (overnight is O.K.).

2. Drain pork chops saving the dressing for later.

3. Place the 1/4 cup oil, chops and onions in a 5 to 6 quart pot and cook over medium high heat until onion is tender and chops are brown on both sides.

4. Add the reserved dressing from step 2 and the 1 cup water. Cook until chops are tender, adding water if necessary. Stir often.

5. Add the mushroom steak sauce and mushrooms with liquid. Taste for seasoning and add salt/pepper if needed. Simmer another 20 minutes.

6. Serve with hot cooked rice and coleslaw.

Cajun Steak Rouille

Rouille is simply a sauce...which may be made several different ways. A thicker sauce than what this recipe makes is often made using mayonnaise and served with fish.

The name is given to it because of its color. In French Rouille means "rust". Here, we present a classic, basic Rouille with crushed red pepper (which gives it a rust shade), onions and vegetable oil. This is a very simple dish that requires little cooking experience to produce great results.

Many people serve Rouille sauce with seafood. Feel free to do so.

Ingredients:

    1 pound tender beef steak cut 1/2 inch thick

    Salt, as needed

    crushed red pepper

    1/4 cup vegetable oil

    1 medium onion, finely sliced

    Water, as needed

Instructions:

    1. Season steak with salt and red pepper on all sides.

    2. In a heavy bottomed skillet, place meat in cold oil over medium heat and cook until most of the liquid has cooked out.

    3. Turn meat, add 1 tablespoon water and cook until meat starts frying, then turn meat and add another tablespoon of water.

    4. Continue with the process of turning, frying and adding water until meat is tender.

    5. Add onion, cook until tender. Add a little water; scrape bottom of skillet to loosen all meat remnants to make a light gravy.

Homemade Tasso (seasoned smoked pork)

Used in a variety of Cajun dishes, Tasso is highly seasoned, intensely flavored smoked pork. You can make your own with this recipe.

The preferred cooking method is to use a smoker and cook on low heat. If you do not have a smoker you can use a grill but keep the meat to the side of of the coals, not directly over the heat. You want to cook long enough to infuse the meat with a smoky flavor without over cooking.

Ingredients:

8-10 pounds boneless pork butt

5 tablespoons salt

5 tablespoons cayenne pepper

3 tablespoons freshly ground black pepper

3 tablespoons white pepper

2 tablespoons paprika

2 tablespoons cinnamon

2 tablespoons garlic powder or granulated garlic

Instructions:

1. Trim the pork of all excess fat and cut it into strips about 1 inch thick and at least 4 inches long.

2. Mix together the seasonings and place in a shallow pan. Roll each strip of pork in the seasoning mixture and place on a tray. Cover with plastic wrap and refrigerate at least overnight (preferable a couple of days).

3. Prepare your smoker. Place the pork strips on a grill or rod and smoke until done, 5-7 hours. Don't let the smoker get too hot.

4. Remove the meat and let it cool completely, then wrap well in plastic and foil.

The Tasso will keep well in the refrigerator for up to 10 days, and it also freezes very well.

Chicken Andouille Gumbo Recipe

If you like chicken and you like gumbo, here's the recipe for you. Yummy Chicken Andouille Gumbo (Andouille is a spicy sausage popular in Cajun cuisine).

Ingredients:

1 large stewing chicken, cut up

1 pound Andouille (Cajun sausage), sliced in 1/4 inch slices

6 large onions, chopped

1 small bunch green onions, chopped fine

1 bell pepper, chopped

1/2 cup chopped celery

1 tablespoon finely chopped parsley

1 clove garlic, chopped

12 oysters (omit if you are not fond of oysters)

12 medium or large shrimp

Salt, black pepper and red cayenne pepper, to taste

1/2 to 3/4 cup all-purpose flour (for roux)

1 cup cooking oil

6 cup hot water

Instructions:

1. Cut up chicken, wash and season with salt, pepper and cayenne.

2. Heat one cup oil in heavy skillet and fry chicken until brown. Remove chicken and set aside

3. Make roux as follows: Pour remaining oil (from frying chicken) into large heavy pot over medium heat. Add 1/2 cup flour and stir until roux just starts to turn brown. When done you

should have a slurry-looking brown paste. If too oily, add more flour a tablespoon at a time. If too thick, add oil.

4. After roux is made, lower heat and add all chopped ingredients, except green onions, garlic and parsley. Cover and simmer until onions are clear and tender, stirring occasionally.

5. Add sliced Andouille and chicken to roux mixture, cover and let simmer about 1/2 hour. Stir often during this process. Keep heat low.

6. Add water, garlic, parsley and green onions. Increase heat until mixture begins to boil; then lower heat to simmer. Cover and cook 1-1/2 to 2 hours or until chicken is tender.

Note: This dish will yield a gravy/sauce which should be served over rice.

Serves 6

New Orleans Chicken Etouffee

Yes it has a fancy sounding name but chicken Etouffee is simply a spicy chicken in a yummy gravy-like sauce. It takes a little while to make but is fairly easy. You can keep any left over's for up to three days and re-heat. Some people think it is better a day or two later.

Ingredients:

6 of your favorite pieces of fryer chicken

Cayenne pepper, to taste

salt and black pepper, to taste

3 tablespoons vegetable oil (for browning chicken

6 tablespoons vegetable oil (for roux)

1/2 to 3/4 cup flour

1 medium onion, finely chopped

1/2 cup celery, diced

1/2 cup bell pepper, diced

1 tablespoon garlic, minced

6 cups chicken or vegetable stock

1 tablespoon sugar

1 tablespoon lemon juice

dash liquid smoke

paprika and or hot sauce, to taste (optional)

Instructions:

1. Season chicken pieces to taste with salt, pepper and cayenne pepper

2. Heat 3 tablespoons oil in heavy bottomed pot over medium high heat.

3. Put chicken in pot and cook on both sides to a golden brown, turning the pieces occasionally.

4. Remove chicken and set aside.

5. For roux: Add 6 tablespoons oil to any oil remaining in pot and heat till bubbly. Add 1/2 cup flour and stir until a light brown paste forms. If too oily, add more flour. If too dry, add oil.

6. Add onion, celery and bell pepper and cook until soft, 2 to 3 minutes.

7. Add garlic and cook another 2 minutes.

8. Add vegetable or chicken stock, sugar, lemon juice and liquid smoke. Take care with liquid smoke...it can be overpowering.

9. Brink mixes back to a boil and add chicken. Reduce heat and simmer for 1 hour or until chicken is "falling off the bone" tender.

10. Remove chicken from pot and strip chicken meat from bones. Return chicken meat to pot, add paprika and hot sauce if desired, to taste

11. Simmer another 30 minutes or until sauce thickens. Taste and add seasoning if needed.

Serve with rice.

Notes:

If liquid in pot gets low, add stock or water as needed. You should end up with at least 2 cups of sauce.

The roux is what thickens the sauce. If sauce is too thin at the end, mix 2 tablespoons cornstarch in 1 cup COLD water and add to mix a little at a time. Stir and watch thickness of sauce for a couple of minutes between each addition of cornstarch mix.

If sauce is too thick, add water or stock.

Pork and Pecan Stir Fry

Stir fry is a little like our kitchen sink vegetable soup. You can put everything you want in it (except maybe the kitchen sink). This recipe gives the basic ingredients but feel free to add any vegetables from the fridge. You can add boc choy, napa cabbage, kim chee, pineapple, mushrooms, water chestnuts or???

Ingredients:

    1 pound pork stir-fry strips (loin, fresh pork leg or tenderloin)

    1 1/2 tablespoons Cajun seasoning

    1 tablespoon vegetable oil

    3/4 cup chopped celery

    1/2 cup chopped onion

    1 clove garlic, crushed

    1 green bell pepper, seeded and cut into 3/4-inch squares

    3/4 cup toasted pecan halves (see note below)

    1/2 cup medium shrimp, cleaned (optional)

    3 cups hot cooked rice

Instructions:

    1. In medium bowl toss together pork strips with Cajun seasoning to coat evenly.

    2. In large nonstick skillet heat oil over high heat, stir-fry pork until nicely browned, about 4-6 minutes.

    3. Add celery, onion, bell pepper, garlic (and shrimp if using) to skillet and cook, stirring often, until onion is almost translucent, about 3-4 minutes.

    4. Add pecans, stir continuously, and cook just long enough to heat through, about 2 minutes. Serve over rice.

Serves four.

Note: To toast pecans, place on a cookie sheet and cook under broiler until the pecans just begin to color. WATCH THE ENTIRE TIME! Do not walk away from them, they will burn quickly!

Pork Jambalaya

Simple, flavorful way to cook pork chops with a Cajun flair. The Holy Trinity and mushroom sauce set the tone for this recipe. Feel free to add a dash of Tabasco sauce to the cooked chops if you like a Cajun spiciness.

Ingredients:

2 pounds boneless pork chops

salt and pepper, to taste

4 tablespoons vegetable oil

1 cup onions, chopped

3/4 cup bell pepper, chopped

1/2 cup celery, chopped

1/2 cup mushrooms, chopped

1 cup water

1 tablespoon cornstarch mixed in 1/2 cup cold water

1 cup green onion tops, chopped

4 cups cooked rice

Instructions:

1. Season pork chops to taste with salt and pepper.

2. Add oil to a large, heavy skillet and brown pork chops on both sides.

3. Remove pork chops from skillet and add onions, bell pepper, and celery. Cook until tender.

4. Pour off oil from the skillet and add 1 cup of water. Stir while scraping bottom of pan and cook to make sauce.

5. Make thickening sauce by mixing 1 tablespoon cornstarch in 1/2 cup COLD water.

6. Put chops back into the skillet. Add thickening sauce (cornstarch mix) and cook on medium heat for about 20 minutes or until sauce thickens and chops are tender.

7. Serve over rice and garnish with onion tops.

Serves 4.

Note: If sauce is too thick, add water. If too thin, add more cornstarch/water mix.

Shrimp Jambalaya

An old Cajun stand-by, shrimp jambalaya is hard to beat for a delicious, filling dish. You can substitute catfish or crayfish for the shrimp if that's what you have. Of course it would no longer shrimp jambalaya. It would be "something else" jambalaya. But I bet you will like it.

Ingredients

* 1 tablespoon canola oil
* 6 ounces Andouille sausage, halved lengthwise and sliced into 1/4-inch-thick pieces
* 1 medium onion, diced
* 1 green bell pepper, ribs and seeds removed, diced
* 3 celery stalks, diced
* 2 garlic cloves, minced
* Coarse salt and ground pepper
* 2 teaspoons paprika
* 4 large tomatoes, chopped
* 3 cups water
* 1 cup long-grain white rice
* 1 pound medium shrimp (about 30), peeled, deveined, and tails removed
* 1/2 cup thinly sliced green onions, for garnish

Directions

1. Heat oil in a large skillet over medium-high heat. Add sausage; cook, turning occasionally, until browned on all sides, 4 to 6 minutes. Add onion, bell pepper, celery, and garlic; season with salt and pepper. Cook, stirring occasionally, until onion begins to soften, 5 to 6 minutes. Stir in paprika; cook until fragrant, about 1 minute.
2. Add tomatoes, rice, and 3 cups water to skillet; cover, and simmer over medium heat until rice is cooked and has absorbed all water, about 15 minutes.
3. Add shrimp to skillet, and cook, covered, until shrimp are opaque throughout, 3 to 4 minutes. Remove from heat; season with salt and pepper, as desired. Garnished with green onions and serve hot

Catfish Jambalaya Recipe

This yummy dish is very easy to make. Serve with hush puppies.

Ingredients

8 oz. catfish fillet

4 medium yellow onions, chopped

2 cloves garlic, chopped

1/2 bell pepper, chopped

1 stalk celery, chopped

1/2 lb. margarine

One 10 oz. can chopped tomatoes

4 oz. fresh mushrooms, sliced

salt and pepper to taste

Directions

1. Put all ingredients except catfish into saucepan and cook until mixture starts to turn light brown. Season to taste with salt and pepper while mixture is cooking (about 5 minutes).

2. Add catfish; break up catfish into chunks with wooden spoon. Cook 15 to 20 minutes longer.

3. Serve over rice. Sprinkle top with freshly chopped onion tops or parsley. Serve hot.

Serves 6

Bayou Beef Stew

Here's a wonderfully tasty and hearty treat made in the Cajun tradition of one-pot cooking. It uses the Cajun "Holy Trinity" minus the bell pepper. Feel free to add a cup of chopped bell pepper if you like.

Ingredients:

- 3 pounds beef chuck, cubed
- salt and black pepper to taste
- Your favorite hot sauce to taste
- 1/3 cup flour
- 1/4 cup vegetable oil
- 1 cup diced onions
- 1 cup diced celery
- 1/2 cup celery leaves
- 1/4 cup minced garlic
- 1 bay leaf
- 2 tbsps Worcestershire sauce
- 1 quart hot water or beef stock
- 1 pound sliced carrots
- 2 pounds quartered new potatoes
- 1 pound sliced mushrooms
- 1 cup sliced green onions
- 1/2 cup chopped parsley

Instructions:

1. Place beef in a large mixing bowl and season with salt, pepper and hot sauce. Sprinkle in flour to coat meat well.

2. In a cast iron Dutch oven (or large pot), heat oil over medium-high heat. Add meat and brown on all sides. Once meat is golden brown and caramelized on bottom of pot, remove and keep warm.

3. Stir in onions, celery, celery leaves and garlic. Saute 3 to 5 minutes or until vegetables are wilted.

4. Return meat to pot and blend well. Add bay leaf and Worcestershire sauce. Pour in hot water or stock, scraping bottom of pot to remove any drippings. Blend in carrots and potatoes. Bring to a rolling boil then reduce to simmer.

5. Cover and cook 1 to 1 and 1/2 hours or until meat is tender.

6. Add mushrooms, green onions and parsley. Adjust seasonings if necessary. Cook 5 to 10 minutes longer. Serve as is or over steamed white rice.

6 Servings

Crawfish Etouffee

The best thing to do with crawfish? Make crawfish Etouffee, of course. Etouffee simply means cooked in its own juices.

Ingredients

1 lb. crawfish

2 tbs. olive oil

3 tbs. parsley flakes

1 cup onion, diced medium

1 cup water

1/2 cup bell pepper, diced medium

1/4 cup celery, diced small

2 tbs. garlic, minced finely

1/2 cup green onion, sliced very thin

1 tsp. Cajun seasoning roux (mix 2 tbs cornstarch in 1/4 cup cold water - mix well)

Hot Sauce to taste

Instructions:

1. Heat olive oil to hot in a 10 inch skillet. Add onion, bell pepper, celery and garlic. Simmer on high until onions begin to wilt.

2. Add Cajun seasoning and parsley and stir in well. Add water and bring to a boil for 3 minutes.

3. Add crawfish and stir in well.

4. Bring back to a boil, add roux slowly to the Etouffee and stir in well on medium high heat until it thickens and is creamy. Simmer on low for 4 minutes covered, stir, and then remove from heat.

Garnish with green onion. Serve over rice. Serves 4

Cajun Seafood Gumbo

Here's a wonderfully tasty recipe for an old Cajun favorite. It takes some time to make but is well worth the effort. This recipe easily serves 6. You may keep any leftover in the refrigerator for 3 days and re-heat before serving.

Ingredients

* 2 Quarts Water
* 2 tablespoons Oil
* 2 tablespoons All-Purpose Flour
* 2 Large Onions (chopped)
* 2 tablespoons Bacon Fat
* 3 Cups Okra (chopped)
* 1 Large Bell Pepper (chopped)
* 3 Stalks Celery, Chopped
* 12 oz. Tomatoes (can or fresh)
* 3 Cloves Garlic, Chopped
* Cayenne Pepper to taste
* 2 pounds Peeled Shrimp
* 1 pound Crabmeat
* 2 dozen oysters (liquor reserved)
* Salt to taste
* Black Pepper to taste
* 1/2 cup Andouille sausage, chopped (optional)

Instructions

1. Peel and wash shrimp. Pick through crabmeat for any remaining shell. Store in refrigerator until needed.

2. In a large pot, bring the 2 quarts of water to a boil.

3. In a medium frying pan, make a roux by heating 2 tablespoons of oil till hot, add flour and stir till dark brown.

4. Take one cup of water from the boiling 2 quarts of water; add to flour (roux) mixture. When well-blended, add back to boiling water.

5. In a skillet, heat 2 heaping tablespoons of bacon fat, fry okra in fat till slime is removed. Add onions, celery and bell pepper to okra and cook until tender.

6. Smash tomatoes and add tomatoes and garlic to okra mixture. Fry about five minutes, add mixture to the 2 quart boiling water/roux mix).

7. Reduce heat and simmer Gumbo for 1 1/2 hours. Add the oysters with oyster liquor, crabmeat and shrimp 15 minutes before serving. Serve hot over cooked rice.

Cajun Spicy Shrimp

This quick and easy shrimp recipe is a favorite of ours. The 1/2 pound of shrimp will make about 3-4 servings. You might want to cook additional shrimp for hearty appetites.

Takes about 30 minutes to prepare and marinate but only minutes to cook. Serve as an appetizer, party finger food or add rice and a salad for a complete meal.

Ingredients:

- 2 teaspoons salt
- 1/2 teaspoon black pepper
- 1/2 teaspoon onion powder
- 1/2 teaspoon garlic powder
- 1 teaspoon cayenne pepper
- 1 teaspoon paprika
- 1/4 teaspoon dried oregano
- 2 tablespoons olive oil
- 1/2 pound uncooked large shrimp, peeled and deveined

Instructions:

1. In a bowl, combine the first 7 (dry seasoning) ingredients and mix well.

2. Add the olive oil to the seasoning mix and stir until well combined.

3. Add the shrimp to the seasoning mix and toss until the shrimp is coated on all sides. Leave shrimp in the seasoning mix and place in the refrigerator for 20 minutes.

4. Thread the shrimp onto skewers. Reserve the seasoning mix.

5. Turn oven on broiler setting.

6. Broil shrimp for 2 minutes with shrimp 4-6 inches from the heat.

7. Turn shrimp over and baste with reserved seasoning mix. Broil 1-2 minutes longer or until the shrimp turn pink.

Note: The cooking times given are guides only. Ovens vary so watch shrimp closely while under the broiler. Do not overcook the shrimp or they will be tough and tasteless.

Cajun BBQ Shrimp

If you love shrimp you will love this. Sinfully delicious! And...It only takes minutes to cook. Cajun means it is a little spicy but if you prefer you can reduce or eliminate the pepper flakes.

Excellent recipe if you do not overcook the shrimp. Remember that shrimp cooks fast. If it is over cooked it is tough and tasteless. Properly cooked shrimp turns pink and curls into a "C" shape. If overcooked the shrimp curls beyond a "C" shape. The secret is to watch the shrimp as it cooks. Do not walk away. The shrimp will go from "perfect" to overcook very fast.

Prep time: 10 min
Cook time: 10 min
Total time: 20 min
Yield: 2 servings

Ingredients

1 cup butter (melted)

1 teaspoon rosemary

1 teaspoon paprika

1 teaspoon oregano

1/2 tablespoon crushed red pepper flakes

1 teaspoon salt

7 garlic cloves, chopped

2 bay leaves

Juice of 1 lemon

12 large (Jumbo) shrimp, shelled and de-veined

Instructions:

1. Melt the butter in a large saucepan and add all ingredients, *except shrimp*.
2. Cook over medium heat for approximately 5 minutes.
3. Add shrimp and cook until orange/pink color, 2-3 minutes on each side (see TIP below). Remove from heat and ladle butter sauce over shrimp.

Shrimp Creole

Shrimp creole is similar to gumbo. It combines shrimp and vegetables in a slightly spicy sauce...yum! If you prefer a little less heat omit the cayenne pepper. However you will find this dish is really not very spicy as is.

Ingredients:

2 tablespoons butter

1/2 cup onion, finely chopped

2 tablespoons all-purpose flour

3 cups water

6 oz can tomato paste

1/2 cup green pepper, finely chopped

1/2 cup celery, finely chopped

1 teaspoon parsley, chopped

1/2 teaspoon salt

1/4 teaspoon hot pepper sauce

dash ground cayenne pepper

1 bay Leaf

2 cups medium shrimp, cooked

2 cups hot cooked rice

Instructions:

1. In a large heavy skillet over medium heat, melt the butter.

2. Add the onion and cook until tender but not browned.

3. Stir in the flour until dissolved. Add all remaining ingredients EXCEPT the shrimp. Cook uncovered over medium low heat for about 30 minutes, or until thickened, stirring occasionally.

4. Add the shrimp and heat through. Remove the bay leaf.

Serve over hot cooked rice.

Makes 4 servings.

Cajun Bayoubaisse

Bayoubaisse is a Cajun seafood dish cooked in a rich tomato based sauce. It is usually served over rice. We like to serve with fresh French bread for dipping in the sauce.

This recipe is only faintly spicy. If you want a little more "kick" just add a couple of chopped jalapeno peppers while cooking the sauce.

Prep time: 20 min
Cook time: 2 hours 21 min
Total time: 2 hours 41 min
Yield: 6 servings

For the sauce:

Sauce Ingredients:

- 1/2 medium onion, chopped
- 2 tbsp. olive oil
- 4 tbsp. butter
- 1/2 stalk celery, chopped
- 1 medium carrot, chopped
- 1 bunch green onions, chopped
- One 10-oz. can Mexican Style tomatoes with chili peppers (see note below)
- One 16-oz. can whole tomatoes, chopped
- 1 tbsp. tomato paste
- 3-1/3 cup water
- 2 tsp. salt
- Freshly ground black pepper (to taste)

1/2 tsp. each of oregano, basil and thyme

4 bay leaves

Cooked rice

**Note: If Mexican style tomatoes are unavailable you may substitute with regular canned tomatoes and add 1 small, chopped Jalapeno pepper.

Instructions for Sauce:

1. Sauté onion in oil and butter over medium heat for five minutes; do not brown.
2. Add celery, carrot and green onions. Cook covered 5 minutes over low heat.
3. Add remaining ingredients. Simmer partially covered 2 hours, stirring occasionally. Add water if liquid gets low.
4. Remove from heat and discard bay leaves.

For the Seafood

Ingredients:

1 lb. shellfish (crawfish, shrimp, oysters and/or crab)

1 lb. catfish or other firm white fish

2 tbsp. flour

1 tsp. garlic, chopped

2 tbsp. olive oil

4 tbsp. butter

1 cup white wine

Green onions, chopped

Parsley

Instructions for Seafood and Combining Sauce:

1. Dust seafood with flour.
2. In a large saucepan, sauté garlic in oil and butter over medium heat for 1 minute. Do not brown.

3. Add all seafood. Sauté over medium-high heat until seafood is golden brown (5-10 min).
4. Add wine, stir, and cook 1 minute.
5. Add the sauce which was previously prepared. Cover. Cook 3-4 minutes over low heat.
6. Serve in large bowls with rice and sprinkled with green onions and parsley.

Irish stew

This is an old recipe for Irish stew. Perfect for your St. Patrick's Day dinner. If you are not fond of lamb you can substitute beef...but don't tell your Irish friends.

Prep time: 20 min
Cook time: 2 hours
Total time: 2 hours 20 min
Yield: 4-6 servings

Ingredients:

3 lbs lamb, shoulder chops, breast

2 large potatoes for each person

2 medium onions per person, thickly sliced

1 or 2 carrot per person

1 tsp. thyme

1 tsp. Tabasco sauce

1 bay leaf

Salt to taste

Water or broth to cover

Instructions:

1. Arrange lamb in alternating layers with potatoes, onions and carrots in a large stew pot.
2. Add the seasonings and just cover with water or broth.
3. Cover pot and simmer on top of stove for 1-2 hours or until meat is tender.
4. Taste for seasoning and add if needed.

Section 7
Southern Barbecue and sauce Recipes

Simple Southern Barbecue Sauce Recipe

This recipe makes a basic, simple Southern Barbecue sauce loaded with flavor. It is made with common BBQ ingredients. You can make a batch (or double batch) of this sauce and store it in a sealed container in the fridge for weeks.

Very good all-around BBQ sauce for pork, beef or chicken. We even used it to make BBQ beans which were very good.

Prep time: 5 min
Cook time: 30 min
Total time: 35 min
Yield: 5 cups

Ingredients:

- 2 cups Coca-Cola (or Pepsi)
- 2 cups ketchup
- 1 cup white vinegar
- 1/2 large onion, finely chopped
- 1 1/2 tablespoons black pepper
- 1/4 cup brown sugar
- 3 tablespoons salt
- 3 tablespoons chili powder

Instructions:

1. Mix all ingredients in a saucepan and bring to a boil.
2. Reduce heat and simmer for 30 minutes or until sauce is reduced and slightly thickened, stirring occasionally.
3. Transfer to a sealable container and store in refrigerator.

Sweet and Sticky BBQ Sauce

This recipe makes a BBQ sauce that uses a little trick of adding equal parts of water to the recipe which tends to keep the sauce from burning off on the grill. The sauce will produces a wonderful shiny glace on meat or chicken.

A lot of ingredients but it makes a good sauce. Be aware that the alcohol in the rum evaporates during cooking so there is no significant alcohol in the sauce. It just adds flavor.

Prep time: 10 min
Cook time: 45 min
Total time: 55 min
Yield: 2 pints

Ingredients:

- 1/2 cup vegetable oil
- 5 garlic cloves, chopped
- 1 medium onion, chopped
- 1 green bell pepper, chopped
- Salt to taste
- 1/4 cup dark rum
- 3 tablespoons chili powder
- 1 tablespoon black pepper
- 1/2 teaspoon allspice
- 1/2 teaspoon ground clove
- 1 cup dark brown sugar
- 2 cups water
- 2 cups ketchup

1/2 cup molasses

1/2 cup cider vinegar

2 teaspoons hot sauce

Instructions:

1. Heat the oil in a large saucepan.
2. Add the garlic, onion, green pepper and a large pinch of salt. Cook over medium heat, stirring occasionally, until onions and peppers are softened, about 10 minutes.
3. Add the rum and simmer 2 minutes.
4. Add the chili powder, black pepper, allspice and cloves. Cook, stirring, 3 minutes.
5. Add the brown sugar, water, ketchup, molasses, vinegar and hot sauce. Simmer until thickened, about 30 minutes.
6. Transfer to a food processor and puree. Season with salt to taste.
7. May be refrigerated up to 2 weeks.

Sauce for BBQ Chicken

This recipe makes a simple BBQ sauce for grilled chicken. May be used as a marinade, brushed on chicken as it cooks or served on the side at the table.

Quick and easy BBQ sauce recipe using ingredients probably already in your kitchen. We found adding a few drops of liquid smoke kicked it up a notch.

Prep time: 10 min
Cook time: 5 min
Total time: 15 min
Yield: 1 1/2 cups

Ingredients:

One whole chicken (or you may use just your favorite chicken parts)

1-1/2 sticks butter

1/4 cup vinegar

1 cup ketchup

1/4 cup Worcestershire sauce

2 cloves garlic, minced

crushed red pepper, to taste

cayenne pepper, to taste

Instructions:

1. Melt all sauce ingredients together on low heat- DO NOT BOIL.
2. Grill chicken, basting with sauce frequently.
3. When chicken is cooked pull off skin and remove meat from bone.
4. Chop meat medium fine (like pulled BBQ pork).
5. Pour sauce over chicken and serve hot

Old Tennessee Sweet BBQ Sauce

We found this recipe in an old church recipe book that was over 40 years old. The original recipe did not use liquid smoke so we added it for a little more "smoky" flavor. This sauce goes well with BBQ beef or pork served on the side at the table.

Prep time: 10 min
Cook time: 15 min
Total time: 25 min
Yield: 2 1/2 cups

Ingredients

    2 cups ketchup

    1/2 cup brown sugar

    6 tablespoons lemon juice

    1 teaspoon vinegar

    3 tablespoons molasses

    1 teaspoon liquid smoke

    2 teaspoons dry mustard (or 1 tablespoon prepared mustard)

    1 tablespoon Worcestershire sauce

    1 teaspoon onion powder

    1/2 teaspoon garlic powder

    1/2 teaspoon black pepper

Instructions:

1. Combine all ingredients in a saucepan and bring to a boil while stirring.
2. Reduce heat, continue stirring and simmer 10 minutes.
3. Serve at room temperature.
4. Store in refrigerator for up to 2 weeks.

Oven Barbecued Ribs

When you want ribs with that outdoor BBQ flavor in the middle of a winter snow storm, this is the recipe for you. Serve with Mom's Cole Slaw and BBQ beans

The secret to these indoor BBQ ribs is the slow cooking. They are literally "fall off the bone" tender. You can substitute beef for the pork ribs but pork tends to be tenderer.

You can cook with sauce on the ribs or add the sauce after cooking at the table.

Prep time: 25 min
Cook time: 4 hours
Total time: 4 hours 25 min
Yield: 6 servings

For the Dry Rub:

Ingredients

- 4 tablespoons paprika
- 2 teaspoons red pepper
- 2 teaspoons white pepper
- 2 teaspoons black pepper
- 2 teaspoons onion powder
- 2 teaspoons garlic powder
- 2 teaspoons salt

Dry Rub Instructions

1. In a small bowl combine all ingredients and mix together thoroughly.

For the Barbecue Sauce:

Ingredients

6 tablespoons chili powder

6 tablespoons salt

2 tablespoons brown sugar

6 tablespoons black pepper

2 tablespoons garlic powder

4 cups ketchup

4 cups white vinegar

4 cups water

1 large onion, diced

1/2 cup sorghum molasses (you may substitute with 1/2 cup honey)

BBQ Sauce Instructions:

1. Combine all sauce ingredients in a large saucepan and bring to a rolling boil. Reduce heat and simmer 1 hour, stirring every 10 minutes.
2. The barbecue sauce will make about 2 quarts of sauce and is best if made a couple of weeks in advance. Store in sterilized canning jars and keep refrigerated. It can be used right away but will develop more flavors over time.

COOKING INSTRUCTIONS FOR RIBS:

1. Sprinkle the dry rub liberally on the ribs and allow ribs to stand 30 minutes at room temperature.
2. Pre-heat oven to 250 degrees.
3. Cook ribs, bone side down, for 2 hours.
4. Turn ribs over and cook 2 more hours.
5. Turn ribs again and baste with the barbecue sauce.
6. Cook another 15 minutes.

Barbecue Beef Brisket Recipe

This simple BBQ Beef Brisket recipe may be cooked indoors in the oven or outside on the grill. Makes a mouth-watering BBQ either way.

The liquid smoke in this recipe gives the meat a strong BBQ flavor so if you prefer a milder taste reduce the liquid smoke to 1 or 2 tablespoons. The low temperature and long cook time is what imparts the entire flavor and makes the meat tender so do not be tempted to rush things by increasing the oven temperature.
Difficulty: Medium

Prep time: 30 min
Cook time: 5 hours
Total time: 5 hours 30 min
Yield: 8 + servings

Ingredients:

   1 (4-6 lb) fresh beef brisket (untrimmed)

   6 oz Cajun Seasoning (buy or make your own)

   4 tbsp mustard

   1 lbs light brown sugar

   1/2 large bottle Italian salad dressing (any brand)

   4 tbsp Liquid Smoke

Instructions:

1. Lay brisket on large piece of aluminum foil.
2. Apply 1/4 of the Cajun Seasoning to each side of the brisket and rub in.
3. Apply 2 tbsp mustard to one side and then apply another 1/4 of the Cajun Seasoning over the mustard and rub in.
4. Turn brisket over and repeat mustard and Cajun Seasoning to the other side.
5. Apply 1/2 of the brown sugar so that it completely covers one side with a layer that is about 1/4 inch thick.
6. Flip meat over and repeat on other side.

7. With fat side of the meat facing up, pour Italian salad dressing over the brisket and seal tightly in the aluminum foil.
8. Cook in oven at 275 degree F for 4 hours (or on outdoor grill).
9. Remove from oven. Pour off drippings (skip this step if on outdoor grill).
10. Pour Liquid Smoke around meat and return to oven for 1 hour (skip this step if on outdoor grill).
11. Remove from oven (or grill) and slice across grain of meat.
12. Serve with your favorite BBQ sauce on the side.

Barbecue Beef Sandwiches
(cooked indoors)

This is one of those recipes where you can spend time preparing once, then have several instant meals available later by freezing the meat (assuming you do not eat all 8 sandwiches initially). The real key to making these sandwiches outstanding is to cook the meat until it is falling apart tender.

It takes longer but we prefer using a slow cooker for the tenderest meat. If you have a pressure cooker you can achieve the same tenderness in a fraction of the time. Oven cooked meat will work but it dries out the meat and does not compare to a pressure cooker or slow cooker for tenderness.

This recipe can be used for beef, pork or chicken.

Prep time: 15 min
Cook time: 8 + hours in crock pot
Total time: 8 hours 15 min
Yield: 8 sandwiches

Ingredients:

(To serve fewer people, simply reduce quantity of meat)

3 lbs chuck roast

1/2 cup chopped onion

1 tsp salt

1 tsp paprika

1/2 tsp black pepper

1 tbsp brown sugar

1 tsp mustard

1 tbsp Worcestershire sauce

1 cup ketchup

1 tbsp lemon juice

1 tbsp vinegar

Instructions:

1. Cook the roast until falling apart tender (8 + hours on low setting in a slow cooker. Shred the meat into bite-sized pieces.
2. Combine all remaining ingredients in a large pot and stir in the meat.
3. Cover and let simmer over medium low heat about 30 minutes.
4. Place heaping portions of meat on your favorite bread. Place left over sauce on table for those that want to add more.
5. Leftover meat may be frozen for later use.

Baby Back Ribs Recipe

Aahhh, Baby Back Ribs, don't we love 'em! No doubt they are one of the real favorites of all barbecue lovers. As with most of our recipes, you can barbecue these ribs with the BBQ sauce on or add sauce afterwards at the table. It seems that most BBQ purest insist on cooking the meat without sauce...but then, that's up to you.

The secret to this recipe is that the ribs are slow cooked in 7-Up or Ginger Ale for a long time which tenderizes even the toughest meat. Then the ribs are grilled for that distinctive BBQ flavor and until the meat is "falling off the bone" tender.

Prep time: 20 min
Cook time: 3 hours 20 min
Total time: 3 hours 40 min
Yield: 3-4 servings per rack of ribs

Ingredients:

pork baby back ribs (1 rack of ribs per 3-4 servings)

large white onions (one onion per rack of ribs)

2-liter bottle Canada Dry Ginger Ale or 7-Up (or enough to completely cover ribs)

your favorite BBQ sauce (or make your own)

Instructions:

1. Place ribs (bone side down) in shallow baking pan(s)
2. Add ginger ale or 7-Up until ribs are completely submerged
3. Cut onions in slices (about 1/4 inch thick).
4. Place onions directly on ribs (one complete sliced onion per rack of ribs)
5. Cover ribs with aluminum foil and bake at 300 degrees for 2-3 hours (see note below)
6. Cool to room temperature (still covered)
7. Place ribs on grill set on medium-high and cook until meat easily pulls off bone (15-20 min). Grill ribs bone side down, do not turn over.
8. Note: You can add BBQ sauce the last 10 minutes of cooking or add at the table whichever you prefer.
9. Note 2: Cooking time in the oven will vary by number of ribs being cooked and due to variation in ovens. You may need to cook up to 3 hours. Just cook ribs in oven until tender and cooked through. You will finish cooking them on the grill.

Making your own barbecue sauce can become an obsessive hobby. Many people take great pride in their personal sauce with a closely guarded secret ingredient. You can make your own personal barbecue sauce with the following tips.

Basic Ingredients for Any Barbecue Sauce

Most all barbecue sauce contains these basic ingredients:

* Tomato (in some form)

* garlic

* vinegar

* salt

It's the other additional ingredients that makes it special, distinctive and "one of a kind".

Let's start with a basic recipe

Ingredients:

* 1 cup ketchup

* 1/2 cup water

* 2 tablespoons vinegar

* 1 clove garlic, chopped fine or 1-2 tablespoon garlic powder

* salt and pepper to taste

Cooking

Combine all ingredients in a small sauce pan, bring to a boil and simmer for 3-4 minutes.

Now for the fun part.

In order to create your own secret sauce, you must accept in the beginning that you are experimenting. At some point, you are probably going to add an ingredient or too much of an ingredient that makes a sauce you do not like. Which means you may need to throw away a few batches of sauce and start over, until you hit that magic formula.

Obviously, it is important to taste as you go. Always begin with a small amount of any ingredient. Then taste the sauce. If you like it, maybe you want to add more of that last ingredient. Be sure to have paper and pen handy and write down the ingredients and amounts as you go. Above all, have fun and when you hit the right formula, take pride in knowing you have your own, personal, secret Barbecue Sauce

Here are some ingredients to experiment with. These ingredients work well with most BBQ sauces. Add any or all, in any amounts you want to the basic recipe above for your experiments.

* Cocoa (powder, unsweetened). Start with 1 teaspoon

* Liquid smoke. Start with 1/2 teaspoon.

* Brown sugar or molasses. Start with 2 tablespoons

* Cola/Pepsi. Start with 1/2 cup.

* Beer. Start with 1/2 cup.

* Orange juice. Start with 1/4 cup

* Different types of vinegar (malt, balsamic, garlic flavored, etc) Start with 2 tablespoons.

* Tomato sauce, tomato paste, whole tomatoes in place of, or in addition to ketchup

* Honey. Start with 1 teaspoon

* Hot sauce (tabasco, etc.) Start with 1 teaspoon

* Anything else you want to try

Additional Tips

* **Thickening your sauce:**
If you want thicker sauce, mix 1 tablespoon cornstarch in 4 tablespoons COLD water. Stir until cornstarch is dissolved. At the end of simmering the sauce, add 1/2 of the cornstarch mixture. Bring sauce back to a simmer while stirring. Watch for 30 seconds (continuing to stir). If you want thicker, add remainder of cornstarch mixture and continue simmering and stirring. If still not thick enough, make another batch of cornstarch mix and just add more of the mix and continue stirring and simmering. Be aware that the sauce will thicken more as it cools.

Most people prefer a smoky flavor with a slightly tomato, slightly sweet, slightly spicy taste. The color should be deep maroon. Most like a thickness that is not watery, yet not too thick, similar to pancake syrup.

* If sauce is bland (tasteless- no kick): add more salt first. If still bland, add more garlic, pepper, ketchup, hot sauce, in that order, tasting after each addition. Even if you do not like spicy sauce, just a touch of hot sauce will liven up the sauce without making it spicy.

To adjust color: additional ketchup or tomato sauce will make a lighter red color. Cocoa or liquid smoke will make a darker color.

So, give it a try and have fun.

Barbecue Ka-Bobs Recipe

This is a flexible recipe that may vary according to ingredients you want to use and number of people you are serving. We provide suggestions but the choice of meat, chicken, seafood or vegetables to use is yours. Just adjust the amount of marinade to ensure you have enough to cover the amount of meat and vegetables you use.

For the meat, we suggest: good cuts of beef, chicken breast or shrimp. Cook at least two ka-bobs for each person.

Prep time: 30 min
Cook time: 20 min
Total time: 50 min plus 1 hour marinade time
Yield: 8 servings

For the Vegetables:

Ingredients:

- 1 medium onion
- 2 medium bell peppers
- 1 dozen mushrooms
- 4 baby potatoes (cut in half)
- 16 cherry tomatoes
- 1 medium zucchini
- 16 sugar peas

For The Marinade:

Ingredients:

In a large flat container (a roasting pan works good) combine:

- 2 cups water
- 1 cup soy sauce

tablespoons sugar

6 cloves garlic (mashed)

1/2 tablespoon horseradish (optional)

4 tablespoons ketchup

1/2 tablespoon ginger powder.

Mix until well combined.

Instructions:

1. Cut all ingredients into bite size pieces (except cherry tomatoes).
2. Place all meat and vegetables in the marinade. Mix well. Place in refrigerator for minimum of 1 hour (overnight is O.K.)
3. Periodically stir to cover all ingredients with marinade.
4. Remove from fridge and push meat and vegetables onto skewers, alternating meat and various vegetables.
5. Cook on BBQ grill until meat is cooked through and vegetables are tender (about 15-20 min).
6. TIPS: It is difficult to cook the meat and potatoes thoroughly before the vegetables burn You can pre-cook the meat and potatoes slightly by placing in boiling water for 10-15 minutes before placing in marinade.
7. Tomatoes tend to turn mushy before everything else is cooked. Therefore, leave a little room at the end of the skewers and push the tomatoes on the skewers the last 10 minutes of cooking time.

Barbecue Pork Spare Ribs Recipe

This is our all-time favorite Barbecue Pork Spare Ribs recipe. By pre-cooking the ribs in the oven you save considerable time and the ribs are tenderized with the oven slow cooking. But you still get that wonderful grill flavor by finishing the final cook on the grill.

Very tender ribs with good barbecue flavor. In bad weather you can cook the ribs entirely indoor in the oven. You lose the smoky grill flavor but still have a yummy BBQ flavor.

Prep time: 20 min
Cook time: 1 hour 50 min
Total time: 2 hours 10 min
Yield: 6 servings

Ingredients:

6 pounds Pork Spareribs

1 (10-3/4 oz) can tomato soup

1 (10-1/2 oz) can condensed beef broth

2 Tbsp light or dark molasses

1/4 cup onion, chopped

1/4 cup cider vinegar

1 tsp chili powder

1 tsp crushed thyme

1 tsp dry mustard

2 cloves garlic, crushed

Dash celery salt

Instructions:

1. Make the sauce first by mixing all ingredients (except spareribs) in saucepan.
2. Simmer the sauce, while stirring, for 10 minutes on medium heat. Set aside.
3. Place the ribs, bone side down, on a rack in a shallow pan. Set the oven for 350 degree F. and cook for one hour.
4. Drain excess fat.
5. Brush sauce over partially cooked ribs.
6. If you want to finish the ribs indoors, continue roasting the ribs 30 to 40 minutes or until the meat is falling off the bone tender, basting with the sauce every 10 minutes.
7. If you want to finish the ribs on the outdoor grill, after step 5, place ribs on the grill 6 inches above gray coals and cook 20 minutes on each side or until ribs are tender. Baste with sauce every 10 minutes while on the grill.

Crock Pot BBQ Pulled Pork
(cooked indoors)

This recipe makes the most flavorful, tender BBQ pulled pork that rivals any BBQ restaurant. You may serve this pork as a stand-alone main course but its real forte is as a BBQ sandwich. If you have left over pork you can freeze it for 6 months and reheat as needed.

We like this recipe for our pulled pork sandwiches. We believe the sandwich bread is almost as important as the pork. Be sure to use big, soft buns that are as fresh as you can get. The right bun can literally turn a good BBQ sandwich into a special sandwich.

All you need for the pulled pork sandwich is the BBQ pulled pork, fresh buns and dill pickles. Complete the meal with a side serving of barbecue beans and slaw.

Prep time: 15 min
Cook time: 12 hours
Total time: 12 hours 15 min
Yield: 8 servings

Ingredients:

* 1 large onion, chopped

* 1 Tablespoon vegetable oil

* 5 garlic cloves, minced

* 1 Tablespoon chili powder

* 1 teaspoon peppercorns

* 1 teaspoon salt

* 1 Cup chili sauce

* 1/4 Cup brown sugar

* 1/4 Cup cider vinegar

* 1 Tablespoon Worcestershire sauce

* 1/2 teaspoon Liquid Smoke

* 3 pound boneless pork shoulder, fat trimmed off

Instructions:

1. Heat oil over medium heat. Add onions, cook until soft but not browned.
2. Add garlic, chili powder and liquid smoke. Cook, stirring, one minute.
3. Add chili sauce, brown sugar, vinegar, and Worcestershire sauce. Bring to a boil while stirring.
4. Place pork in crock pot (slow cooker). Pour sauce from previous step over top of pork. Cover and cook on low 10-12 hours or until pork is falling apart tender.
5. Transfer meat to cutting board and shred.
6. Return shredded meat to crock pot and stir to coat in sauce while re-heating for 5 minutes.

Add water and stir well if additional sauce is needed

Classic BBQ Chicken Recipe

This recipe is so simple but you will be pleasantly surprised when you taste the BBQ chicken. We combine ketchup, coca cola and simple spices to get a barbecue flavor. The coca cola marinade tenderizes the chicken with just a 2-4 hour soak.
Very easy marinade for chicken made with ingredients you probably already have in your kitchen. We added a dash of liquid smoke for a little extra kick.

Prep time: 20 min
Cook time: 2 hours
Total time: 2 hours 20 min plus 4 hour marinade
Yield: 4 servings

Ingredients:

- 1 cut up chicken fryer
- 1 cup ketchup
- 12 oz Coca Cola or Pepsi (not diet)
- 1/2 tsp black pepper
- 1 tsp garlic powder
- 1/2 tsp cayenne powder (omit if you do not like spicy)

Instructions:

1. Combine Coca Cola, ketchup and all dry ingredients in a shallow dish.
2. Place chicken in marinate, turn to coat on all sides and refrigerate for 2 to 4 hours.
3. Cook on BBQ grill until meat starts to separate from bone.
4. May be cooked indoor in oven at 300 degrees for 2-3 hours or until meat easily pulls off bone.

Barbecue Salmon Recipe

Some might argue that this dish should more properly be called "grilled salmon", not BBQ, since no BBQ sauce or rub is used. We will leave that to the BBQ enthusiast to figure out. What we do know is that this is one of the best ways to cook salmon. .
While frozen salmon (or previously frozen) is more available and somewhat cheaper, if you can get fresh salmon it will make "good" turn into "unbelievable". If you are accustomed to frozen salmon or have never tasted "fresh", you will not believe the difference. They are almost like two different types of fish.

Having said that, do not think you must have fresh salmon to enjoy this recipe. Frozen also makes an excellent, tasty grilled salmon. Fresh is simply better.

Prep time: 20 min
Cook time: 20 min for salmon 2 inches thick
Total time: 40 min plus 1 hour refrigeration
Yield: 8 ounce (1/2 pound) per serving

Ingredients:

1 whole salmon, cleaned (plan on 8 oz. per person)

2 to 3 lemons, sliced

2 to 3 limes, sliced

tarragon sprigs (as needed)

dill sprigs (as needed)

Instructions:

1. Place the fish on a double layer of foil.
2. Cover the salmon with herbs (tarragon and dill) and arrange alternate citrus slices over the fish (lime/lemon/lime/lemon, etc.) so that the herbs and citrus are on both sides of fish.
3. Seal the fish in the foil and refrigerate for 1 hour
4. Preheat barbecue on medium high (propane) or grey coals (charcoal)
5. Cook the salmon 10 min for each inch thickness of salmon (1/2 to 1 inch = 10 min. 2 inch = 20 min.)
6. If additional browning is desired, remove salmon from foil and continue cooking if desired. Be careful not to overcook which will produce a tasteless, poor texture fish.
7. Serve with additional fresh citrus slices on the side. Good hot or cold.

Barbecue Shrimp Recipe

This recipe may be cooked on the outdoor grill or indoor stove. For a unique twist cook the shrimp in a wok for an Oriental BBQ touch.

This recipe will make BBQ shrimp that is sweet or spicy. We like a combination of both. To adjust flavor (sweet or spicy) just use the suggestions in the ingredients list to add or subtract honey and/or hot pepper sauce.

Prep time: 20 min
Cook time: 6 min
Total time: 26 min
Yield: 8 servings (4 oz. each)

Ingredients:

2 pounds LARGE shrimp, uncooked (vein, tail and shell removed)

1 cup olive oil

1/2 teaspoon liquid smoke

1/4 cup honey *Note - If making spicy BBQ, use 1 teaspoon honey

juice of 1 lemon

2 tablespoons hot pepper sauce (Tabasco or similar - omit for sweet BBQ)

1 tablespoon chili powder (Omit for sweet BBQ)

3 cloves garlic, minced

4 tablespoons ketchup

1 teaspoon salt

1 teaspoon ground black pepper

Instructions:

1. In a large bowl, mix together all of the ingredients. Marinate shrimp at least 4 hours in bottom of refrigerator, turning occasionally (overnight O.K.).
2. Heat grill, skewer shrimp and BBQ for about 2-3 minutes on each side.
3. You can make kabobs by adding chunks of onion and bell pepper to skewers, alternating shrimp, onion, bell pepper the length of the skewer.
4. Note: Shrimp cooks very fast so take care not to overcook. Over cooked shrimp is tough and chewy. Proper cooked shrimp will curl into a "C" shape. When it curls much beyond this shape it is over cooked.

Coal-Fired Pico De Gallo

Yields: 2 cups servings
Cook time: 5 minutes **Prep time:** 10 minutes

Ingredients

1 banana pepper

1 medium white onion

2 cloves crushed garlic

2 jalapeño peppers

6 plum tomatoes

½ lime juiced

½ teaspoon sugar

¾ teaspoon salt

⅓ cup cilantro

Instructions

1. Build a charcoal fire for direct grilling. While the grill is heating cut the onion into round slices, each ½-inch thick. Cut the peppers in half and remove the seeds and veins. Place the prepared vegetables and whole tomatoes directly over the hot coals (approximately 500°F) and cook for 5 minutes turning once or until they char and start to soften.
2. Remove the vegetables from the grill and dice. Combine the diced vegetables, cilantro, garlic, salt, sugar and lime juice into a small bowl. Let the Pico de Gallo sit for 30 minutes so the flavors will meld together. Serve or refrigerate and serve chilled.

Grilled Hawaiian Hot Sauce

Ingredients

½ pineapple cored, peeled, quartered

1 cup apple cider vinegar

1 cup water

1 mango peeled, quartered

1 papaya peeled, quartered

2 tablespoons honey

2 tablespoons sea salt

½ sweet onion peeled, roughly chopped

4 Jamaican hot peppers whole

Instructions

1. Grill fruit over direct medium-high heat approximately 3 minutes per side. Remove from heat and place in a pot along with additional ingredients and bring to a boil. Reduce heat and allow it to simmer for one hour. Remove hot peppers and place remaining ingredients in a blender. Blend until smooth adding peppers individually until desired level of heat is obtained.

Memphis BBQ Sauce

Ingredients

1 tablespoon garlic powder

1 tablespoon chili powder

1 tablespoon onion powder

2 cups ketchup

⅔ cup apple cider vinegar

3 tablespoons Worcestershire sauce

½ cup brown sugar

½ cup molasses

½ cup yellow mustard

½ tablespoon ground black pepper

½ tablespoon salt

Instructions

1. Mix all ingredients together in a medium sauce pan and bring to a simmer. Cook over medium low heat for 30 minutes stirring frequently to avoid scorching. Remove from heat and place in the fridge to cool.

East Carolina BBQ Sauce

Ingredients

    1 cup vinegar

    1 teaspoon coarse black pepper

    1 teaspoon red pepper flakes

    1 teaspoon salt

    2 tablespoons brown sugar

    ¼ cup ketchup

    ½ cup water

Instructions

1. Mix all ingredients well and refrigerate for a minimum of 24 hours to allow the flavors to meld.

Southern Slaw Dressing

Prep time: 1 hour

Ingredients

- ¼ cup apple cider vinegar
- 1 cup mayonnaise
- ½ teaspoon pepper
- 2 tablespoons sugar
- ¼ teaspoon mustard powder

Instructions

1. Mix all ingredients and refrigerate for at least one hour.

Mint Pesto sauce

Prep time: 15 minutes

Ingredients

½ cup mint leaves

½ cup parsley

2 tablespoons grated Parmesan

2 tablespoons pine nuts toasted

2 cloves garlic minced

½ tablespoon lemon juice

½ cup extra virgin olive oil

Instructions

1. Combine all ingredients in a blender and blend until smooth.

Pink Peppercorn Cream Sauce

Yields: 1 servings
Cook time: 5 minutes **Prep time:** 5 minutes

Ingredients

½ cup beef stock

½ cup heavy cream

2 tablespoons unsalted butter

1 teaspoon cracked pink peppercorns

Instructions

1. Pre-heat grill to medium.
2. Heat butter, cream and beef stock in a medium skillet and reduce by half (approximately 5 minutes).
3. Add pink peppercorns, stir and pour directly over steak.

Cranberry Relish

Yields: 1 servings
Cook time: 15 minutes **Prep time:** 5 minutes

Ingredients

- 8 ounces fresh cranberries
- ¼ cup maple sugar
- Juice of one squeezed lemon
- Juice of one squeezed orange
- ½ teaspoon lemon zest
- 1 teaspoon chili powder
- ¼ teaspoon allspice
- 2 tablespoons fig preserves

Instructions

1. Combine all ingredients minus cranberries, simmer approximately 10 minutes until thickened.
2. Add cranberries over medium high heat and cook for 5 minutes stirring frequently.
3. Remove from heat, cool and serve.

Creole Mustard Marinade

Prep time: 5 minutes

Ingredients

- 3 tablespoons Creole mustard
- 3 tablespoons extra virgin olive oil
- 3 tablespoons red wine vinegar
- 2 tablespoons Worcestershire sauce
- 2 teaspoons minced garlic
- 1 teaspoon dried thyme
- ½ teaspoon kosher salt
- ½ teaspoon ground black pepper

Instructions

1. In a small bowl, whisk all of the ingredients until smooth.

Green Apple Salsa

Yields: 2 servings
Cook time: 10 minutes **Prep time:** 10 minutes

Ingredients

1 green apple cored, finely chopped

1 lime halved

1 tablespoon chopped cilantro

½ jalapeño deseeded, minced

2 green onions

salt to taste

pepper to taste

Instructions

1. Preheat grill to medium.
2. Grill green onions and lime halves (cut side down) approximately 10 minutes until lightly charred.
3. Remove from the grill, finely chop green onion and mix together with lime juice, green apple, jalapeno, and cilantro.
4. Add salt and pepper to taste.

Chimichurri Marinade

Prep time: 15 minutes

Ingredients

½ cup roughly chopped parsley

4 cloves garlic peeled

½ tablespoon red pepper flakes

half lemon juiced

3 tablespoons red wine vinegar

½ cup olive oil

Salt and pepper to taste

Instructions

1. Add parsley, garlic, red pepper, lemon juice and vinegar to a food processor or blender and pulse to blend well.
2. Slowly add in olive oil to create a smooth, vibrant green sauce, remove and chill until ready to use.

Southern Style Salsa

Ingredients

Two 10-ounce cans diced tomatoes and green chills, such as Rotel
One 28-ounce can whole tomatoes with juice
1/2 cup fresh cilantro leaves (or more to taste!)
1/4 cup chopped onion
1 clove garlic, minced
1 whole jalapeno, quartered and sliced thin, with seeds and membrane
1/4 teaspoon ground cumin
1/4 teaspoon salt
1/4 teaspoon sugar
1/2 whole lime, juiced

Directions

Combine the diced tomatoes, whole tomatoes, cilantro, onions, garlic, jalapeno, cumin, salt, sugar and lime juice in a blender or food processor. (This is a very large batch. I recommend using a 12-cup food processor, or you can process the ingredients in batches and then mix everything together in a large mixing bowl.)

Pulse until you get the salsa to the consistency you'd like. I do about 10 to 15 pulses. Test seasonings with a tortilla chip and adjust as needed.

Refrigerate the salsa for at least an hour before serving.

Cilantro Lime Hot Sauce

This tangy hot sauce is delightful on Southern Greens, black eyed peas and fried fish. It is spicy but not red hot. Very easy recipe that seldom fails to please. If you want to kick it up a notch do not remove the seeds and membrane from the peppers in step 1.

Prep time: 20 min
Cook time: 12 min
Total time: 32 min
Yield: 1 pint

Ingredients:

4-6 jalapeno peppers (hot do you want it?)

6 garlic cloves

1 small onion

2 cups apple cider vinegar

1/4 cup chopped Cilantro

2 teaspoons salt

juice of 2 limes

1 teaspoon black pepper

Directions:

1. Remove the seeds and ribs (membrane inside) from the jalapeno peppers and cut into medium chunks.
2. Roughly chop the onion and garlic and put all the chopped ingredients into a small saucepan. Pour in the vinegar and bring to a boil. Reduce heat and simmer 10 minutes.
3. Roughly chop the Cilantro and put into a blender or food processor with the salt, pepper and lime juice. When the jalapeno mixture is cooked, allow to cool 10 minutes, then add to the blender.
4. Turn the blender on low for 10 seconds, then increase to highest setting and puree for 2-3 minutes or until a smooth sauce is obtained.
5. If you want a pure liquid sauce, strain through a medium hole strainer. If you like the pulp in the sauce, do not strain.
6. Pour into a sterilized jar and refrigerate.

Gravy, Turkey

Here's an easy recipe for turkey gravy that only takes a few minutes to make. When you take your turkey out of the oven you should let it rest for 15 or 20 minutes before carving. This seals in the juices and makes a moister, tender turkey. You can make this gravy while you are waiting.

Prep time: 10 min
Cook time: 25 min
Total time: 35 min
Yield: 4 1/2 cups gravy

Ingredients:

1/2 cup melted butter

1/4 to 1/2 cup all-purpose flour, as needed

4 cups chicken or turkey stock (canned O.K.)

1 tablespoon dried thyme seasoning

1/2 teaspoon dried sage seasoning

1/2 cup (or more if desired) pan drippings from roast turkey

Salt and black pepper to taste

Instructions:

1. Heat the butter over low heat until it just starts to bubble (about 5 min).
2. Add flour a little at a time and stir constantly another 2-3 min until flour is completely dissolved and a thin paste (roux) forms. There should be no liquid butter or lumps of flour showing. Set aside on low heat.
3. In a separate soup pot bring chicken (or turkey) stock to a boil. Add thyme, sage and pan drippings. Reduce heat and simmer 5 min.
4. Whisk the roux (from step 2) into the simmering stock.
5. Simmer over low heat until the desired thickness is reached, about 5-10 minutes.
6. Season with salt and pepper to taste.
7. Remove from heat and strain to remove any solids that might have been in the pan drippings.
8. If gravy is not thick enough in step 5, dissolve 1 tablespoon cornstarch in 1/2 cup cold water and slowly stir into the gravy. The longer you cook, the thicker it will get.

Gravy, Sausage

Although this recipe makes sausage gravy you can substitute bacon, chopped ham or leave the meat out. We found making the roux the only difficult part but we got the hang of it quickly. The secret is, as the recipe says, to make the roux so there is no visible oil or lumps of flour showing.

Prep time: 5 min
Cook time: 15 min
Total time: 20 min
Yield: 4-6 servings

Ingredients:

12 ounces ground pork sausage

1/4 cup bacon grease or cooking oil, as needed

1/4 cup diced onion

2-4 tablespoons all-purpose flour

1-2 cups milk (see instructions)

salt and pepper to taste

parsley for garnish (optional)

Instructions:

1. In a skillet over medium heat, add the sausage and onion to the bacon grease. Cook while stirring until sausage is brown and onion tender. Remove sausage and onion and set aside (or if using a large pan, push to one side).
2. To make roux: Add one tablespoon of flour to the bacon grease while stirring constantly. Watch the consistency of the roux and add more flour as necessary to obtain a thick, dull colored paste. There should be no visible liquid grease or lumps of flour in the roux. You must get the roux consistency correct now. You can NOT add flour or grease after this point
3. If you want white gravy, go to the next step (adding milk) just as the roux begins to show color. If you want brown gravy cook the roux until it turns a rich brown color (just before burning). You must constantly stir the roux.
4. Add 1/2 cup milk while stirring. As the roux dissolves and the milk begins to boil, add more milk a little at a time while watching the thickness of the gravy. The thickness will be determined by how much milk you add and how long you cook it. When the gravy is removed from the heat and cools, it will become a little thicker.

5. As you approach the thickness you want, add the sausage/onion mix back into the gravy if they were removed. Add salt and pepper to taste and cook one minute.
6. If you want the gravy spicy, add a dash of crushed red pepper flakes in the previous step.
7. Pour the steaming hot gravy over biscuits and garnish with chopped parsley

Homemade Mustard

If you wish your store bought mustard was a little sweeter or tart or..??? Why not make your own? You can with this recipe and adjust the flavors to whatever you like.

We tested this recipe with varying results, but it will certainly make mustard. Our results were a little thicker than store bought mustard but it did had a very good flavor.

Be very careful with turmeric; it will stain practically everything it contacts (counter tops, utensils) and is very difficult to remove.

Don't be afraid to experiment with additional or less vinegar and sugar to alter sweetness or tartness.

Prep time: 15 min
Cook time: 3 min
Total time: 18 min
Yield: about 1 pint

Ingredients:

1/2 cup dry mustard (powdered spice)

1/2 cup all-purpose flour

1 teaspoon salt

1 tablespoon sugar

1/2 cup white vinegar

1/2 cup water

2 eggs

teaspoon horseradish (optional - add only if you want spicy)

1/2 teaspoon turmeric (for color)

1 tablespoon softened margarine

Instructions:

1. Mix all ingredients EXCEPT MARGARINE in a medium sauce pan.
2. Place on low heat and stir constantly until mixture thickens and begins sticking to bottom of pan (about 2-3 minutes). Mix will be lumpy.
3. Remove from heat and stir in margarine.
4. Use a potato masher or electric mixer set on slow to beat mustard until you have a smooth consistency. You may need to add additional margarine to get a thinner, creamier mix.
5. Transfer to a sealable jar and store in refrigerator.

Homemade Ketchup

"This ketchup does come close to those name brands in terms of taste, texture and color. I've never had tomato paste-based ketchup that I liked, so I decided to cook down crushed tomatoes instead. By using the slow cooker, we take most of the labor out of the process."

Makes 3 cups

- 2 (28 ounce) cans peeled ground tomatoes
- 1/2 cup water, divided
- 2/3 cup white sugar
- 3/4 cup distilled white vinegar
- 1 teaspoon onion powder
- 1/2 teaspoon garlic powder
- 1 3/4 teaspoons salt
- 1/8 teaspoon celery salt
- 1/8 teaspoon mustard powder
- 1/4 teaspoon finely ground black pepper
- 1 whole clove

Directions

Pour ground tomatoes into slow cooker. Swirl 1/4 cup water in each emptied can and pour into slow cooker. Add sugar, vinegar, onion powder, garlic powder, salt, celery salt, mustard powder, black pepper, cayenne pepper, and whole clove; whisk to combine.

Cook on high, uncovered, until mixture is reduced by half and very thick, 10 to 12 hours. Stir every hour or so.

Smooth the texture of the ketchup using an immersion blender, about 20 seconds.

Ladle the ketchup into a fine strainer and press mixture with the back of a ladle to strain out any skins and seeds.

Transfer the strained ketchup to a bowl. Cool completely before tasting to adjust salt, black pepper, or cayenne pepper.

Section 8
Vegetables

Stove Top BBQ Beans (cooked indoors)

We believe this is the best BBQ beans recipe around. These are not your ordinary beans. The BBQ flavor really stands out in these tender beans.

Very good recipe that makes beans with a lot of BBQ flavor. We placed them on the stove and just sort of forgot about them for a couple of hours and they were delicious. We did have to add water occasionally as it evaporated.

Prep time: 10 min
Cook time: 2 hours 10 min
Total time: 2 hour 20 min plus overnight bean soak
Yield: 4 + servings

Ingredients:

    1 lb red kidney beans

    1/2 cup ketchup

    1 large onion, finely chopped

    4 cloves garlic, minced

    2 bell pepper, cored, seeded, chopped

    1 stalk celery, finely chopped

    4 slices bacon

    3 jalapeno peppers, seeded and diced

    2 cups your favorite barbecue sauce

    1 cup brown sugar (adjust to your taste)

    1/2 cup mustard

    1/2 teaspoon liquid smoke

    salt and ground black pepper to taste

    1 tbsp cornstarch dissolved in 1/4 cup cold water (if needed in step 5)

Instructions:

1. Cover beans with water and soak overnight.
2. Cover beans with water and bring to a boil on high heat, Reduce heat and simmer beans 1 hour.
3. Add all other ingredients **EXCEPT cornstarch** and cook until beans, celery and peppers are tender (about 30 min to 1 hour).
4. Add water as necessary to keep beans from drying out.
5. When beans are done you should have about 1 cup of thick sauce in the bottom of the pot. If not, add water as necessary to obtain 1 cup of a liquid in the pot. To thicken, dissolve 1 tablespoon cornstarch in 1/4 cup cold water, add to beans and cook another 10 minutes.
6. When beans are cooked and tender, cool 2 full spoons of beans and taste. Add salt, pepper and brown sugar as needed to taste.

Southern Vegetable Soup

This is the simplest soup you will ever make, because...you can put almost anything you want in it. Use the ingredients and quantities given here as just a guide. Feel free to put more or less of any ingredient, but taste as you go and adjust to your personal taste.

My mom made soup like this when I was growing up and I don't think it ever came out the same. I think she just cleaned out the refrigerator and made soup out of it (the kids called it "Clean out the fridge soup"). But, it was always good!
Be sure any meat added is able to be cooked in the one hour soup cook time.

Prep time: 20 min
Cook time: 1 hour
Total time: 1 hour 20 min
Yield: 8 servings

Ingredients:

    2 (or 3) carrots, chopped in bite-size chunks

    1 medium onion, quartered

    1 cup cabbage, chopped

    1-2 cups meat of choice, chopped (beef, pork, ham)

    2 potatoes, peeled and cut in 2 inch chunks

    1 stalk celery, chopped

    1 cup white beans, cooked (optional)

    2 tablespoons white vinegar

    1 small can tomato paste or large can of tomato sauce

    6-8 cups water, as needed

    1 large tomato, cubed (optional)

    1 teaspoon oregano

    salt and pepper to taste

    anything else left over in the fridge that you want to add

Instructions:

1. Pretty simple...throw everything in a large pot and bring to a boil. Reduce heat and simmer about an hour or until vegetables are tender and any added meat is cooked.
2. If you use tomato sauce, start with about 1/2 large can. If you use tomato paste, start with 4 tablespoons. Add more or less water and tomato sauce/paste according to your preference for a thick or thin soup and how strong a tomato flavor you like. Stir and taste occasionally. Add salt and pepper to taste.

Black Eyed Peas

Serving black eyed peas on New Year's Eve is an old tradition in the South. The "old timers" say it brings good luck for the coming year. True or not, it's a good excuse to dine on this classic Southern treat.

Black eyed peas are easy to cook but a few tips make them special. The onion and bacon (or ham hock) are standard ingredients but a touch of vinegar and hot sauce puts them on a different level. While these two items are not traditional they put a little "kick" in the peas that is worth trying.

Prep time: 10 min
Cook time: 40 min
Total time: 50 min
Yield: 4+ servings

Ingredients:

    2 1/2 cups dried black eyed peas

    water, as needed

    1 tablespoon salt

    1/2 tablespoon black pepper

    1 medium onion, sliced in half

    2 slices bacon (or ham hock)

    1 clove garlic, minced

    1/2 tablespoon white vinegar

    dash hot sauce (Tabasco)

    1/4 cup green bell pepper, diced (optional)

Instructions:

1. Place all ingredients in a large cooking pot and bring to a boil.
2. Reduce heat and simmer 40 minutes or until peas are tender. Add additional water if needed to keep peas covered. If all the water boils away the peas will burn quickly, so watch closely.
3. Taste peas and add vinegar, hot sauce, salt or pepper as needed to suit your taste.

Bourbon Sweet Potatoes

These yummy sweet potatoes are very easy to make. Note that the bourbon only provides flavor. There is no significant alcohol in the dish since the alcohol evaporates during cooking. You can substitute yams for sweet potatoes if that is what you have available.

These creamy sweet potatoes flavored with a touch of bourbon are sweet and creamy enough to serve as a side dish or even as dessert. Note the instruction concerning the shape of the potatoes in step #2.

Prep time: 30 min
Cook time: 1 hour
Total time: 1 hour 30 min
Yield: 6 servings

Ingredients

* 6 medium sweet potatoes

* 1/4 cup butter

* 3 tablespoons bourbon

* 3 tablespoons milk

* 1 tablespoon firmly packed brown sugar

* 1/2 teaspoon nutmeg

* salt and black pepper to taste

* 1/4 cup miniature marshmallows

* 6 pecan half's

Instructions

1. Bake the sweet potatoes for 50 minutes in a 400 degree F. oven, or until they can be easily pierced with a fork.
2. According to the shape of the potatoes, either cut a slice off the top of each potato or cut in half lengthwise. And scoop out the inside taking care not to break the shell.
3. In a bowl, mash the potatoes then add the butter, bourbon, milk, brown sugar and nutmeg. Beat together until well blended, then add the salt and pepper to taste.
4. Spoon the mixture into the shells. Garnish with the pecan halves and miniature marshmallows.
5. Set the oven heat to 350 degrees F. and return the potatoes to the oven. Bake the potatoes until the marshmallows just start to brown (about 5 to 10 minutes).

Candied Yams (Sweet Potatoes)

The name "yams" and "sweet potatoes" are often used interchangeably and many people think they are the same or related. They are not the same and, in fact, are not even remotely related. Sweet potatoes are what you most often see in stores. Frequently they are labeled as yams. Sweet potatoes are oval shaped with a pointed, tapered end. Real yams are rounder without the tapered end and can grow much larger.

Yams are sweeter and more moist that sweet potatoes. The confusion began years ago when a sweet potato was developed that was sweeter making it more like a yam. This sweet potato began to be called and labeled as a "yam"...when actually it was a sweet potato.

If that confused you we will now simplify it. You can use either yams or sweet potatoes in this recipe. You probably will not notice much difference either way.

This is candied yams like my mom made when I was a child. Very easy to make and good served with any meat dish.

Prep time: 10 min
Cook time: 47 min
Total time: 57 min
Yield: 4 servings

Ingredients:

    5 large yams, peeled, chopped into 2-3 inch chunks

    1/2 cup sugar

    2 tablespoons cinnamon

    1/4 teaspoon ground cloves

    1/2 teaspoon salt

    water, as needed

    1 cup miniature marshmallows

Instructions:

1. Place all ingredients in a large pot.
2. Add enough water to cover yams 2 inches.
3. Simmer on medium heat until yams are tender and liquid is syrupy, about 30-45 minutes. Add water if necessary. Do NOT allow to get dry. You should end with about 1 cup of syrupy liquid in pot. If too watery, add a couple more spoons of sugar the last 15 minutes of cooking.
4. After yams are cooked, place in a pan and cover with miniature marshmallows. Place in over set on broiler. Watch continually and remove as soon as marshmallows are melted (just 1 or2 minutes).

Collards Turnip Greens

There's nothing like the smell of cooking greens coming from the kitchen. This same recipe may be used for turnip, collard or mustard greens. Better yet, combine all three in one pot and serve with fried chicken, black eyed peas and cornbread.

Some people like greens with a firm texture and cook their greens about an hour. I like greens very tender and limp so I cook my greens much longer. As long as 2-3 hours. Remember to watch the greens closely and make sure all the liquid does not boil away and scorch the greens making them uneatable.

We tried the suggestion of combining turnip, collard and mustard greens and they were delicious.

Prep time: 10 min
Cook time: 1 hour 7 min
Total time: 1 hour 17 min
Yield: 4 servings

Ingredients:

2 1/2 lbs turnip, collard or mustard greens, washed and chopped into 1-in. pieces

3 slices bacon, cut into 1-inch pieces or ham hock

2/3 cup chopped onions

1 or 2 dashes cider or red wine vinegar

salt and pepper to taste (start with 1 tablespoon salt and 1/4 teaspoon pepper)

dash hot sauce (Tabasco), optional

Instructions:

1. Fry the bacon in a pot large enough to cook the greens. If you substitute a ham hock for the bacon, just use 2 tablespoons of bacon grease or cooking oil and lightly brown the ham hock before going to step 2 (about 5 min).
2. Add the greens along with onions.
3. Cook on low heat, stirring with wooden spoon, until greens are coated with bacon fat (or cooking oil if ham hock used) about 2 minutes. Pour off excess fat.
4. Cover the greens with water and season with salt and pepper.

5. Bring to a boil. Cover the pot, reduce heat, and simmer until tender (time will vary, about 1 hour). Stir occasionally and add water if they threaten to scorch.
6. When done, increase heat to med-high, stir often. Boil off nearly all the cooking liquid.
7. Add vinegar and stir. Taste and add salt and pepper if needed.
8. Serve very hot with hot sauce to be added at the table if desired.

Collards with Cajun Tasso

Collard greens are a staple in The South and something we've enjoyed all our lives. I learned to love them at an early age and have never lost my taste for them; in fact I probably love them more now than I ever did, now that I know how nutritious they are. Collards are said to contain high levels of anti-carcinogens among their many benefits, which include high levels of vitamin C and strong antiviral and antibacterial properties.

Traditionally, pots of collard's are seasoned with a cured and smoked ham hock, or bits of country ham, sometimes even crackling's. This is the first time I am making them with Tasso, so we will see how they turn out. A pot of collards is extremely easy to make, however certain steps are necessary for it to turn out "just right". These steps I will explain along the way.

Not very many ingredients are needed. The garlic is one of two "secret ingredients" that I was taught to use in order to make a pot of collards above and beyond delicious.

Ingredients
* 2 pounds collard greens
* 1 onion, diced
* 1 pound Tasso, chopped
* 1 heaping teaspoon kosher salt
* 1 heaping teaspoon black pepper
* 3 cloves garlic
* 1/2 to 3/4 cup cider vinegar (to taste)
* 1/4 cup molasses to 3/4 cup

Directions

The first thing we need to do is to cut off most of the stems. Then, on the outer darker leaves, we have to trim off the thicker portion of the stem since it gets woody and tough in cooking. The thinner stems on the more tender inner leaves can be left on. These thick stems should be saved in the refrigerator and boiled along with other vegetable trimmings and odd beef, pork or chicken bones to make homemade stock.

After trimming, the leaves need to be rinsed in cool water. Just run a sink full of cold tap water and swish them around for a minute or so, then drain.

Here's the fun part! The thick leaves need to be cut up for the pot. To do this, layer several leaves upon one another, then roll them up like a taco. Once rolled, slice them into pinwheels as in the picture and you have perfect pieces for the pot.

Once the collards are cut up, they go into the pot they will be cooked in. This is set aside (with no water in it). Meanwhile, in a smaller pot, put 1 gallon cold tap water over high heat. Add 1 diced onion and the Tasso. Bring to a boil, then reduce the heat to obtain a slow boil for about an hour or until 1/4 to 1/3 of the liquid has been reduced.

After the onion and Tasso boiled for about 30 minutes I tasted the broth. I was surprised. The Tasso was not as salty as I thought it would be and far from anything like country ham. So adding salt was going to be necessary.

Here I have 1 heaping teaspoon of coarse ground kosher salt and the same amount of black pepper plus 4 garlic cloves which get dumped on top of the waiting collards.

Now we pour the hot Tasso/onion broth on top of the dry collards. I always do this in the sink since having an unfortunate accident a long time ago. The accident involved two friends, a large dog and a Frisbee as I was combining the pots on the stovetop. Be very careful as steam burns are a possibility as well.

Stir this mixture with a wooden spoon and set on the stove over high heat. Once it comes to a boil, reduce the heat to the lowest setting and let gently cook down, uncovered. This way, the pot can stay on the stovetop all day long until supper time. If you turn up the heat, then it will cook faster, obviously.

If you feel this is too much liquid in the pot, just cut down the initial water by 1 quart. My favorite way of eating collards is in a bowl over a thick chunk of cornbread to soak up all that extra delicious juice.

To this pot the next step is to add 1/2 cup cider vinegar. You can add more or less depending on how you like it. I add the 1/2 cup now and another 1/4 cup at the very end, just before serving. My second "secret ingredient" is molasses. Long time ago someone taught me that adding about 1/4 cup molasses to the pot made the whole thing richer, deeper and tastier. They were correct. I have always done it this way and folks rave about my collards.

Once the collards are tender and the liquid and ingredients made friends and joined together into deliciousness, it is ready.

Nothing better on a cold wintry day!

Corn Fritters

I think of corn fritters as a cross between cornbread and pancakes infused with whole kernel corn. This is a very simple, easy recipe that may be served in place of cornbread.

Prep time: 10 min
Cook time: 20 min
Total time: 30 min
Yield: 6 servings

Ingredients:

* 1 and 1/2 cups all-purpose flour

* 1/4 cup cornmeal

* 3 teaspoons baking powder

* 1/2 teaspoons salt

* 1 egg, slightly beaten

* 1 cup milk

* 1 tablespoon melted shortening

* 2 cups whole kernel corn (drain liquid if using canned)

* oil for frying (enough for about a 3/4 inch depth in your frying pan)

Instructions:

1. In a medium size bowl, combine all of the ingredients except the corn and frying oil. Mix until smooth.
2. Add the corn and mix well. The batter should look like a thick cornbread or pancake batter. You may need more or less than the 1 cup milk. You should be able to compress a small handful and have it hold it's shape without crumbling or running through your fingers.
3. In a large skillet, heat the frying oil until very hot (365 degrees F.). If you do not have a thermometer, place the handle of a wooden spoon or other wooden utensil into the oil. You should see bubbles rise around the wooden handle immediately. If not, wait for oil to get hotter.

4. Drop the batter by the tablespoon into the hot grease and fry until browned on both sides, Serve Hot!

Fried Summer Squash

This is just too good to be so simple. But it's also easy to mess it up if not cooked right. The secret is in the cooking time. When properly cooked it should resemble a goulash, with about half brown and half yellow coloring. The onions and squash should be slightly caramelized.

The squash has a very subtle flavor that can be overpowered by tomato, so if you add tomato, do not use very much.

The squash must be stirred frequently; especially the last few minutes or it will burn. Do not add water, the squash will release all the moisture needed.

Prep time: 20 min
Cook time: 23 min
Total time: 43 min
Yield: 2 servings

Ingredients:

- 1 lb Yellow Summer Squash with skin, coarsely chopped
- 2 medium onions, chopped course
- 3 tablespoons bacon grease (or as needed)
- 1 fresh tomato, chopped (optional)
- Salt to taste
- Black pepper to taste

Instructions:

1. Wash the squash and chop course (bite size), with the skins intact.
2. Chop onion course.
3. In a 10 or 12 inch cast iron skillet, cook 3-4 slices of bacon to obtain about 3 tablespoons of bacon grease.
4. Remove bacon. Pour off 2 tablespoons of the bacon grease and save.
5. Add chopped squash and onions.
6. Bring to a slow simmer on medium low heat, stirring frequently.

7. If additional grease is needed, add the saved bacon grease (from step 4) a little at a time.
8. Cook until the squash is about half brown and half still yellow (about 15-20 minutes). The squash and onions will be very tender and resemble a stew.
9. If using tomato, add now. Add salt and pepper to taste and cook another 3 min. Serve steaming hot.

Fried Green Tomatoes

One of the most traditional Southern dishes, fried green tomatoes are so famous they even had a movie named after them. Properly cooked, they should be crispy on the outside and tender on the inside.

When slicing the tomatoes remember that thicker slices will have more soft insides while thin cuts will be crisp all the way through.

Prep time: 10 min
Cook time: 8 min
Total time: 18 min
Yield: 4 servings

Ingredients:

4 Green Tomatoes

2 cups White Corn Meal

1/2 cup Flour

Cooking oil (enough to provide about 1 inch deep in pan)

1 egg

1/2 cup milk

Salt and Pepper to taste

Instructions:

1. Place cooking oil in large frying pan and place on medium heat.
2. Wash and slice tomatoes (slice about 1/4 inch thick)
3. Combine egg and milk in medium sized bowl and beat enough for good mix
4. Place corn meal and flour on a separate large plate and mix with dash of salt and pepper
5. Dredge tomato slices in cornmeal mix, shake off excess
6. Dip tomato slices in egg/milk wash
7. Dredge in the cornmeal mix again to coat thoroughly
8. Placed coated slices in frying pan without sides touching
9. Cook until golden brown on both sides (about 3-4 minutes per side)
10. Remove and place on paper towels to absorb oil.
11. Serve HOT!

Hoppin John's

Hoppin John is an old Southern dish said to be popular in Georgia and the Carolinas. So...what is "Hoppin John", you ask? In its simplest form, black eyed peas and rice. However, like many old recipes, there are a variety of ways to make Hoppin john. It can be made with a Cajun flavor of spiciness or the more traditional peas and rice with a little onion and tomato.

While Hoppin John can be traditional, seasoned peas and rice...this recipe leans toward the spicier Cajun style. We found that the ingredients are somewhat flexible and if you are missing one or two it will still come out good. And, the aroma of this dish cooking is heavenly.

Prep time: 20 min
Cook time: 2 hours
Total time: 2 hours 20 min
Yield: 8 + servings

Ingredients:

    1 pound package dry Black Eye Peas

    3/4 cup ham, bacon or sausage, chopped and cooked (we prefer ham)

    1 medium onion, diced (about 1 cup)

    2 cloves garlic, minced

    bell pepper, chopped (about 1 cup)

    1 cup celery, diced

    1 jalapeno pepper (diced with seeds removed)

    1 cup tomatoes, diced

    1 teaspoon Cajun seasoning

    1/2 teaspoon ground Thyme

    1/2 teaspoon ground cumin

    1/2 teaspoon black pepper

    6 cups vegetable or chicken stock (you can substitute water but will loss some flavor)

    2 Tablespoons canola oil

2 cups long grain white rice, cooked

Instructions:

1. In a 6 quart soup pot, heat the canola oil on medium high heat. Sauté the onion, bell pepper, garlic and celery until the onion is tender.
2. Add the vegetable or chicken stock. Add the tomatoes, seasonings, jalapeno, ham and black eye peas.
3. Bring to a boil. Lower heat to medium low and cover. Simmer for one and one half (1 1/2) hours stirring occasionally. Check frequently and add water if needed to keep covered in liquid.
4. During the last 1/2 hour, cook the rice according to package directions.
5. Spoon out some rice in a deep bowl. Cover liberally with the Hoppin John and serve hot with cornbread.

Mashed Potatoes

Such a simple dish, mashed potatoes, and yet there are so many different ways to prepare them. This is a basic recipe which includes a list of optional additives to make them special.

We used several different types of potatoes for this recipe and found that Russet and Yukon Gold worked the best.

You can mash the potatoes with an electric mixer but we found that an old fashioned potato masher gave us better control of the consistency. Be careful adding milk while mixing so you do not end up with soupy potatoes. You can add more milk but you cannot take it out.

Prep time: 15 min
Cook time: 20 min
Total time: 35 min
Yield: 4 + servings

Ingredients:

    2 pounds of potatoes

    1 teaspoon of salt

    1 cup of half and half or regular milk

    6 tablespoons of butter

    Salt and pepper, to taste

Instructions:

1. Peel and quarter the potatoes
2. Add the potatoes to a large pot with enough cold water to cover them by an inch or so. Add 1 tsp. salt and bring the water to a boil. Cook until the potatoes are tender when pierced with a fork (about 15-20 minutes).
3. Drain the potatoes, return them to the pot and cook the drained potatoes over low heat for a couple of minutes to evaporate some of the water still in the potatoes.
4. Mash by your method of choice (electric mixer of hand potato masher).
5. Blend in the butter, half and half (or milk) and any additives from the list below.
6. Season with salt and pepper to taste.

Optional Additives:

Garlic (two crushed cloves)

Diced dill or sweet pickles (1/4 cup)

Bacon bits (1/4 cup)

Cream Cheese (1/4 cup)

Grated Cheddar Cheese (1/4 to 1/2 cup)

Chopped shallots or green onions (1/4 cup)

Worcestershire sauce (1 tablespoon)

Regular or Dijon mustard (1 tablespoon)

Dried dill weed (or fresh if you have it) (1 tablespoon)

Fancy Mashed Potatoes

Most everyone has their favorite mashed potatoes recipe but this one provides a variety of optional additives to make your mashed potatoes special. We like to add dill weed and just a touch of horseradish.

Prep time: 25 min
Cook time: 35 min
Total time: 1 hour
Yield: 4 + servings

Ingredients:

* 2-3 pounds potatoes (about 7-8 medium size potatoes for 4 people)

* salted water

* 1/2 to 3/4 cup warm milk

* 6 tablespoons melted butter

* salt and pepper to taste

Instructions:

1. Peel potatoes and cut into large pieces.
2. In a large pot, add potatoes, cover with water, add a dash of salt and bring to a boil.
3. Cook until tender and a fork easily penetrates the potatoes (about 20 minutes).
4. Drain potatoes and place in a large mixing bowl.
5. Combine milk and butter in a cup and heat in microwave (or stove top) until butter melts. Set aside.
6. Mash potatoes until no lumps remain.
7. Add any or all of the "fancy ingredients" below.
8. Add milk/butter mixture in small amounts to potatoes, beating after each addition, until desired consistency is reached.
9. Add salt and pepper to taste. Continue beating until mashed potatoes are light and fluffy.

Fancy Ingredients (Use one or any combination. Add in step 7)

* 1/3 cup onions, minced

* 1/3 cup mushrooms, minced

* 1/2 tablespoon dill weed

* 1 tablespoon prepared mustard

* 1 teaspoon horseradish sauce

* 1/3 cup cucumber, diced

* 1/3 cup dill pickle, diced

* 1/2 tablespoon garlic powder

* 1/3 cup cooked bacon, crumbled

* 1 cup shredded cheddar cheese

* 1 package (8 ounce size) cream cheese, cubed

* 1 cup sour cream

Southern Potato Salad

Your family will love this mouth-watering recipe for Southern Potato Salad. Be sure to include it at any picnic. Serve the potato salad cold and keep it refrigerated since it contains mayonnaise and can spoil if left out too long.

This recipe make quite a lot (serves 6-8). If you want a smaller portions just half the ingredients. To adjust yield, allow 1 large potato per person in the recipe. It's better to make too much than to run short...especially if the one who wants more is your sister's six year old with nerve shattering vocal cords.

Prep time: 30 min
Cook time: 20 min
Total time: 50 min
Yield: 6-8 servings

Ingredients:

    8 Large (or 10 medium) potatoes

    1 cup mayonnaise

    1/2 cup sour cream

    1/4 cup chopped celery

    1/4 cup chopped onion (red onion adds a lot of color)

    2 tsp sweet pickle relish

    1 tsp mustard

    1/4 lb cooked bacon, crumbled

    3 hard-boiled eggs, sliced

    1 tsp celery seed

    1/2 tsp garlic powder

    1/4 tsp dill weed

    1/4 tsp paprika

    Salt and pepper to taste

Instructions:

1. Peel potatoes and cut into large bite sized chunks.
2. Boil potatoes until a fork pushed in a potato goes in with a slight resistance (about 15-20 min). Do not overcook. Set aside and allow to cool.
3. When cool add all other ingredients, except eggs and paprika, to the potatoes and mix thoroughly. Mix gently to avoid breaking up potatoes and ending up with mashed potatoes. Add salt and pepper to taste as you mix.
4. Garnish top with sliced boiled eggs and sprinkle **lightly** with paprika.
5. For variety, use small red potatoes instead of regular potatoes and leave the skin on. Also, use red onions instead of regular onions.

Pineapple Upside down Sweet Potatoes

This dish not only tastes good it is such a pretty presentation. When you invert the pan the pineapple and brown sugar are on top giving the appearance of a pineapple upside down cake.

Very novel treatment of this Southern favorite. We were tempted to add melted marshmallows to the top but resisted and were happy with what this recipe produced.
Difficulty: Medium

Prep time: 30 min
Cook time: 45 min
Total time: 1 hour 15 min
Yield: 8 servings

For The Topping

Ingredients:

- 2 tablespoons margarine, melted
- 1 tablespoon brown sugar, packed
- 1 tablespoon maple syrup
- ground cinnamon (as needed)
- 8-10 whole pineapple slices OR 1 1/2 cups pineapple chunks (canned or fresh)

For The Filling:

Ingredients:

- 1 can (18 oz.) sweet potatoes (or if you cook your own: 2 1/4 cups)
- 1 1/2 teaspoons vanilla extract
- 3/4 teaspoon ground cinnamon
- 1 tablespoon brown sugar, packed

Instructions:

1. Preheat oven to 350 degrees F.
2. Lightly oil (or use nonstick spray) a 9-inch pie pan
3. Prepare Topping: Combine melted margarine, brown sugar and maple syrup in a small bowl and mix well. Spread mix evenly over the bottom of the prepared pie pan.
4. Sprinkle lightly with cinnamon. Arrange pineapple slices (or chunks) evenly over the margarine mix in pie pan.
5. Prepare Filling: In a large bowl, combine all of the filling ingredients. Mash with a fork or potato masher until smooth and completely combined.
6. Spoon sweet potato filing mix over the pineapple in the pie pan and smooth with the back of a spoon.
7. Cover with aluminum foil and bake 45 minutes.
8. Remove from oven and let sit 2 minutes. Remove foil, run a knife around the edge of the pan and invert onto a serving plate.

Rice and Okra

Like bacon and eggs, okra and rice just go together for a nice blend of complimentary flavors.

Although brown rice is healthier, we substituted white rice because we just prefer the flavor. We liked the idea of frying the okra separate so it does not impart that sticky texture to the dish that many people dislike.

This recipe makes a Cajun-like stew that performs well as a main course with hot cornbread on the side.

Prep time: 10 min
Cook time: 40 min
Total time: 50 min
Yield: 4 servings

Ingredients:

- 1 cup brown rice
- 3 cups chicken stock
- 1 tomato, seeded and chopped
- 1/2 teaspoon curry powder
- 2 tablespoons butter or margarine
- 1/2 pound okra, cut into 1 inch pieces
- salt and ground black pepper, to taste
- dash red pepper flakes, optional

Instructions:

1. In a large saucepan, combine the rice, stock, tomato and curry. Cook over medium heat, stirring occasionally, until the rice is tender, about 20-25 minutes. Add more stock, if needed, to keep rice from sticking.
2. In a small fry pan over medium heat, melt the butter and fry the okra for 4-5 minutes or until lightly browned.
3. Add the okra to the rice and cook another 10 minutes, stirring occasionally. Add a dash of crushed red pepper flakes if you want it a little spicy. Add salt, to taste. Remove from heat and serve hot.

Southern Fried Okra

Burn the okra? That's what the recipe says. Believe it or not it gives the okra a super crunch with a toasty unique flavor. It's nothing like boiled okra or okra in soups. Another bonus is that this recipe works well with fresh or frozen okra.

Prep time: 20 min
Cook time: 30 min
Total time: 50 min
Yield: 4 servings

Ingredients:

Vegetable Cooking oil, enough to cover okra completely in frying pan

4 cups cut up okra (or one bag frozen)

1 egg

1/2 cup milk

1 cup cornmeal (we prefer white but use yellow if that's what you have)

2 tablespoons flour

1 teaspoon salt

1/2 teaspoon black pepper

Instructions:

1. Heat oil in large frying pan on medium heat. Use a pan large enough not to crowd the okra.
2. Chop okra into 1 inch pieces (if using frozen, you can buy it already chopped).
3. Beat egg lightly in a bowl, add milk and stir well.
4. Add okra to the egg/milk wash. Stir to coat okra with mixture and let sit for 5 minutes in the wash.
5. Place the cornmeal, flour, salt and pepper in a separate large bowl and mix
6. Dredge the okra in the cornmeal mix to cover all sides of okra with mix.
7. Place one piece of coated okra in the hot oil and check that it immediately bubbles and sizzles. If not, the oil is not hot enough. Increase heat until you get the bubbles when adding one piece of okra.
8. If oil temperature is O.K., add all the okra to the skillet.

9. Cook the okra, stirring frequently, until it is one shade from burnt (about 15 minutes). When done, the okra should **not** be bright green. It should be brown with a few black (burned) edges. (See pictures below)
10. Place cooked okra on paper towels to absorb some of the oil but do NOT cover. If you need to keep the okra hot place it in an oven set on low. The okra will be VERY CRUNCHY! Serve hot.
11. Note: If you do not want the okra very crunchy, just cook until golden brown like picture on left below.

Southern Green Beans

The cooking time for these green beans may not be what you are accustomed to but they definitely will not taste like bland canned beans.

You will be surprised at how simple this green beans recipe is. But these are not your average green beans. The secret is in the cooking time. You will find this Southern Style Green Beans recipe to be a little different. The beans are cooked until they are very tender and a dark green color.

Served with fried chicken and collard greens these beans were the hit of the meal.

Prep time: 15 min
Cook time: 2 hours
Total time: 2 hours 15 min0 min
Yield: 6 servings

Ingredients

6 cups fresh, snapped green beans (do not cook them whole!)

1 tablespoon salt

1/2 teaspoon black pepper

1 slice bacon

1 medium size onion

1 tsp garlic powder

Instructions

1. Place the snapped beans in a large pot. Cover beans with at least 2-4 inches water (over top of beans).
2. Place all other ingredients in the pot (slice onion in half)
3. Place pot on medium heat and bring to a slow boil.
4. Cook the beans until they are very tender and have a dark green color. When cooked properly, they will NOT be bright green or crunchy. This should take from 1 to 2 hours.
5. Monitor the water in the pot very closely. You want to boil the water down to about 1/2 cup or so, BUT DO NOT ALLOW ALL THE WATER TO BOIL AWAY! The beans will burn very quickly if dry and just a few burnt beans in the bottom of the pot will affect the flavor of all the beans.

Sorghum Baked Beans

Think beans are just beans? Not so. These are not your ordinary beans. These flavor loaded beans are a little sweet, a little spicy and a lot yummy.

The hot sauce is optional but you should include it to taste since it adds a little kick to these special beans. For a real treat serve these sorghum beans with your next barbecue.

Prep time: 10 min
Cook time: 2 hours 20 min
Total time: 2 hours 30 min
Yield: 6 servings

Ingredients

* 2 cups cooked beans (kidney, red beans, pinto - canned beans O.K.)

* 5 slices bacon

* 1 onion, coarsely chopped

* 3 tablespoons catsup

* 1 teaspoon prepared mustard

* 1/4 cup water

* 1/2 cup sorghum molasses

* hot sauce to taste (optional)

Instructions

1. Cook the beans until tender (or use canned). Set aside.
2. Preheat oven to 350 degrees F.
3. Fry the bacon until done, but not crisp. Cut bacon into 2 inch strips.
4. Combine bacon with all remaining ingredients in an oven-safe medium casserole dish. Stir well.
5. Cover and bake for twenty minutes
6. Reduce heat to 250 degrees F, and continue to cook for two hours. Check the beans every 20-30 minutes to make sure they do not dry out. If dry, add a little water. You should end up with a thick sauce in the beans.

Kitchen Sink BBQ Beans

These slow cooked barbecue beans owe their explosive flavor to the fact that they include nearly everything...except the kitchen sink.

If you cannot find Chinese BBQ pork in your area you can substitute 3 or 4 slices of bacon. Do not be tempted to speed up the cooking time by increasing the heat. It's the slow cooking that makes these beans so good.

If you prefer you can cook the beans in a pot on the stove top instead of a crock pot. Just cook on low heat and keep the beans covered with water.

Prep time: 30 min
Cook time: 4 hours
Total time: 4 hours 30 min
Yield: 6 servings

Ingredients

 2 cups kidney beans (you can substitute pinto or red beans)

 1/2 cup Chinese BBQ pork, chopped (see note)

 1 medium onion, diced

 4 cloves garlic, minced

 1/2 cup brown sugar

 1/2 cup barbecue sauce (see below to make your own)

 1/2 cup ketchup

 1 tbsp liquid smoke

 1/4 cup Worcestershire sauce

 1 tbsp unsweetened cocoa powder

 1/3 cup cider vinegar

 1 tbsp hot sauce (Tabasco)

 1 tbsp salt

1/2 tbsp black pepper

water, as needed (see directions)

Instructions

1. Combine all ingredients in a slow cooker (crock pot).
2. Cover and cook on high setting for 4 hours or until beans are tender (may take much longer).
3. VERY IMPORTANT!! When the beans are tender, taste and add any ingredients needed. Some people like more brown sugar and/or BBQ sauce. The liquid in the pot should be reduced to a thick sauce. If still watery dissolve 1 tbsp cornstarch in 1/2 cup cold water and add to beans. Continue cooking until the liquid is a slightly thick sauce.

Sage Roasted Potatoes

This recipe presents a pleasant change from French fries and is much healthier. Just a little sage, salt and pepper are all you need. So simple but very tasty.

This very simple recipe is excellent to accompany and meat main course, especially roast beef. We used small whole red potatoes with the skin on. Very flavorful treatment of the common potato.

Prep time: 20 min
Cook time: 45 min
Total time: 1 hour 5 min
Yield: 4 servings

Ingredients:

2-3 pounds potatoes (Yukon Gold or red potatoes recommended)

1/4 cup olive oil

1/4 cup fresh sage (use dried if fresh unavailable)

salt and black pepper to taste

Instructions:

1. Heat the oven to 350 degrees F.
2. If using Yukon Gold or red potatoes, wash and leave skin on. If using russet potatoes, peel skin.
3. Cut potatoes into 1/2 inch wedges or 1 inch cubes.
4. Drizzle potatoes with olive oil and toss to coat.
5. Sprinkle with sage, salt and pepper (start with 1 teaspoons salt and 1/2 teaspoon pepper)
6. Toss to cover potatoes evenly with sage, salt and pepper
7. Place potatoes on a cookie sheet in a single layer.
8. Bake, turning occasionally, until tender and evenly browned, about 45 minutes.

Salt and Vinegar Potato Bites

Roasted potatoes with a salt and vinegar tanginess. Easy to make and ideal as an appetizer or side dish.

This recipe may work for some but the vinegar was a little over-powering for our taste. Perhaps milder vinegar such as rice vinegar would blend in a little better.

Prep time: 40 min
Cook time: 45 min
Total time: 1 hour 25 min
Yield: 8 servings

Ingredients

    6 medium red or yellow potatoes

    2 tablespoons vegetable oil

    1 cup malt vinegar

    salt, as needed

Instructions:

1. Soak potatoes in cold water for 30 minutes. Drain and pat dry.
2. Preheat oven to 425 degrees F.
3. Cut potatoes into bite sized chunks.
4. Toss potatoes with oil on a baking sheet, spread in a single layer.
5. Roast potatoes 45 minutes or until golden and crisp, turning 2 or 3 times as needed.
6. Bring vinegar to just under a boil in a saucepan over medium heat, stirring occasionally. Do not bring to a full boil.
7. Lightly drizzle a light coating of malt vinegar over the hot potatoes and serve the remaining vinegar at the table on the side for dipping.
8. Sprinkle potatoes with salt to taste and serve hot.

Vidalia onion Pie

If you have never had Vidalia Onions, try this recipe and you will be a Vidalia fan for life. This prize onion is only available for a short time of the year so watch for them at your store or buy online and have them shipped to your door.

This is a vegetable pie to be served as a main course. It is not a dessert-type pie, even though the Vidalia onions are as sweet as apples. We loved this sweet, cheesy pie with its crunchy crust.
Difficulty: Medium

Prep time: 20 min
Cook time: 55 min
Total time: 1 hour 15 min
Yield: 6-8 servings

Ingredients:

　　1 cup soda cracker crumbs

　　5 tablespoons melted butter

　　2 1/2 cups thinly sliced Vidalia onions

　　2 tablespoon vegetable oil

　　3/4 cup milk

　　1 teaspoon dried dill

　　1 teaspoon garlic powder

　　2 eggs

　　1 1/2 cups shredded cheese (cheddar or your favorite)

　　1/2 teaspoon of salt

Instructions:

1. Make a pie shell by mixing the cracker crumbs with the melted butter in the bottom of a pie pan. Use a fork to work up the sides. You may need a little more or less than 5 tablespoons of melted butter.
2. Bake the cracker crust at 350 degrees F until it is partially cooked (about 8 minutes). Remove from oven and sit aside.
3. Sauté onions in 2 tablespoons vegetable oil until translucent (about 3-4 minutes) and spread evenly in partially baked pie shell.
4. Beat the milk, dill, garlic powder, salt and eggs together in a small bowl then pour over the Vidalia onions in the pie shell.
5. Sprinkle shredded cheese on top.
6. Bake at 350 degrees F. for 45 minutes or until firm.
7. Serve hot.

Southern Vegetable Succotash

This tasty dish is great with almost any dinner. Full of fresh vegetables makes it a healthy addition to any meal.

Ingredients:

1lb. Speckled Butter Beans

1 lb. Baby Lima beans (may be little less depending where you get them)

1 lb. Butter peas

1 lb. Corn (yellow or white)

1 lb. Okra

1 very large onion (yellow or white)

1 28oz can of diced tomatoes

6 cloves of minced garlic

1 Tbsp. hot sauce (this adds zest you can add as much or as little as you desire)

1 cup chicken broth

3 tsp. salt

3 tsp. black pepper

2 tsp. sugar

3 strips of bacon (if you desire, it adds more flavor)

4 Tbsp vegetable oil   (2 Tbsp. oil if you use bacon)

Heat oil and bacon in a heavy pot. Add onion and cook till onion start to brown, then add garlic. Cook for about 3 minutes, then add tomatoes cook for about 5 minutes. Now stir in add all the spices then add all the other ingredients and cook for 20 to 30 minutes over medium heat. Lower heat when succotash starts to boil.

Section 9
Salads/Soups/Side Dishes/Appetizers

What Are Chitlins and Cracklins

Chitlins and Cracklins have been popular in the South as long as the South has existed. Supposedly, they became popular when poor Southerners had to use every scrap of available food in order to have anything at all to eat. Anyone lucky enough to have a pig took great effort to avoid wasting any portion of it. Thus, everything was eaten; feet, ears, skin, intestines...it all wound up on the table.

Chitlins and Hog Maw are pig intestines and stomach. Cracklins are made from pork fat. Chitlins are called Chitterlings if you go looking for them in a store. We use the terms "Chitlins" and "chitterlings" interchangeably in this book. They are generally boiled or fried and while they may not sound appetizing, if you have never tried them they are quite tasty.

Chitlins are typically served as a side dish while Cracklins may be used as a side dish, appetizer or in cooking. Cracklins are very popular in Cracklin Cornbread (recipe).

Here's our Cracklins Recipe

It is very important to thoroughly wash Chitlins prior to cooking. While it is a time consuming process, it is not difficult.

Here's how:
1. Soak your pork Chitlins (chitterlings) in cold water for 15 minutes.

2. Using your hands, one by one gently roll the chitterlings open in your hands. Use a knife and your fingers to remove any remaining fat or foreign matter from inside the chitterlings.

3. Place the chitterlings in a large pot of plain water and bring to a rolling boil. Then remove from heat immediately.

4. Pour the chitterlings into a strainer and run cold water over them.

5. Repeat the cleaning process in step two again.

So, if you have never tried Chitlins or Cracklins, give 'em a try. You may be pleasantly surprised.

How to Make Cracklins

While this recipe is not difficult it does take a practiced eye to determine when the pork belly is cooked to the proper degree of browning. Unless you like chewy Cracklins it is better to overcook than to under cook for a crunchy texture.

In addition to Cracklin cornbread we added this to our breakfast gravy in place of sausage and everyone loved it.

Prep time: 20 min
Cook time: 1 hour
Total time: 1 hour 20 min
Yield: 1 pound Cracklins

Ingredients:

* 5 pounds pork belly (should include part of the skin, a thick layer of fat and a small amount of meat)

* Cooking oil, as needed

* Cajun seasoning, as needed (optional)

Instructions:

1. Slice pork into small pieces. For cornbread, cut about 1/4 inch square cubes.
2. Heat about 4 cups of cooking oil to 350 degrees F. in a large cast iron pot.
3. Add pork belly and fry, stirring often, until golden brown (about 50 minutes). Add additional oil as needed to prevent the pork belly from sticking.
4. Increase heat to 375 degrees F. and continue cooking until the pork belly starts making a crackling, popping sound. Continue cooking another 5 minutes.
5. Remove from heat and drain on paper towels.
6. While still hot you may sprinkle with any desired seasoning to taste (salt, pepper, garlic powder, Cajun seasoning)
7. The Cracklins will not develop the desired crunchy texture until fully cooled.

Fried Chitlins

Also known as chitterlings, Chitlins are a popular soul food ingredient for cornbread, stews and other Southern dishes.

We call them chitterlings but they are also called Chitlins. They are an acquired taste but very popular with some families in the South. Chitterlings may be boiled or fried and served with greens, beans or any other vegetable. This recipe provides the complete cleaning procedure which you should follow closely.

Prep time: 45 min
Cook time: 2 hours 30 min
Total time: 3 hours 15 min
Yield: 6 servings

Cleaning Procedure:

Regardless of frying or boiling, you should clean the chitterlings as follows:

1. Soak your pork Chitlins in cold water for 15 minutes.
2. Using your hands, one by one gently roll the chitterlings open in your hands. Use a knife and your fingers to remove any remaining fat or foreign matter from inside the chitterlings.
3. Place the chitterlings in a large pot of plain water, add 1 tablespoon of baking soda and bring to a rolling boil. Then remove from heat immediately.
4. Pour the chitterlings into a strainer and run cold water over them.
5. Repeat the cleaning process in step two again

For Fried Chitlins:

Ingredients

* 2 pounds chitterlings

* 1 onion, chopped

* 2 bay leaves

* 2 teaspoons salt

* 1/2 teaspoon black pepper

* 2 cloves garlic, minced

* 1 egg, lightly beaten

* 1 tablespoon water

* fine cracker crumbs, as needed

* oil for deep frying, as needed

Instructions:

1. Clean chitterlings per above instructions.
2. Place chitterlings in a large pot and cover with water.
3. Add chopped onions, bay leaves, salt, pepper and garlic.
4. Bring to a boil and simmer for 2 hours or until chitterlings are tender
5. In a small bowl, beat egg with 1 tablespoon water until light and frothy.
6. Cut boiled chitterlings into bite-sized pieces and dip each piece into egg mixture then roll in cracker crumbs.
7. Fry in about 2 inches of oil on medium heat until golden brown.

For Boiled Chitlins:

Ingredients

* 10 lbs. chitterlings

* 3 lbs. hog maws (pig stomach)

* 1 1/2 tsp. peppercorns

* 1 1/2 tsp. salt

* 1 med. whole onion

* 1 large green pepper

Instructions:

1. Clean chitterlings and hog maws per the procedure above.
2. Cut up chitterlings and maws into large bite size pieces, cover with water in a large pot.
3. Add peppercorns, salt, onion and green pepper.
4. Bring to a boil, and then simmer for 4 to 6 hours until chitterlings and maws are tender.

Ambrosia

Serve this delightful fruit salad as a side dish or as a dessert.

Not just for special occasions. Serve this treat every day.

My mom served Ambrosia once a year at Christmas. An entire dish made of fruit was beyond our budget to serve often those days. Now you can afford to serve this delightful treat any time. Even every day.

Prep time: 30 min
Cook time: 0 hr 0 min
Total time: 30 min
Yield: 4-6 servings)

Ingredients:
* pineapple chunks: 1 (20 oz.) can
* mandarin orange segments: 1 (11 oz.) can
* Sliced banana: 1 large
* seedless grapes: 1 & 1/2 cups
* miniature marshmallows: 1 cup
* flaked coconut: 1 cup
* pecan halves: 1/2 cup
* sour cream OR plain yogurt: 1 cup
* brown sugar: 1 tablespoon

Directions:

1. Drain pineapple and orange segments.
2. In large bowl, combine pineapple, orange segments, grapes, marshmallows, coconut and nuts.
3. In a separate bowl, combine sour cream and brown sugar.
4. Stir sour cream mix into fruit mixture.
5. Refrigerate, covered, 1 hour.
6. Add sliced bananas to ambrosia just before serving (if bananas are allowed to sit very long they will turn an unsightly brown. You can spray with lemon juice to slow the color change but they will still eventually change color).

Southern Potato Salad

Your family will love this mouth-watering recipe for Southern Potato Salad. Be sure to include it at any picnic. Serve the potato salad cold and keep it refrigerated since it contains mayonnaise and can spoil if left out too long.

This recipe make quite a lot (serves 6-8). If you want a smaller portions just half the ingredients. To adjust yield, allow 1 large potato per person in the recipe. It's better to make too much than to run short...especially if the one who wants more is your sister's six year old with nerve shattering vocal cords.

Prep time: 30 min
Cook time: 20 min
Total time: 50 min
Yield: 6-8 servings

Ingredients:

8 Large (or 10 medium) potatoes

1 cup mayonnaise

1/2 cup sour cream

1/4 cup chopped celery

1/4 cup chopped onion (red onion adds a lot of color)

2 tsp sweet pickle relish

1 tsp mustard

1/4 lb cooked bacon, crumbled

3 hardboiled eggs, sliced

1 tsp celery seed

1/2 tsp garlic powder

1/4 tsp dill weed

1/4 tsp paprika

salt to taste

pepper to taste

Instructions:

Peel potatoes and cut into large bite sized chunks.

Boil potatoes until a fork pushed in a potato goes in with a slight resistance (about 15-20 min). Do not overcook. Set aside and allow cooling.

When cool add all other ingredients, except eggs and paprika, to the potatoes and mix thoroughly. Mix gently to avoid breaking up potatoes and ending up with mashed potatoes. Add salt and pepper to taste as you mix.

Garnish top with sliced boiled eggs and sprinkle **lightly** with paprika.

For variety, use small red potatoes instead of regular potatoes and leave the skin on. Also, use red onions instead of regular onions.

Asian Salad

No it's not Southern but it goes well with many Southern dishes such as fried chicken. This spicy Asian salad uses the old Chinese technique of combining sweet and sour with an added touch of spiciness.

If you are not fond of spicy food you may want to eliminate or reduce the amount of the jalapeno pepper. However, it does provide that little kick that makes this salad special and...a little different.

As a side dish this recipe will serve 4 people but for a party appetizer you can double or triple the recipe.

Ingredients

* 2 carrots, sliced into match stick sized pieces

* 2 large cucumbers, thinly sliced

* 1/2 a medium red onion, thinly sliced

* 1/2 a green bell pepper, thinly sliced

* 1 jalapeno pepper, seeded and sliced into thin rounds (optional)

* 1 teaspoon finely minced ginger

* 2 teaspoons salt

* 1/4 cup rice vinegar

* 4-5 teaspoons sugar, depending on your taste

* black pepper to taste

Directions

1. Mix the sliced cucumbers, onions, peppers and carrots into a bowl along with the salt. Mix well and add enough water to cover. (The water should be slightly salty to your taste. Add an additional teaspoon of salt if needed).

2. Allow the vegetables to marinate in the salty water for 30 to 60 minutes. The vegetables will soften slightly during this time.

3. While the vegetables are marinating, make the dressing as follows:

4. In a glass bowl mix the rice vinegar, sugar, black pepper and ginger together. Stir the mixture until the sugar is completely dissolved and the dressing is clear.

5. Thoroughly drain the vegetables though a colander and transfer to a large bowl.

6. Combine the dressing and marinated vegetables in a large bowl and stir well. Cover and place in the refrigerator overnight.

May be served, as is, for a side salad or used on sandwiches or as party finger food.

Grilled Cheese Sandwich

Who doesn't love a grilled cheese sandwich? They are quick and easy to make...and filling. Even though it's a simple recipe, there are a few tips to making the "best" grilled cheese. Read on to discover all those tips.

Who would have though there are so many right and wrong ways to make a grilled cheese. But try the tips presented here and you will find that it does make a difference. It's true that slow cooking will make the most perfect toasting of the bread that you could ever want.

Prep time: 5 min
Cook time: 8 min
Total time: 13 min
Yield: 1 sandwich (repeat as needed)

Ingredients: (per sandwich)

2 slices of bread (you can use any kind...but fresh, plain, white bread works best)

good quality margarine (enough to cover one side of each slice of bread)

1/2 cup cheese, grated (cheddar melts great and is our favorite but you use can use American or your choice)

Instructions:

Heat a non-stick frying pan on LOW HEAT (about number 3 on my stove)

Spread margarine on one side of each slice of bread.

Place one slice of bread in the frying pan, margarine side down.

Place as much cheese as you want on top of the bread

Place the other slice of bread on top of the cheese, margarine side up

Cook 2 or 3 minutes then lift the sandwich with a spatula and peek at the bottom. If it's already dark brown or burnt, turn down the heat. If you have the correct heat the margarine should be melted and the bread should just be taking on color.

Continue this process of cooking for a minute then taking another peek. When the bread is golden brown, flip the sandwich over and repeat the process. It should take about 4 minutes per side to obtain a golden brown. If it takes much less, your stove is too hot.

Serve immediately.

TIPS:

Use fresh white bread and fresh cheese. Whole wheat may be healthier but regular white bread toasts much better.

Use good margarine, not real butter. Butter burns easily which will impart an off-flavor to the sandwich. Margarine withstands heat better and browns the bread better for this application.

Some advocate melting the margarine and brushing it on the bread. We believe the old fashioned way of spreading the margarine directly on the bread (not melted) works better.

Always use a non-stick pan that is big enough to provide room around the sandwich to get a spatula easily under the sandwich (at least 10 inch pan).

Grate the cheese and use plenty of it (we like about 1/2 cup per sandwich, but use as much or as little as you like).

HERE'S THE SECRET to a perfect grilled cheese. Cook on low heat. This does two things...it toast the bread perfectly and it gives the cheese time to melt properly. If you use the correct temperature, it should take about 4 minutes per side. ...and, of course, serve it hot right from the stove.

Want To Rev It Up A Notch?

Add sliced tomato with the cheese.

Add sliced olives and or sliced jalapeno pepper.

Add sliced mushrooms

Coat the bread with peanut butter before adding the cheese (goes on the side of the bread opposite of the margarine...in other words...inside the sandwich with the cheese).

Shrimp, Baked, Spicy

This Cajun, spicy, baked shrimp recipe is quick and easy to make. Excellent as an appetizer but can be a main dish using large or jumbo shrimp.

There are about 30-35 medium size shrimp in a pound so adjust the number of shrimp for the number of people you are serving. In general, you should plan on about 1/3 pound per person.

Be aware that shrimp is highly perishable and should not be used if the aroma of ammonia is present. In general, it is safer to buy frozen shrimp and keep it frozen. Defrost in the bottom of the refrigerator prior to cooking.

This recipe is adjustable to the number of servings you require. We found it simple to adjust for 12 people. You can remove the shells of the shrimp before cooking or cook with the shells intact. We prefer to cook with shells and remove them at the table because there is less tendency to overcook.

Over cooked shrimp is tough and tasteless so we cook just until the shrimp turn pink and curl into a "C" shape. If they curl beyond a "C" shape, they are over cooked.

Prep time: 15 min
Cook time: 12 min
Total time: 27 min
Yield: 6 servings

Ingredients:

2 lb fresh shrimp, with tails intact (adjust as needed for number of servings)

olive oil, as needed

1/4 cup Worcestershire sauce, or as needed

2 teaspoons sea salt, or as needed (regular salt may be substituted)

pinch of powdered cayenne pepper, to taste

juice of one medium lime

Instructions:

Preheat oven to 350 degrees F.

Place shrimp in an oven safe baking dish

Cover shrimp generously with Worcestershire sauce. Adjust amount according to how much shrimp you are cooking. Mix well to cover all sides of shrimp.

Add olive oil (about 3 or 4 tablespoons) and mix well.

Add lime juice and mix well.

Sprinkle salt and cayenne pepper over top of shrimp. Be careful with the cayenne pepper, it is very hot.

Bake in preheated oven about 10-12 minutes

Mom's Cole Slaw

If it's a barbecue, fish, fried chicken or a picnic, slaw seems to go with just about everything. Especially if it's as good as this sweet, tart Cole slaw.

This cole slaw is definitely not mild and bland. It packs a punch with a tart and sweet vinegary flavor.

Prep time: 25 min
Cook time: 5 min
Total time: 30 min
Yield: 6 servings

Ingredients:

* 6 cups finely chopped cabbage

* 1 cup bell pepper, chopped

* 1 cup onion, chopped

* 1 medium carrot, shredded

* 2 tablespoons celery seed

* 1 cup white vinegar

* 1 cup sugar

* 1 tablespoon olive oil

* 2 tablespoons salt

* 1/4 tablespoon black pepper

* 1/4 cup mayonnaise

Directions:

1. Mix chopped cabbage, bell peppers, onion and carrot in a large bowl. Set aside.

2. In a small saucepan, bring vinegar, sugar and salt to a boil, stirring until sugar is completely dissolved (about 5 min).

3. Allow vinegar/sugar mix to cool 5 minutes then pour over cabbage mix.

4. Stir in black pepper, olive oil, celery seed and mayonnaise. Mix well.

5. Adjust ingredients to taste. If too sweet, add vinegar. If too much vinegar, add sugar and oil. If bland, add salt.

6. Refrigerate for 30-45 minutes. Pour off excess liquid before serving.

Old West Cole Slaw

It's a little sweet, a little tangy and mighty good; this buttermilk slaw goes great with chicken, meat or seafood. And...It's always a big hit at any picnic.

Not sure why it is called "Old West" but it is a catchy title. This slaw is a little tart, probably due to the buttermilk in addition to the vinegar. If you prefer a sweet slaw, add an additional couple tablespoons of sugar. Just taste as you goes and makes adjustments according to your taste.

Prep time: 20 min
Total time: 20 min
Yield: 6 servings

Ingredients:

1/2 cup mayonnaise

1/3 cup buttermilk

1/3 cup sugar

2 tablespoons white vinegar

1/2 teaspoon salt

1 teaspoon celery seed

1 pound (16 oz) cabbage, shredded

1/2 cup carrots, shredded

1 whole green onion, chopped

1 teaspoon dill seed or ground dill weed

Instructions:

Combine all ingredients in a large serving bowl and mix thoroughly.

Cover and refrigerate at least 4 hours, stirring occasionally (overnight O.K.).

Before serving, pour off excess liquid.

Cha-Cha Relish

This Cha-Cha recipe is a Southern relish that was made popular in the 1800's by the African American communities of the South. Probably just as popular today if not more so.

Cha-Cha is unique in that it may be made in a wide variety of ways with significantly different ingredients. This is a basic recipe with the understanding that each cook may wish to revise ingredients to fit their own preferences. Hot and spicy, or mild you can obtain either with this recipe.

Prep time: 20 min
Cook time: 30 min
Total time: 50 min
Yield: 1 1/2 pints

Ingredients:

* 4 cups cabbage, grated

* 4 cups green tomatoes, chopped (you can substitute red tomatoes)

* 1 large onion, chopped

* 1 large bell pepper, chopped

* 1/2 Tbsp. pickling spice (see note 3 below to make your own)

* 1/3 Tbsp. dried dill weed

* 2 tbsp sugar

* 1/3 cup vinegar (add an additional 2 tablespoons vinegar if using red tomatoes)

* 1 tbsp salt

* Tabasco Sauce or jalapeno pepper (optional - see note below)

Instructions:

Place all ingredients in a large pot and bring to a boil.

Reduce heat and simmer 15 to 30 minutes or until vegetables are tender, stirring frequently.

Cool and store in refrigerator. If you do not expect to consume within 2 days, place hot relish in sterilized canning jar and process in a boiling water bath 10-15 minutes. If processed you do not need to refrigerator until opened.

Notes:

If you like hot and spicy Cha-Cha, add 1-2 tbsp. Tabasco Sauce or 1 chopped jalapeno pepper (to taste) to the above recipe.

The traditional Cha-Cha is made with green tomatoes. We prefer red since they are more available. You can also substitute Mexican tomatillo, which are generally available most of the year in large supermarkets.

Pickling spice is available at most supermarkets but you can make you own if you have a well-equipped spice rack. Just combine as many of the following ingredients as you have available and grind them into a powder with a food processor.
One bay leaf
1/2 tsp chili powder
1/4 tsp cloves
1/3 tsp ground cinnamon
1/3 tsp ginger
1/2 tsp allspice
1/2 tsp mustard seed
1/2 tsp coriander
1/2 tsp black pepper
1 tsp dill seed
these measurements are "ballpark" so taste and adjust as you like.

Serve Cha-Cha with any meat or vegetable.

Deviled (stuffed) Eggs

There are many ways to make deviled (stuffed) eggs and everyone seems to have their own favorite recipe. Here's our favorite.

Top notch recipe! We substituted chopped hot garlic dill pickles for the relish to get a little spiciness and it was a big hit at our table.

Prep time: 20 min
Cook time: 12 min
Total time: 32 min
Yield: 12 servings

Ingredients:

6 eggs, hard boiled

1 tablespoon mustard

1 to 3 tablespoon mayonnaise, or as needed

1/2 teaspoon dill weed

1/4 cup chopped onion

1/4 cup FINELY chopped celery

1/4 tablespoon salt (adjust to taste)

1/4 tablespoon black pepper

1 1/2 teaspoons sweet pickle relish, all liquid pressed out (or 1/4 cup diced dill pickle)

Dash paprika

Instructions:

Place eggs in a sauce pan and cover eggs with 2 inches of **COLD** water. Do not stack eggs.

Bring water to a rolling boil

Turn off heat and cover pot with a tight lid.

Allow eggs to sit undisturbed (12 min for medium size eggs, 17 min for large eggs, 19 min for jumbo).

Remove eggs from hot water and place in a deep bowl of cold water to cool.

When eggs are cool enough to handle, peel eggs then slice lengthwise.

Carefully remove yokes from eggs into a mixing bowl. Set egg halves (white shells) aside.

Add all remaining ingredients, except paprika, to egg yolks and mash into a paste with a fork. When adding mayonnaise, add 1 tablespoon at a time until you get the consistency you want. You may need more or less than 1-3 tablespoons mayonnaise.

Gently, stuff the egg white half's with the egg yolk mixture.

Shake a light dusting of paprika on the top of the stuffed eggs. Refrigerate if not eaten within 30 minutes.

Crab Cakes

The delicate flavor of fresh crab fried with tender insides and a crunchy crust.

While some may not view crab cakes as traditional Southern food, my mom served them often when I was growing up in Alabama. This recipe makes a tasty crab cake just like I remember my mom making.

Prep time: 20 min
Cook time: 10 min
Total time: 30 min
Yield: 4 servings

Ingredients:

2 - 6-1/2 oz. cans crab meat or 3/4 lb. fresh crab meat (about 2-1/2 cups)

2 tablespoons mayonnaise

1 tablespoon Worcestershire sauce

Several drops hot pepper sauce (Tabasco)

4 green onions, chopped

2 tablespoons dry mustard

Salt and freshly ground pepper to taste

2 egg whites

1 cup cracker crumbs

Olive oil spray

Instructions:

Drain crab meat and flake with a fork, picking out any shell or cartilage.

Put crabmeat in a bowl. Add the mayonnaise, Worcestershire sauce, hot pepper sauce, green onions, dry mustard, pepper and salt.

Blend in the egg whites.

Using hands shape into 4 cakes about 4 inches across.

Place cracker crumbs on a plate and season with salt and pepper.

Roll crab cakes in crumbs, making sure both sides are coated.

Heat a nonstick skillet on medium heat. Spray with olive oil spray. Add crab cakes and cook 5 minutes. Turn and cook 5 more minutes or until golden brown on both sides.

Apple/Walnut Salad

Creamy, nutty and fruity, this apple salad may be served as a healthy dessert or refreshing salad.

My mom always made this Apple Salad for summer picnics. She called it the poor man's Waldorf salad because if you added grapes, celery and lettuce you would, indeed, have a Waldorf. This recipe is simpler and somewhat more economical.

Prep time: 20 min
Cook time: none
Total time: 20 min
Yield: 4+ servings

Ingredients

6 medium size apples (cored, peeled and chopped into bite size)

1 cup chopped walnuts

1 cup sugar

1/3 cup raisins

2 tablespoon lemon or lime juice (I prefer lime)

1/2 tablespoon salt

1/2 cup mayonnaise

Instructions

Combine all ingredients in a large bowl and mix well. Taste as you go and adjust flavor to your preference. I like a combination of slightly sweet, slightly tart, which the above recipe makes. If you want it sweeter, add sugar. If you like tart, add salt and lemon juice.

Flavor will improve if chilled for 20 min. in refrigerator before serving.

Macaroni and Cheese

Pretty straight forward recipe for this all-time kid's favorite. Nothing fancy or difficult here, just good mac and cheese.

To kick it up a notch, try adding chopped ham, a teaspoon garlic powder and 1/2 teaspoon honey in step 6.

Prep time: 20 min
Cook time: 20 min
Total time: 40 min
Yield: 6-8 servings

Ingredients:

1 (8 oz) box elbow macaroni

3 tablespoons butter

2 tablespoons flour

1/2 cup milk

salt and black pepper to taste

1 cup grated cheddar cheese

grated Parmesan cheese as needed (optional)

Instructions:

Cook one box (8 oz.) elbow macaroni according to box instructions. Set aside.

In a saucepan, melt 3 tablespoons butter over medium heat.

Add 2 tablespoons flour and stir until dissolved and all lumps removed.

Pour in 1/2 cup milk and cook until thickened.

Season with salt and pepper. Add 1 cup grated cheese and stir until melted.

Add **cooked** macaroni and stir.

Pour mixture into 2 qt. casserole dish. Bake for 20 minutes at 350 degrees.

Remove from oven and sprinkle top with grated Parmesan cheese (optional)

Chicken Pot Pie Recipe

This yummy homemade pot pie has a few ingredients but is easy to make. If you are good at working with dough, make your own crust.

Ingredients

2 pie crusts - unbaked (store bought or homemade)
1 1/2 lbs. boneless, skinless chicken breasts
2 cups chicken broth
1 1/2 tablespoons vegetable oil
1 medium onion, finely chopped
3 medium carrots, peeled and sliced 1/4 inch thick
2 stalks celery, sliced 1/4 inch thick
4 Tablespoons butter
1/2 cup flour
1/2 cup whole milk
1/2 teaspoon ground dried thyme
3 Tablespoons dry sherry (optional)
1/4 cup frozen peas, thawed

Directions

Heat oven to 400 degrees, place oven rack in middle position.
2. Place chicken and broth in a stock pot over medium heat. Cover, bring to a simmer and simmer 10 min.
3. Transfer the chicken to a large bowl; reserve the broth in a separate bowl.
4. Place oil in the stock pot, turn heat to medium high.
5. Add the carrots, onion and celery. Sauté until just tender (about 5 min.). Season to taste with salt and pepper.
6. Shred the chicken meat into bite-sized pieces, then place the cooked vegetables into the bowl with the chicken and set aside.
7. Heat the butter in the empty stock pot over medium heat. Once melted, add the flour and cook 1 minute.
8. Whisk in the chicken broth, milk and thyme. Bring to a simmer, continuing to simmer until sauce thickens (about 1 min.). Season with salt and pepper, stir in the sherry.
9. Pour the sauce over the chicken-vegetables mixture, stir well. Stir in the peas.
10. Line a 9x13 inch pan with one of the pie crusts. Roll the dough to fit the pan.
11. Pour the chicken mixture into the pan and top with second crust.
12. Bake in preheated oven until pie crust is golden brown and the filling is bubbly,

about 30 minutes.

Option: If you can find single serve pie pans, you can use them instead of the one large pie pan. Should make about 4 single serves, according to the size pie pans you have available.

Cream of Chicken Soup

This easy cream of chicken soup recipe is perfect for those cold winter days...or anytime at all actually. Great for the kids after school snack.

Ingredients

4 tablespoon butter
* 4 tablespoons flour
* 1 quart chicken stock or broth
* 1 cup light cream or half and half
* 1/4 teaspoon salt (to taste)
* 1/8 teaspoon white pepper (to taste)
* 1/2 teaspoon dried chicken seasoning
* 1 tablespoon minced parsley, chives or green onion
* 1 cup cooked, diced chicken
* 1/3 cup thinly sliced, cooked carrots (optional)

Directions

Note: If you want to add carrots, they should be pre-cooked until just tender.
1. Melt the butter in a large heavy saucepan over moderate heat and blend in 4 tablespoons flour.
2. Add broth and 1 cup light cream and heat, stirring constantly, until thickened and smooth
3. Mix in salt, pepper, chicken seasoning, parsley or chives, cooked carrots (if using) and diced, cooked chicken. Cover and let simmer over low heat until heated through (about 5 minutes). Note: If too soup is too thick, add broth or water. If too thin (watery) simmer longer until desired thickness is obtained.
Serve hot.

Chicken Corn Chowder

Here's a tasty recipe for chicken corn chowder soup to warm your tummy on cold winter nights. Actually it's pretty good any time of the year. Lot of ingredients but easy to make.

Ingredients

1 Tbsp butter or olive oil
* 1/2 large sweet onion, peeled and chopped into large dice
* 4 cups chicken broth (see Note)
* 2 red potatoes, peeled and cut into 1-inch pieces
* 1/2 tsp oregano
* 1/2 tsp poultry seasoning
* 1/2 tsp chili powder
* Salt and freshly ground pepper to taste
* 3 cups fresh or frozen corn kernels
* 1 (4 ounces) can chopped mild green chilies, drained
* 1 large raw chicken breast cut into 1-inch bites
* 1 cup heavy cream or half-and-half
* 2 cups Mexican 4-cheese blend shredded cheese
* 1 roasted red pepper, cut into 1-inch strips (jarred is fine)
* 1 Tbsp chopped fresh Cilantro
* Hot sauce to taste
* Shredded cheese, chopped green onions, toasted cashews and additional chopped Cilantro for garnish
* Bread bowls for serving (optional)

Directions

In a large Dutch oven, sauté the chopped onions in butter or olive oil until they begin to turn translucent and fragrant. Add the chicken broth, potatoes, oregano, poultry seasoning, chili powder, salt, and freshly ground pepper to taste. Bring to a low boil and simmer about ten minutes, until potatoes are just barely tender. Add the corn and simmer until corn is heated through.

2. Remove about 1-1/2 cups of the chowder and puree in a blender or food processor. Return puree to the chowder and add green chilies and chicken. Simmer about 5 minutes to cook chicken. Add cream and shredded cheese. Stir until incorporated and cheese has melted. Gently stir in red pepper, Cilantro, and hot sauce to taste.

3. Serve in bread bowls or regular soup bowls with additional shredded cheese and Cilantro for garnish.
Yield: 6 servings

Chicken Noodle Soup

Chicken noodle soup, an all-time favorite...good for whatever ails you. At least that's what mom always said. Here's a simple, basic recipe for chicken noodle soup.

Ingredients

2 carrots, peeled and sliced thin
* 2 tablespoons butter
* 3 chicken breasts, cubed
* 2 garlic cloves, minced
* 4 cups chicken broth
* chicken bouillon cubes, to taste
* water, as needed (start with 2 cups)
* 1 pkg elbow pasta or fettuccine (or use your favorite)
* salt and pepper, to taste
* onion powder to taste
* 4 bay leaves

Directions

In a large soup pot, boil carrots in water until tender. Pour off water and remove carrots.
2. In the same pot, melt butter, add chicken and cook until browned on all sides.
3. Add garlic and cook till tender but not brown.
4. Add chicken broth simmer slowly for 1/2 hour.
5. Add bouillon cubes and water. Add paste, carrots and all remaining ingredients. Simmer until paste is tender.
6. Remove bay leaves and serve hot.

Notes: You can make a heartier soup by adding other vegetables. You may want to add potatoes (pre-cooked), broccoli or tomatoes.

Chicken Tortellini Soup

This makes a fairly thick soup but by watching the consistency in the last step you can adjust to the thickness you want. See note.

Ingredients

3 tablespoons olive oil
* 6 skinless, boneless chicken breasts, chopped
* 2 cloves garlic, minced
* 1 cup celery, chopped
* 1 large onion, chopped
* 3 cans chicken broth (10-1/2 ounces size cans)
* 1 1/2 cups broccoli, chopped (or one 16 ounce package frozen)
* 1 package tortellini pasta (9 ounces)
* black pepper, to taste
* 1 teaspoon basil or 3 fresh basil leaves
* 1/2 tablespoon Italian seasoning
* 1 cup sour cream
* parsley and chopped tomatoes for garnish (optional)

Directions

In a large soup pot, heat the olive oil. Add the chicken and brown on all sides. Add the garlic, onion and celery. Cook until the garlic is tender, but not browned.
2. Add the chicken broth and simmer 15 minutes.
3. Add all remaining ingredients EXCEPT the sour cream. Bring back to a boil, reduce heat and simmer 15 minutes.
4. Slowly add the sour cream, a little at a time. Watch the thickness of the soup and stop when you have the thickness you like.
Garnish with chopped parsley and tomato if desired.
Note: If the soup is too thick, add more water or chicken broth. If too thin, add more sour cream and/or milk and cook longer.
Makes 8 to 10 servings

Lemon Chicken Soup

Here's an easy recipe for a tangy chicken soup with a hint of lemon. You can use any type pasta you prefer but we like the small elbow pasta.

Ingredients

8 cups chicken broth
* 1 boneless, skinless chicken breast, chopped bite size
* 2 carrots, peeled and diced
* 1 stalk celery, chopped
* 1/2 cup onion, chopped
* 1 bay leaf
* black pepper, to taste
* 1 cup elbow pasta (or your favorite)
* juice of 1 large lemon

Directions

Place all of the ingredients except the lemon juice in a large soup pot. Cover and bring to a boil over high heat. Reduce the heat to low, cover and simmer, stirring occasionally, for 30 minutes or until the vegetables are tender.
2. Add the lemon juice, stirring well. Cook 5 minutes.
3. Remove and discard the bay leaf. Serve hot.

Mexican Chicken Soup

Here's a hearty chicken soup with a south of the border flavor. Great for cold winter days.

Ingredients

8 medium potatoes (2-1/2 pounds)
* 1 chicken (4 pounds), cut into pieces
* 3 large stalks celery, each cut into thirds
* 3 carrots, peeled and cut into thirds
* 2 medium onions, cut into quarters
* 10 cups water
* 10 whole sprigs Cilantro plus additional 1/4 cup chopped Cilantro
* 2 bay leaves
* 1 teaspoon whole black peppercorns
* 1 can (15-1/4 to 16 ounces) whole-kernel corn, drained
* 2 teaspoons salt
* 1/4 cup fresh lime juice (about 2 large limes)
* 2 ripe medium avocados, cut into 1/2-inch pieces
* Tortilla chips
* Lime wedges

Directions

Peel 3 potatoes. In 8-quart soup pot, combine chicken, peeled potatoes, celery, carrots, onions, water, Cilantro sprigs, bay leaves, and peppercorns. Heat to boiling over high heat. Reduce heat; cover and simmer until chicken loses its pink color throughout and vegetables are tender, 35 to 45 minutes. Transfer chicken and potatoes to separate bowls.
2. Strain broth through sieve into large bowl; discard vegetables.
3. Skim and discard fat from broth; return broth to same soup pot. Mash cooked potatoes with 1 cup broth; stir mashed-potato mixture into broth soup pot.
4. Peel and chop remaining 5 potatoes. Add potatoes to broth; heat to boiling over high heat. Reduce heat; cover and simmer until potatoes are tender, about 10 minutes.
5. When chicken is cool enough to handle, discard skin and bones from chicken; cut chicken into bite-size pieces.
6. Stir chicken, corn, and salt into broth; heat through.
7. Just before serving, stir lime juice and chopped Cilantro into soup.
8. Serve with avocado, tortilla chips, and lime wedges on the side. Yield: about 8 servings

Mulligan Stew

This recipe has a lot of ingredients but don't let it discourage you. The recipe is only a guide to get you started. It's really a "clean out the fridge" soup. So, use whatever you want or add whatever appeals to you.

Ingredients

4 ribs celery, chopped in 1/2-inch chunks
* 4 peeled carrots, chopped in 1/2-inch chunks
* 1 medium onion, cut into large dice
* 2 Tablespoons butter or olive oil
* 1 quart (or three 14-ounce cans) chicken broth
* 1 cup water
* 1 package chicken gravy mix powder
* 1 teaspoon garlic powder
* 1 teaspoon onion powder
* 1 teaspoon salt, or to taste
* 1/2 teaspoon black pepper (or to taste)
* 1/2 teaspoon poultry seasoning
* 1/2 teaspoon dried oregano
* 1/2 teaspoon dried basil
* 1 (19-ounce) can white cannellini beans, undrained
* 1 (14-1/2-ounce) can petite-cut tomatoes, undrained
* 1/4 cup real bacon bits
* 1/2 cup elbow pasta (about 1/2-inch long)
* 1/2 cup rice
* 2 medium potatoes, peeled and chopped bite size
* 1/2 cup frozen green peas
* 2 boneless, skinless chicken breast halves, cut into 1-inch chunks

Directions

> In a large soup-pot, gently sauté celery, carrots, and onion in the butter about 5 minutes. Add chicken broth, water, chicken gravy mix, garlic powder, onion powder, salt, pepper, poultry seasoning, oregano, and basil. Bring to a boil, while stirring to combine.
> 2. Add cannellini beans, tomatoes, bacon bits, pasta, rice and potatoes. Return to a boil, then lower heat and simmer until potatoes, pasta, rice, and vegetables are tender, 10 to 15 minutes.
> 3. Add peas, and chicken. Return to a boil, then lower heat and simmer an additional 5-10 minutes or until chicken is cooked through.
> 8 servings. Serve with sourdough bread. May be kept in refrigerator up to 5 days.

Buffalo wings

Some call them hot wings, spicy wings or BBQ wings...we just call them yummy.

Some Buffalo wings are more BBQ flavored than spicy but this recipe makes very noticeably spicy wings. An absolute necessity for your next party.

Prep time: 20 min
Cook time: 15 min
Total time: 35 min plus 1 hour refrigeration
Yield: 4 servings

Ingredients

* 20 chicken wings, tips removed

* vegetable oil (enough to cover chicken in oil while frying)

* 1 cup all-purpose flour

* 1/2 tsp. paprika

* 1/2 tsp. cayenne pepper

* 1/2 tsp. salt

* 1/2 cup butter

* 1/2 cup Hot Sauce (Tabasco or your favorite)

* 1/4 tsp. ground pepper

* 1/4 tsp. garlic powder

Directions

Combine the flour, paprika, cayenne pepper, and salt in small bowl.

Wash wings and leave damp.

Place wings in a large bowl and sprinkle the flour mixture over them, coating each wing generously.

Refrigerate wings for one hour.

Combine the butter, hot sauce, ground pepper, and garlic powder in a small saucepan over low heat.

Heat, stirring often, until the butter is melted and the spices are well-blended.

Deep-fry chicken, 8-10 pieces at a time; in 375 degree vegetable oil for 10 to 15 minutes or until some of the wing edges begin to turn dark brown.

Remove wings and place on paper towels to drain oil.

Place the wings in a large bowl. Add the hot sauce (from step 6) and stir, coating all of the wings evenly.

Good served hot or cold.

Cajun Chicken Wings #1 (Baked)

Very simple and yummy deep fried chicken wings recipe. Although the recipe says chicken wings, we like to add legs and other inexpensive chicken parts.

Ingredients:

2-1/2 pounds Chicken wings, tips removed (or legs)

3/4 cup Plain yogurt

2/3 cup Louisiana hot sauce

2 teaspoons Garlic powder

1 cup Flour

1/2 cup Cajun seasoning

Oil (for frying)

Instructions:

1. In a bowl, mix together yogurt, hot sauce and garlic. Add chicken and marinate overnight in the refrigerator. If you can't wait, marinate at least 2 hours.

2. The following day, mix together flour and Cajun seasonings in a bowl. Remove chicken from the marinade and coat evenly in flour mixture.

3. In a wok or deep fryer, heat oil to 370 degrees F. If using a wok, heat over medium high heat (or use thermometer for 370 degrees F.)

4. Use enough oil to cover 4 to 5 chicken wings at a time. Deep fry wings for approximately 8 minutes or until golden brown.

6. Drain on paper towel.

Serves 2 to 4

Cajun Spicy Hot Wings

Hot wings are a big hit at any party, especially these Cajun spicy wings. Very easy to make and most of the time required is the marinating procedure.

The marinade is for about 60 wings (roughly 10 wings to the pound). Start with any amount of wings you want but make the full marinade recipe.

Prep time: 20 min
Cook time: 1 hour
Total time: 1 hour 20 min
Yield: 12 servings

Ingredients:

chicken wings up to 3 pounds

For The Marinade:

Ingredients:

2 tablespoons Canola oil (you can use any mild flavor vegetable oil)

juice of 2 lemons

3 teaspoons garlic, minced

1 1/2 tablespoon Worcestershire sauce

1/3 cup ketchup

3 green onions, chopped

1 tablespoon Tabasco sauce

1/2 teaspoon dried thyme

1 teaspoon ground cayenne pepper (you can substitute red pepper flakes)

2 tablespoons brown sugar, packed

1/2 teaspoon black pepper

For The Basting Mix

Ingredients:

reserved left over marinade
2 tablespoons honey
1/2 teaspoon cayenne pepper

Directions:

Wash chicken wings and pat dry. Cut wing tips off at the joint and discard.

In a large sealable plastic bag, combine all the marinade ingredients and mix well. Add the chicken wings and shake to coat the wings thoroughly. Seal the bag and marinate in the refrigerator for 4 hours.

Heat the oven to 375 degrees F.

Line a roasting pan with aluminum foil and place a wire rack in the bottom of the pan.

Remove the wings from the marinade and place the chicken wings on the wire rack in the roasting pan. Save the marinade.

Pour the saved marinade into a saucepan and add 2 tablespoons of honey and 1/2 teaspoon cayenne pepper. Heat the marinade while stirring; just until the honey is dissolved (do not boil).

Bake the chicken wings for 50 to 60 minutes, turning about halfway through, and basting occasionally with the marinade.

Serve hot or cold. Refrigerate any leftover wings within one hour of cooking.

Chicken Bacon Kabobs

Here's an easy BBQ chicken bacon kabob recipe to serve as an appetizers at your next party.

Very simple recipe for chicken kabobs. You can add additional items to the skewers if you like, such as bite size chunks of pineapple, red and yellow bell pepper, lemon and/or mushrooms.

Prep time: 20 min
Cook time: 11 min
Total time: 31 min
Yield: 6-8 servings

Ingredients:

* bamboo or metal skewers, as needed

* 3 large boneless, skinless chicken breasts (about 1 lb), cut into 1 inch pieces

* 4 large green onions, cut into 2 inch pieces

* 1 package (2.1 oz, 15 pieces) bacon, cooked

* 1/2 cup your favorite barbecue sauce, or more as needed

Instructions:

Cook the bacon first. Do not cook crispy. You want to leave it tender so it will not crumble when pushed on the skewers.

If using bamboo skewers, soak them in water at least 30 minutes.

Cut each chicken breast into 1-inch pieces. Cut onions into 2-inch pieces. Cut bacon slices in half crosswise.

Heat gas or charcoal grill.

Push 1 skewer through end of 1 bacon piece, then through middle of 1 chicken piece and back through other end of bacon piece. Add 2 onion pieces. Repeat with another bacon piece and chicken piece. Repeat to make remaining kabobs.

Place kabobs on grill over medium heat. Cover grill; cook 5 minutes. Turn kabobs; brush with half of the barbecue sauce. Cover and cook another 5 minutes. Turn kabobs and brush with remaining sauce. Cover and cook about 1 minute longer or until chicken is no longer pink in center.

Serve with additional BBQ sauce on the side.

Chicken Liver Pate'

Use this quick, easy recipe for Chicken Liver Pate' to serve as an appetizer at your next gathering.

Ingredients

1/2 cup peanut oil
* 1/2 cup onion, diced
* 1 pound cooked chicken livers
* 1 hard-boiled egg
* 1 teaspoon salt
* 1/8 teaspoon pepper

Directions

Heat peanut oil in a heavy skillet, add diced onion and saute' until transparent, about 5 minutes. Allow to cool in skillet
2. Grind or chop together the cooked chicken livers, egg and onion from skillet. Stir in salt and pepper.
3. Chill until ready to serve.
Yield= 1 1/2 cups spread.

Chicken Quesadillas

Easy chicken quesadillas "bites" to serve as appetizers at your next party or as a snack anytime.

Ingredients

2 10-inch flour tortillas
2 tablespoons butter, softened
1 cup diced chicken
1/3 cup shredded Monterey jack cheese
1/3 cup shredded cheddar cheese
1/2 medium tomato, chopped
2 teaspoons diced onions
1 teaspoon diced canned jalapeno
1/4 teaspoon finely chopped cilantro
1 dash salt

Toppings: Sour cream (as needed)
Guacamole (as needed)
Salsa

Directions

Heat a large frying pan over medium heat. Spread half of the butter on one side of each tortilla.
2. Put one tortilla, butter side down, in the hot pan, then spread cheese and cut up chicken strips in the center of the tortilla, leaving about an inch all the way around the edges.
3. Sprinkle the tomato, onion, and jalapeno over the chicken and cheese.
4. Sprinkle the cilantro and a dash of salt over the tortillas.
5. Top off the quesadilla with the remaining tortilla, being sure that the buttered side is facing up.
6. When the bottom tortilla has browned, about 1 to 1 1/2 minutes, flip the quesadilla over and grill the other side for the same amount of time.
7. Remove the quesadilla from the pan, and, using a sharp knife or pizza cutter, cut the quesadilla three times through the middle like a pizza, creating 6 equal slices.
8. Serve hot with sour cream, guacamole, and salsa on the side.

Chicken Kabob's

This chicken kabob's recipe is so easy to make. Serve them as appetizers at your next party. You can even do the marinating the previous day if you want. Just leave then in the fridge until ready to grill.

Not something we would make every week but these kabob's are worth the effort and time for those week-end BBQ's when something a little special is called for.

Prep time: 30 min
Cook time: 11 min
Total time: 41 min plus 1 hour marinate
Yield: 6-10 kabobs

Ingredients:

bamboo skewers (at least 6 inches long), as needed

2 cloves garlic, finely chopped

1/4 cup onions, finely chopped

1/2 teaspoon paprika

1 tablespoon chopped fresh parsley (or dried if fresh not available)

1/2 teaspoon crushed red pepper flakes

1/2 teaspoon ground cumin

1/4 teaspoon salt

1/4 cup olive oil

2 tablespoons lemon juice

1 lb boneless skinless chicken breasts (about 3 pieces), cut into 1-inch bites

1 bell pepper, cut into 2 to 3 inch pieces (for color, try red or yellow peppers)

Instructions:

Combine garlic, onion, paprika, parsley, red pepper flakes, cumin, salt, lemon juice and 2 tablespoons of the olive oil in a sealable plastic bag. Shake to mix well.

Add chicken, seal bag and shake to coat with marinade. Refrigerate for at least 1 hour, turning occasionally.

Heat gas or charcoal grill.

Soak the skewers in water for 30 minutes.

Thread chicken and bell pepper pieces on skewers (and any other items from the tip below).

Place kabobs on grill over medium heat. Cook 9 to 11 minutes, turning occasionally; brushing with remaining 2 tablespoons of oil, until chicken is no longer pink in center.

TIP: Want to jazz it up a little? Add bite size wedges of onion and cherry tomatoes. You can also add broccoli, chunks of pineapple or thinly sliced carrots.

You can use metal skewers if you have them and skip the soak

Mexican Chicken Strips

Here's a zesty chicken appetizer recipe with salsa served on the side. Very easy to make.

Ingredients

1/4 cup sour cream
* 3/4 cup fresh salsa
* 1 pound boneless, skinless chicken breasts (about 3 pieces)
* 1 egg
* 4 cups plain (original) Fritos chips
* 1 teaspoon chili powder
* 1 teaspoon dried dill weed
* vegetable oil as needed for frying

Directions

Make the salsa dip by combining sour cream and salsa in a small bowl, mix well. Refrigerate, covered, until ready to serve.
2. Cut chicken into approximately 24 strips.
3. Beat egg in a shallow bowl. In another shallow bowl, crush Fritos and stir in chili powder and dill weed.
4. Dip chicken strips in egg, then coat with seasoned crushed Fritos.
5. In a deep, heavy skillet, heat oil to 375 degrees F. Fry chicken strips a few at a time until golden brown. Drain on paper towels. Serve hot with salsa dip on the side.

Note: The image on the right of this page was our first attempt where we fried a whole chicken breast using this recipe. We found that cutting the chicken into strips resulted in a crunchier, tastier result.

Slightly Spicy Chicken Bites

Easy, quick recipe for a must-have appetizer at your next party.
This slightly spicy chicken bites appetizer will be a big hit at any party. You can double or triple the recipe by simply preparing more cut up chicken and adds remaining ingredients as needed

Prep time: 30 min
Cook time: 3 min
Total time: 33 min plus 30 min refrigerate
Yield: 4-6 servings

Ingredients

* 1 pound boneless, chicken breasts (about 3 pieces)

* 1 egg

* 1/2 cup milk

* 1/8 teaspoon garlic salt

* 1/2 teaspoon black pepper

* 2 tablespoons red pepper

* 1 cup flour

* Vegetable oil, as needed for frying

Directions

Cut chicken breasts lengthwise, then into bite size cubes.

Combine milk and egg in a bowl and beat until well mixed.

Combine garlic salt, black pepper, red pepper and flour into a separate bowl and mix well.

Drop chicken cubes into egg/milk mix and coat on all sides.

Transfer chicken cubes to flour mix and stir to coat on all sides.

Place chicken in refrigerator for 30 minutes to 1 hour.

Deep fry chicken in oil at 375 degrees F for 3 minutes or until no pink color shows inside.

Drain on paper towels and serve hot or cold.

Too Hot Chicken Bites

If you like spicy, this is the appetizer for you. You can make it hotter or you can tone it down by adjusting the amount of red pepper you use. This recipe uses 2 pounds of chicken but you can make as many or as few as you want. Just adjust the amount of flour/spice coating you need.

Ingredients

2 pounds boneless chicken breasts (about 6 pieces)
* 1/8 teaspoon garlic salt
* 2 tablespoons crushed red pepper flakes
* 1/2 teaspoon black pepper
* 1 cup flour
* Vegetable oil as needed for frying

Directions

Cut chicken breasts lengthwise into 1-inch pieces, then into 2 inch bites. Wash chicken and blot excess water with paper towels leaving chicken slightly damp.
2. Combine garlic salt, crushed red pepper, black pepper and flour in a sealable plastic bag (1 gallon size). Place chicken in the bag and shake bag to coat chicken on all sides with flour/spice mix. Seal bag and place in the refrigerator for 1 hour.
3. Remove chicken bites from bag and deep fry, stirring occasionally, in oil at 375 degrees F for 3 minutes or until chicken has no pink inside. Drain on paper towels. Serve hot or cold.

Chicken Salad

Here's an easy chicken salad recipe. This old favorite is great for sandwiches or as a side dish.

Ingredients

2 cups cooked, cold, shredded chicken
* 1 cup celery, chopped
* 1 Tablespoon lemon juice
* Salt and pepper to taste
* 3/4 cup mayonnaise
* 2 hard-boiled eggs, chopped

Directions

> Mix chicken, celery, lemon juice, salt and pepper.
> 2. Add mayonnaise, mix well.
> 3. Fold in chopped eggs, blend gently.
> May be served as a chicken salad sandwich, in a hollowed out tomato, or on a bed of crisp lettuce leaves.

Cashew Chicken Salad

This cashew chicken salad recipe is made simple by using some pre-made ingredients from the store.

Ingredients

2 skinless, boneless chicken breast, cooked, chopped into cubes
* 12-ounces cole slaw, store bought or make your own
* 1 (8.5-ounce) can mandarin oranges in light syrup, drained
* 1/3 cup cashews, chopped, separated
* 1 tablespoon olive oil

Directions

Cook the chicken first any way you like it (fry, boil, bake or broil), allow the chicken to cool and cut into bite size cubes.
2. In a bowl, toss together all ingredients. Save a few cashews to spread over the top.
3. Refrigerate 30 minutes and serve. How simple can it get?

Optional: Add a handful of cherry tomatoes and 1 cup of shredded lettuce.

Curry Chicken Salad

It looks complicated but this yummy recipe is really easy to make.

Ingredients
2 pounds chicken breasts (skinless and boneless)
* 1 cup mayonnaise
* 2 1/2 teaspoons curry powder
* 1 stalk celery, finely chopped
* 1 1/2 teaspoons mango chutney (or orange marmalade)
* Sea Salt and freshly ground black pepper (to taste)
* 1 medium to large papaya, cut lengthwise, seeds removed
* Mixed greens, for garnish
* Paprika, for garnish

Directions

In a medium saucepan, bring 3 cups of water to a boil, reduce heat and add chicken. Add garlic, salt and pepper to taste. Simmer for 10 to 12 minutes or until fork tender. Remove chicken from saucepan and allow chicken to cool. When cool, dice into bite size pieces.
2. In a medium bowl, combine the mayonnaise, curry powder, chopped celery and mango chutney. Add the diced chicken, season with salt and pepper, to taste, and stir until ingredients have mixed completely. Cover and refrigerate for at least 1 hour.
3. Cut a medium papaya lengthwise and remove all seeds. Chill in fridge for 30 min.
4. Prepare a plate with a layer of greens. Place the chilled half papaya in the center of the plate, surrounded by the greens. Place a generous scoop of chilled curried chicken salad into the center of the papaya, and sprinkle with paprika, for garnish.

Asian Chicken Salad

Easy chicken salad with an Asian flavor. Goes well with any main dish.

Ingredients

1 large carrot, peeled and sliced thin
* 3 cups shredded napa cabbage (sometimes called Chinese cabbage)
* 3 cups shredded romaine lettuce
* 3 tablespoons dried basil (use fresh basil if you have it)
* 1 red bell pepper, seeded and de-veined, thinly sliced
* 2 cups cooked chicken breast, chopped bite size.
* 1 tablespoon toasted sesame seeds

Dressing Ingredients:
* 1/4 cup peanut or canola oil
* 2 tablespoons soy sauce
* 2 tablespoons rice vinegar
* 1/2 teaspoon sugar
* salt and black pepper (to taste)
* 1/2 cup chow Mein noodles, for garnish

Directions

In a large bowl, combine the carrot, cabbage, lettuce, pepper, basil, chicken, and sesame seeds.
2. Prepare the dressing: In a small bowl, whisk together the oil, soy sauce, vinegar, and sugar until smooth. Season with salt and pepper, to taste.
3. Pour the dressing over the salad and toss well. Spread the chow Mein noodles over the top.
Can be served immediately of refrigerate 30 minutes to develop flavors before serving.

Chicken Salad Stuffed Tomato

Here's an old recipe that everybody likes but is often forgotten. Somehow we just don't think of stuffed tomatoes. Surprise your family tonight with this delightful salad.

Ingredients

1 whole chicken, cooked, meat shredded or diced
* 1/2 small red onion, diced
* 2 tablespoons freshly chopped tarragon leaves (or dried)
* 1 celery rib, chopped
* 2 tablespoons white wine vinegar
* 3/4 cup mayonnaise
* salt and freshly ground black pepper, to taste
* 6 large beefsteak tomatoes
* 1 head lettuce
* black olives for garnish

Directions

Mix the first 7 ingredients in a large bowl then place in refrigerator for 30 minutes.
2. Core tops of tomatoes with a paring knife then use a melon baller to scoop out the insides of the tomatoes.
3. Lay a leaf of lettuce in each tomato so it sticks out the top or, optionally, prepare a bed of lettuce underneath the tomatoes.
4. Fill the tomatoes with a large scoop of the chicken salad, top with an olive and serve.

Chicken Taco Salad

Here's the ever popular chicken taco salad recipe. It has a lot of ingredients but is really easy to make. The kids love this tasty and healthy salad.

Ingredients

1/4 cup plain low fat yogurt
* 1/2 cup chunky salsa
* 2 tablespoons olive oil
* 1/2 onion, finely chopped
* 1 red bell pepper, seeded and finely chopped
* 2 cloves garlic, chopped
* 1/2 jalapeno pepper, seeded and finely chopped (optional)
* 1 pound (about 3 pieces) cooked chicken breast, shredded or cubed
* 1/2 cup sliced black olives
* 1 tablespoon chili powder
* 1 teaspoon ground cumin
* 1 (15-ounce) can kidney beans, drained and rinsed
* 1 head romaine lettuce, chopped
* 1 cup cherry tomatoes, sliced in half
* 1 cup tortilla chips, crushed
* 1/2 cup shredded Monterey Jack cheese
* 1/2 cup shredded Cheddar cheese
* 1/4 cup cilantro leaves, chopped
* salt and black pepper, to taste

Directions

Lightly mix the yogurt and salsa together in a small bowl and set aside.
2. Heat the olive oil in a large skillet on medium heat. Add the onions, bell peppers, garlic and jalapeno and sauté until tender, 3 to 4 minutes.
3. Add the chicken and sauté until browned. Stir in the chili powder and cumin. Add the beans and olives. Cook until warmed through.
4. In a large salad bowl, combine the chopped lettuce, cherry tomatoes, tortilla chips, cheese, and Cilantro.
5. Stir in the sautéed chicken and bean mixture.
6. Top individual servings with the yogurt/salsa mix and serve immediately.

Mediterranean Chicken Salad

Break out the grill and serve this yummy chicken Mediterranean salad with your next Italian dinner...or anytime at all.

Ingredients

1 boneless, skinless chicken breast (use two if you love lot's of chicken)
* Oil as needed, for the grill grates
* Salt and freshly ground pepper
* 1/4 cup olive oil
* 1 teaspoon Italian seasoning
* 1 teaspoon sugar
* Juice of 1 lemon
* zest of half a lemon
* 8 ounces frozen green beans, thawed
* 1/4 cup sliced black olives
* 1/2 cup crumbled feta cheese
* 1/2 medium red onion, sliced
* 1 large head romaine lettuce, cleaned and torn into bite-size pieces
* 4 or 5 cherry tomatoes, sliced in half

Directions

Preheat the grill to medium-high heat.
2. Slice the chicken breasts horizontally to get 4 large, thin pieces.
3. When the grill is hot, brush the grill grates with cooking oil to prevent the chicken from sticking. Sprinkle the chicken pieces with salt and pepper and grill for 4 minutes per side. Let rest for a few minutes, and then slices into 1 inch wide strips.
4. In a large bowl, whisk together the olive oil, Italian seasoning, sugar, lemon juice, lemon zest and season with a pinch of salt and pepper (to taste). Reserve 2 tablespoons of the dressing to drizzle over the top of the salad.
5. Add the green beans, olives, cheese, onions and lettuce to the remaining dressing, and toss to coat evenly.
6. Divide the salad evenly among 4 plates and top with the sliced chicken strips. Place several cherry tomato slices on each plate. Drizzle with the reserved dressing.

Crab Salad

Cajun Crab Salad is distinguished by the salad dressing which may be made a variety of ways. Some make it spicy, some much milder. We believe the milder version is more authentic Cajun. We are providing both versions here.

Ingredients:

For each individual salad:

6-8 crisp lettuce leaves

1 hardboiled egg, sliced

4 cherry tomatoes

1/4 cup chopped green onion

1 lemon wedge

1/2 cup crab meat

Instructions:

1. Place crab meat on a bed of lettuce leaves or shred lettuce if preferred.

2. Place cherry tomatoes and lemon wedge on side of plate

3. Sprinkle top with chopped green onion and boiled egg slices

4. Pour 1/4 cup dressing over entire salad (see dressing recipes below)

Note: Cajun Crab Salad is frequently served with a wedge of cantaloupe

For Mild Dressing:

Ingredients:

1 cup mayonnaise

1 cup heavy cream

1/4 cup chili sauce

1 teaspoon Worcestershire

2 tablespoons lemon juice

1/4 cup chopped bell pepper

1/4 cup finely chopped celery

salt and pepper to taste

Instructions:

Mix all ingredients well in a medium bowl and chill 30 minutes before use. Makes enough for 4 salads with a little extra for the table.

For Spicy Dressing:

Ingredients:

1 med. garlic clove

1 cup mayonnaise

1 tbsp. ketchup

2 tsp. mustard

2 tsp. prepared horseradish (real horseradish, not horseradish spread)

1/2 tsp. ground dried tarragon

1/2 tsp. ground dried oregano

1/4 tsp. Worcestershire sauce

1/8 tsp. cayenne pepper

Salt to taste

Instructions:

Same as above for mild dressing makes enough for 4 salads

Baked Crab Dip

With a little horseradish spiciness and toasted almond crunch this dip will be a favorite for your parties or picnics. Very easy to make and may be served with any cracker or chip.

Ingredients

8 oz pkg cream cheese, softened

1 tablespoon milk

6-1/2 oz can (or fresh, if available) flaked crab meat

3 tablespoons minced onions

1/2 teaspoon creamed horseradish

1/4 teaspoon salt

1 tablespoon picante sauce

Toasted almonds

Instructions:

Mix all ingredients except almonds until well blended, Pour into 1-quart casserole dish. Sprinkle with toasted almonds. Bake at 375 degrees F. for 15 minutes.

Serve with any type cracker for dipping.

Dirty Rice

Dirty rice takes its name from the dark color produced by using chicken liver. Well, we like dirty rice but we don't like liver. So this recipe uses the typical dirty rice ingredients but substitutes sausage for the liver. So, we call it "not dirty...dirty rice".

Some Cajun Dirty Rice recipes include ground beef, liver, sausage, chicken or pork. Some people like to use a combination of two meats like sausage and chicken.

The recipe here is slightly spicy so it is important to taste as you add the seasonings and adjust to your liking of mild vs. spicy.

Ingredients:

1 tablespoon cooking oil

1 lb sausage (you can use Tasso, spicy sausage or mild)

1 bell pepper, chopped (green or red or combine both)

1 medium onion (chopped)

3 celery stalks, diced

2 cloves garlic, minced

2 teaspoons Cajun seasoning (to taste)

1/2 tsp. cayenne pepper (to taste)

salt and black pepper (to taste)

2 green onions, chopped (for garnish)

4 cups cooked white rice

Instructions:

1. Cook rice according to package instructions (use a rice cooker if you have one).

2. While rice cooks, heat 1 tablespoon cooking oil in a large skillet over medium heat. Add sausage and brown lightly.

3. Add bell pepper, onion, celery, garlic and Cajun seasoning, cayenne pepper and cook until sausage is cooked through and vegetables are tender (about 5-7 minutes). Add salt and black pepper to taste.

4. Place servings of cooked rice on plates and cover liberally with sausage/vegetable mix.

5. Garnish top with chopped green onions and serve hot.

Makes 4 servings

Additional Optional Ingredients (add in step 3):

* 1 minced jalapeno

* 1 teaspoon hot sauce

* 1/2 cup chopped tomato

* 1/2 cup chopped parsley

* 1 teaspoon dried thyme

Acadiana Rice and Black-eyed Peas

Just good down home Southern food that is simple and easy to make. This is the definition of "comfort food" to most Cajuns. Feel free to spice it up with a little hot sauce if you like (we won't tell). You can keep left over's in the fridge for 3 days and reheat to serve.

Ingredients:

2 cups black eyed peas, cooked (recipe for cooking black eyed peas)

One 10-ounce can tomatoes, drained

3 cups rice, cooked

1/2 teaspoon garlic salt

2 tablespoons olive oil

1/2 cup onion, minced

1/2 cup bell pepper, minced

1 teaspoon garlic, minced

1/2 cup green onions, chopped

Instructions:

1. Preheat oven to 350F.

2. Combine first 4 ingredients in large bowl

3. Heat oil in small pan. Add next 3 ingredients to hot oil. Sauté 5 minutes.

4. Add to rice/peas mixture. Stir well.

5. Transfer to 8 inch oven safe casserole dish, sprayed with non-stick cooking spray. Sprinkle green onions on top. Cover. Bake until heated through, about 25-30 minutes.

Serves 6.

Stewed Corn-n-Tomatoes with Okra

This is a spicy vegetable dish that makes a great side to accompany any meat or seafood. Very easy to make. Adjust the jalapeno peppers used to accommodate your tolerance for heat.

Ingredients:

1 onion, chopped

1 fresh jalapeno pepper, chopped (with seeds)

1 large green bell pepper, coarsely chopped

1/2 teaspoon salt

3 tablespoons butter

1 pound tomatoes, coarsely chopped

3 cups corn kernels

1 cup okra, chopped

Instructions:

1. Cook onions, jalapeno, bell pepper, and 1/2 teaspoon salt in butter over medium heat, stirring occasionally, until onions are translucent (7 to 9 minutes).

2. Stir in tomatoes and continue cooking, stirring occasionally, until tomatoes form a sauce (about 15 minutes).

3. Add corn and okra and cook, stirring occasionally, until just tender (about 15 minutes).

Cajun Green Beans

These Cajun green beans are a little sweet, a little tangy and a little spicy. We cook the beans longer than you may be used to cooking beans so be sure to heed the warning to keep the beans covered in water. Burnt beans are totally uneatable and will leave an odor in your kitchen that takes some effort to eliminate.

Ingredients:

1 pound fresh snap beans (cut/snapped into 1 inch lengths)

3 tablespoons bacon drippings

1 small onion, cut in half

1 teaspoon honey

1/2 teaspoon salt

1/4 teaspoon black pepper

1 tablespoon white vinegar

1/2 teaspoon crushed red pepper flakes

Instructions:

1. Combine all the ingredients in a medium soup pot. Add enough water to cover beans by about 4 inches

2. Cover with a tight fitting lid and cook over medium heat 5 minutes.

3. Reduce heat; cook about 1 hour longer until beans are very tender and turn a dull green color.

> Watch carefully and add water if needed to keep at least 2 inches of water in bottom of pot at all times.

Serves 4

Collard Greens Recipe

It doesn't get more Southern than this. Add some spicy chops and black eyed peas and you're living Cajun. This same recipe may be used for turnip greens or mustard greens. For variety, try mixing all three.

Ingredients:

2 1/2 lbs turnip, collard or mustard greens, washed and chopped into 1-in. pieces

3 slices bacon, cut into 1-inch pieces

2/3 cup chopped onions

1 or 2 dashes cider or red wine vinegar

salt and pepper to taste (start with 1/2 tablespoon salt and 1/4 teaspoon pepper)

Instructions:

1. Fry the bacon in a pot large enough to cook the greens.

2. Add the greens along with onions.

3. Cook on low heat, stirring with wooden spoon, until greens are coated with bacon fat (about 2 minutes). Pour off excess fat.

4. Cover the greens with water and season with salt and pepper.

5. Bring to boil. Cover the pot, reduce heat, and simmer until tender (time will vary, about 1 hour).

> Stir occasionally and add water if they threaten to scorch. When done, increase heat to med-high, stir often. Boil off nearly all the cooking liquid. Watch closely that all the liquid does not boil away.

6. Add vinegar. Taste and add salt and pepper if needed. Serve very hot.

Serves 4

Okra Gumbo Recipe

For okra lovers, here's a way to prepare okra other than frying or boiling alone. In addition to flavor, the okra provides a natural thickener to the gumbo. If you have any leftover you can refrigerate in a sealed container for 3 days and reheat when ready to serve.

Ingredients:

1 chicken, cut into serving pieces

4 quarts chicken stock

1 stick butter

2 pounds okra, cut into 1/2 inch lengths

1 green pepper, chopped

1 large onion, chopped

1 clove garlic, minced

1 and 1/2 cups fresh tomatoes, diced

Instructions:

1. Boil chicken in plain water in a large pot until tender.

2. Drain water, and remove chicken from pot.

3. After cooling, remove meat from bones in bite sized chunks.

4. In the same pot, melt butter and sauté okra, onion and green pepper until tender.

5. Add garlic and cook for 2 minutes.

6. Add chicken stock, and tomatoes. Cook over medium heat for 30 minutes, stirring frequently.

Serve with rice and cornbread

Makes 6-8 Servings.

Red Beans and Rice

Normally, we would not salivate over the thought of plain old beans and rice. However, add a little Cajun seasoning and smoked sausage and now you have a real meal packed with flavor. Be sure to keep the beans covered with liquid or they will burn quickly.

Love this recipe. Add the crushed red pepper flakes a little at a time, cook a few minutes and then taste for spiciness. It takes a minute for the full effect of the pepper to kick in.

Prep time: 20 min
Cook time: 2 hours
Total time: 2 hours 20 min plus 1 hour bean soak
Yield: 8-10 servings

Ingredients

1 pound red beans

4 cups water

4 cups chicken broth

2 clover, garlic minced

1 (15 oz) can tomatoes, chopped (with liquid)

1 large bell pepper, chopped

1 large onion chopped

2 stalks of celery, chopped

1/2 pound smoked sausage, sliced bite size

Salt, to taste

Crushed red pepper flakes and black pepper, to taste

Cooked rice

Instructions:

In a large pot, cover beans with water and bring to a rolling boil for two minutes. Remove from stove; cover; let stand for 1 hour. Drain and rinse beans.

Return beans to pot; add all the remaining ingredients except salt and pepper. Bring to a boil, then reduce heat to low and simmer approximately one and one-half hours or until sauce thickens.

3. Season to taste with salt crushed red pepper flakes and black pepper. Remove cover and cook down until liquid is thick. (20-30 minutes).

Serve over hot rice.

Section 10

Dessert Recipes

Never-Fail Pie Crust

We call it "no-fail" because you will make a good pie crust every time with this recipe...but ONLY if you follow all the recipe instructions exactly. If you cut corners you risk failure just like any recipe.

With this recipe you can, indeed, make a good pie crust every time. However, it does require a minimal degree of experience working with dough.

The recipe makes a little over one 9 inch pie crust. If you are good at rolling the dough very thin, you can get two crusts. However, for a two crust pie it is easier to double the recipe...and have a little left over.

Prep time: 30 min
Total time: 30 min plus 30 min refrigeration of dough
Yield: 1 + pie shell

Ingredients:

2 cups all-purpose flour

1 teaspoon salt

1 tablespoon sugar

6 tablespoons soft margarine or butter (do not use unsalted)

6 tablespoons shortening (Crisco)

7 tablespoons ice water

Instructions:

Allow the butter or margarine to reach room temperature.

In a large bowl (or stand up mixer bowl) combine flour, salt and sugar.

Add butter (or margarine), shortening and ice water

Mix by hand or on low speed with mixer until dough comes together in a ball. It should be slightly tacky but not sticky. You may be tempted to add more ice water at this point to make it stick together. DON'T! Just keep working it and it will form a dough.

Wrap with plastic wrap and refrigerate for a minimum of 30 minutes. If you skip this step the dough will be difficult to roll out properly.

Remove from fridge and place on lightly floured cutting board or flat surface.

Using a rolling pin, roll out the dough until it is about 1/8 inch thick (about the thickness of a U.S. quarter).

Place the rolling pin at one edge of the dough and roll the dough up on the rolling pin.

Transfer to your pie pan and unroll the dough off the rolling pin into the pan.

Cut excess from around the edge and crimp the pie shell around the edge.

Pie crust may be refrigerated for a day before use or frozen for a month or more.

Cooking time for the crust will vary according to what you do with the crust. A pie shell alone, with no filling, should take about 20 min at 350 degrees F.

Apple Brown Betty

Apple Brown Betty may be made several different ways but all seem to be very simple and easy. You can use any type apple but the tart cooking apples work best and hold their texture better than sweet eating apples.

This is an old recipe that has been a Southern favorite for many years. It is very simple and down to earth without a lot of creamy fluff. The brown sugar and apples flavor dominate this dish with their earthiness.

Prep time: 25 min
Cook time: 45 min
Total time: 1 hour 10 min
Yield: 6 servings

Ingredients

* 4 cups bread crumbs (store bought or make your own with dried out bread in a food processor)

* 4-5 cups baking apples (tart like Granny Smith), peeled, cored, sliced

* 1 cup brown sugar

* 1 teaspoon cinnamon

* 1/4 tsp salt

* 3 tablespoons lemon juice

* 1/4 cup water

* 4 tablespoons margarine (or butter)

Directions

Pre-heat oven to 350 degrees F.

Grease a 11 x 9 baking dish. (or a 9" pie plate will work).

Sprinkle approximately 1/3 of the bread crumbs over the bottom of the baking dish.

Place 1/2 of the apples in the dish over the bread crumbs.

Mix together the sugar, cinnamon, and salt. Put 1/2 of this sugar mixture over the apples.

Add another 1/3 of the bread crumbs and the rest of the apples.

Sprinkle with the remainder of the sugar mixture.

Top with the final 1/3 of the bread crumbs.

Sprinkle the lemon juice and water over the top of the Apple Brown Betty.

Cut the margarine (or butter) into small chunks and spread around the top.

Cover with aluminum foil and bake in the pre-heated oven at 350 degrees F. for 30 minutes.

Remove cover and bake an additional 15 minutes or until top is brown and juice is bubbly.

Serve hot or cold. Good with ice cream or whipped cream on top.

Classic Apple Pie

Store bought pies are convenient but they do not compare to a classic homemade apple pie.

This classic apple pie is like mom used to make. It is not difficult but if you are uncomfortable working with dough feel free to use a pre-made crust from the store. And, of course, serve with a big scoop of vanilla ice cream.

Prep time: 45 min
Cook time: 1 hour
Total time: 1 hour 45 min
Yield: 6 servings

For the Crust:

Ingredients

* 2 cups all-purpose flour

* 3/4 cup shortening

* 1 teaspoon salt

* 4 tablespoons cold water

Instructions

Combine flour and salt in a bowl; cut in shortening with a fork until a cornmeal consistency. Gradually add cold water, 1 tablespoon at a time, stirring lightly until dough forms a ball.

Chill dough for 30 minutes.

On a floured surface, roll out half of the dough into a 10-in. circle, as thin as you can make it. Place into a 9-in. pie pan (This is the bottom crust. The top will be added later).

For the Filling:

Ingredients

* 7 cups thinly sliced peeled apples

* 2 tablespoons lemon juice

* 1 1/4 cups sugar

* 1/4 cup all-purpose flour

* 1/4 teaspoon ground nutmeg

* 2 teaspoons ground cinnamon

pinch of salt

Instructions

Filling: Place apples in a bowl, add lemon juice and stir to cover apples with juice.

Combine sugar, flour, nutmeg, cinnamon, and salt; add to apples and toss.

Assemble and Cook

You will need 2 tablespoons butter or margarine, 1 egg yolk and 1 tablespoon water

Pour apple mixture into the bottom crust and dot with butter or margarine.

For top crust: Roll out remaining pastry to fit top of pie; place pastry over filling; cut 4 one inch slits in pastry top; seal and flute edges.

Beat egg yolk and water together then brush over pastry top.

Bake at 425 degrees F for 15 minutes. Reduce heat to 350 degrees F; bake additional 40-45 minutes more or until crust is golden brown.

Note: Watch pie the last 20 minutes of baking. If edges of crust begin to burn, cover (edges only) with aluminum foil for remainder of baking time.

Bread Pudding

Bread pudding has been around forever and there are many ways to make it. Here's my mom's recipe that I enjoyed as a child.

We call it "shoestring" because my mom made this when we could not afford more costly pies and cakes. She would say, "I'll make bread pudding for dinner because we are on a shoestring budget

Very classic and very old dessert, bread pudding is a filling dish that kids love. You should use real vanilla extract rather than imitation if possible. It enhances the flavor immensely.

Prep time: 25 min
Cook time: 25 min
Total time: 50 min
Yield: 8 servings

For the pudding:

Pudding Ingredients:

* 9 slices bread

* 1 cup sugar

* 1 large can evaporated milk

* 2 cup milk

* 1 teaspoon vanilla

* 4 egg yolks

* 1/3 cup melted margarine

Pudding Instructions:

Preheat oven to 450 degrees F.

Break bread in small pieces in a large mixing bowl.

In separate bowl, mix sugar, milk, egg yolk, and melted butter. Pour over bread pieces, and then pour in pan sprayed with non-stick spray.

Bake about 20 minutes or until set in middle.

For the Meringue:

Meringue Ingredients:

* 4 egg whites

* 1/4 teaspoon cream of tartar

* 1/4 cup sugar

Meringue Instructions:

Beat 4 egg whites and cream of tartar until soft peaks form.

Add: 1/4 cup sugar gradually, and continue beating, until stiff peaks form.

Layer on top on pudding and bake until lightly browned (3-5 minutes).

Brownie Walnut Pie

This yummy dessert provides the flavor of brownies in the form of a pie. The optional caramel topping really sets off the pie and is highly recommended.

Prep time: 30 min
Cook time: 55 min
Total time: 1 hour 25 min
Yield: 6 servings

Ingredients

1/2 cup butter or margarine

3 ounces unsweetened chocolate, cut up

3 eggs, lightly beaten

1 1/2 cups sugar

1/2 cup all-purpose flour

1 teaspoon vanilla extract

1 cup chopped walnuts

caramel ice cream topping (optional)

1 9-inch unbaked pie shell

Instructions

Preheat oven to 350 degrees F.

In a heavy, small saucepan, melt the chocolate and butter over low heat, stirring frequently. Cool for 20 minutes.

In a large bowl, combine eggs, sugar, flour and vanilla.

Stir in chocolate mixture and nuts. Pour into pastry shell and bake for 50-55 minutes or until a knife inserted in center comes out clean. Cool 1 hour on wire rack before serving.

Serve with ice cream and caramel topping. May be stored 2-3 days in refrigerator.

Caramel Candy

Making homemade candy can be a challenge but with a little skill the average cook should have success with this recipe.

This recipe can be difficult without a candy thermometer or some experience in recognizing the "soft boil stage" of candy making. If you have a thermometer this recipe makes some very good candy.

Prep time: 20 min
Cook time: 20 min
Total time: 40 min
Yield: 15-20 servings

Ingredients:

*1 cup heavy cream

* 1 cup sugar

* 1/2 cup corn syrup

* 1/4 teaspoon salt

* 4 tablespoons butter

* butter, as needed, to grease pan

* 3/4 teaspoon vanilla

Instructions:

Prepare a 10 inch square pan by greasing it liberally with butter.

Place all ingredients except for the butter and vanilla into a heavy, tall-sided saucepan.

Stir the mixture over medium heat with a wooden spoon until the sugar dissolves.

Add the 4 tablespoons of butter and stir until it melts and is well-incorporated and the mixture begins to boil.

Continue to cook **without stirring** until the syrup is just above 248 degrees F, the firm-ball stage, as measured with a candy thermometer. Continuously scrape mixture off the sides of the saucepan **without stirring the mixture**.

Remove from heat and add the vanilla, mix well, then immediately pour the mixture into the greased 10 inch pan.

Allow to cool, then cut into 1-inch squares.

Store in an airtight container at room temperature, between layers of waxed paper.

TIPS:

Note that cook times listed are approximate.

It is possible to make caramel by using the "drop in cold water technique" to determine the firm-ball stage. However we **strongly recommend you use a candy thermometer** for best chance of success.

The "Drop in Water Technique: Drop a little of the mixture in cold water and if you have the correct temperature of the candy the drop will form a firm ball in the water. It will not flatten on its own when you take it out of the water. It should remain soft and hold its shape but will flatten when squeezed.

It is important **not to stir** the mixture after it begins to boil but continuously scrape the mixture off the sides of the pan.

Perfect Chocolate Cake

This chocolate cake, made from scratch, is perfect in our opinion. May not be recommended for the inexperienced cook but not difficult for the average cook.

As you might expect, making a cake from scratch is not as simple as a cake mix. However, made from scratch does not contain preservatives and strange ingredients that you cannot pronounce. If you prefer the wholesome goodness of a homemade cake, this is the recipe for you.

Prep time: 40 min
Cook time: 40 min
Total time: 1 hour 20 min
Yield: 10 servings

For the Cake:

Ingredients

* 1 cup unsifted unsweetened cocoa powder

* 2 cups boiling water

* 2 1/4 cups sifted all-purpose flour

* 2 teaspoons baking soda

* 1/2 teaspoon baking powder

* 1/2 teaspoon salt

* 1 cup butter or margarine, softened

* 2 1/2 cups granulated sugar

* 4 large eggs

* 1 1/2 teaspoons vanilla extract

For the Frosting:

Ingredients

* 1 pkg. (6 oz.) semisweet chocolate pieces

* 1/2 cup light cream

* 1 cup butter or margarine

* 2 1/2 cups unsifted confectioner's sugar

For the Filling:

Ingredients

* 1 cup heavy cream, chilled

* 1/4 cup unsifted confectioner's sugar

* 1 teaspoon vanilla extract

For the Cake: Instructions:

In a medium bowl combine cocoa with boiling water. Mix until smooth. Cool completely.

In another bowl, sift flour with baking soda, baking powder and salt.

Preheat oven to 350 degrees F.

Grease and lightly flour three 9" x 1 1/2" layer cake pans.

In another large bowl, with electric mixer at high speed, beat butter, sugar, eggs and vanilla until light (about 5 minutes), scraping bowl occasionally.

At low speed, beat in flour mixture (in fourths) alternately with cocoa mixture (in thirds), beginning and ending with flour mixture. Do not over beat.

Divide batter evenly into prepared cake pans. Smooth top. Bake 25-30 minutes or until surface springs back when gently pressed with fingertip. Cool 10 minutes. Carefully loosen sides with spatula, remove from pans, cool completely on wire racks.

For the Frosting: Instructions:

In a medium saucepan, combine chocolate pieces, cream and butter; stir over medium heat until smooth. Remove from heat.

With whisk, blend in 2 1/2 cups confectioner's sugar. Set mixture on top of another bowl filled with ice, beat until frosting holds its shape.

For the Filling: Instructions

Whip cream with confectioner's sugar and vanilla until smooth. Place in refrigerator 20 minutes.

Assemble Cake

1. On plate, place a layer, top side down; spread with half of cream filling. Place second layer, top side down, on top of first layer and spread with remainder of cream filling. Place third layer, top side down, on top of second layer.

Frost Cake

1. With spatula, frost sides first, covering with whipped cream filling. Frost top with remaining frosting, swirling decoratively.
2. Refrigerate at least 1 hour before serving. To cut, use a thin-edged sharp knife with a sawing motion.
Serves 12

Cheesecake (no cook)

This is a very simple recipe that requires no cooking. You might want to make two since one will not last long if you have a sweet tooth in the house.

This is a very simple recipe that is quick and easy to make. Really hard to fail. It is tart yet sweet and creamy as cheesecake should be.

Prep time: 20 min
Total time: 20 min
Yield: 6 servings

Ingredients:

* 1 graham cracker crust (homemade or store bought)

* 1 - 16 ounce package of cream cheese, softened

* 1 cup powdered sugar

* 1 package Dream Whip

* 1/2 cup cold milk (for Dream Whip)

* 1 teaspoon vanilla (for Dream Whip)

* 1/2 tsp lemon juice (optional)

* dash of salt

Instructions:

Prepare whipped cream mix (Dream Whip) according to package instructions.

Gently fold in softened cream cheese, powdered sugar, dash of salt and lemon juice until totally blended.

Pour into graham cracker crust.

Chill in refrigerator for at least 4 hours.

Serve as is or garnish top with any of the following: fresh strawberries, blueberries, sliced bananas, raspberries, chocolate chips or crumbled cookies.

Peanut Butter Cookies

It's hard to believe a recipe can be this good and yet so simple and fail-proof. But this one is.

About the only way to fail with this recipe is to overcook the cookies. The finished cookies should be soft and chewy, not hard and crunchy. Watch closely while baking and remove from oven when the tops just turn a light tan. Do not cook until the tops are golden brown.

Prep time: 30 min
Cook time: 12 min
Total time: 42 min plus 1 hour dough chill down
Yield: about 1 doz. cookies

Ingredients:

1/4 cup shortening (Crisco)

1/4 cup butter or margarine (softened)

1/2 cup peanut butter (smooth recommended but you can use chunky if you prefer)

1/2 cup white sugar

1/2 cup brown sugar (pack down in measuring cup to get a good, full 1/2 cup)

1 egg

1 1/2 cups all-purpose flour

3/4 tsp baking soda

1/2 tsp baking powder

1/4 tsp salt

Instructions:

Combine shortening, softened butter, peanut butter, sugar, brown sugar, and egg. Blend well.

In a separate bowl, mix together flour with baking soda, baking powder and salt. Add to peanut butter mixture. Mix well.

Cover and chill for at least an hour.

Roll dough into one inch balls - a little smaller than golf balls.

Place dough balls on greased cookie sheets. Leave a 2 inch space between the balls.

Use a fork to mash the balls out flat like cookies. Make a crisscross pattern on the cookie tops with the fork. Mash one direction. Turn the fork and mash the other direction. If the fork is sticking to the dough, dip the fork lightly in flour.

Bake at 375 degrees F for 10 to 12 minutes. Cookies should be very lightly browned. Don't overcook, or the cookies will be hard instead of soft and chewy.

Peanut Butter Pie (Easy)

This is one of those "never-fail" recipes that is so simple a child could probably make it. No cooking is required for this treat and your family will love it. Better make two because they do not last long

This is one of the easiest recipes we've tried. It really is difficult to mess up this delightful pie. If you are fond of peanut butter and sweets, you will love this combination.
Difficulty: Easy

Prep time: 30 min
Total time: 30 min
Yield: 6-8 servings

Ingredients:

1 (8 ounce) package cream cheese (softened)

1 cup creamy peanut butter

1 tablespoon unsalted butter (softened)

1 cup sugar

1 teaspoon vanilla extract

1 cup heavy whipping cream

1 (9-inch) graham cracker pie crust

1/4 cup chocolate syrup (ice cream topping)

Instructions:

Let the cream cheese and butter come to room temperature.

Mix together the butter, cream cheese, peanut butter, sugar, and vanilla until smooth.

In a separate bowl, whip the heavy cream until smooth and thick.

Pour the heavy cream into the peanut butter mixture and blend gently with a spoon until incorporated.

Spoon filing into pie crust.

Refrigerate for 3 hours

Drizzle chocolate topping syrup over top of pie before serving.

Note: The graham cracker crust may be used with or without baking. Baking provides a somewhat crunchier texture. If you choose to bake, place in a 375 degrees oven 8-10 minutes or until lightly browned. Refrigerate for 30 minutes before filling

Pineapple Upside Down Sweet Potatoes

This dish not only tastes good it is such a pretty presentation. When you invert the pan the pineapple and brown sugar are on top giving the appearance of a pineapple upside down cake.

Very novel treatment of this Southern favorite. We were tempted to add melted marshmallows to the top but resisted and were happy with what this recipe produced. Difficulty: Medium

Prep time: 30 min
Cook time: 45 min
Total time: 1 hour 15 min
Yield: 8 servings

For The Topping

Ingredients:

2 tablespoons margarine, melted

1 tablespoon brown sugar, packed

1 tablespoon maple syrup

ground cinnamon (as needed)

8-10 whole pineapple slices OR 1 1/2 cups pineapple chunks (canned or fresh)

For The Filling:

Ingredients:

1 can (18 oz.) sweet potatoes (or if you cook your own: 2 1/4 cups)

1 1/2 teaspoons vanilla extract

3/4 teaspoon ground cinnamon

1 tablespoon brown sugar, packed

Instructions:

Preheat oven to 350 degrees F.

Lightly oil (or use nonstick spray) a 9-inch pie pan

Prepare Topping: Combine melted margarine, brown sugar and maple syrup in a small bowl and mix well. Spread mix evenly over the bottom of the prepared pie pan.

Sprinkle lightly with cinnamon. Arrange pineapple slices (or chunks) evenly over the margarine mix in pie pan.

Prepare Filling: In a large bowl, combine all of the filling ingredients. Mash with a fork or potato masher until smooth and completely combined.

Spoon sweet potato filing mix over the pineapple in the pie pan and smooth with the back of a spoon.

Cover with aluminum foil and bake 45 minutes.

Remove from oven and let sit 2 minutes. Remove foil, run a knife around the edge of the pan and invert onto a serving plate.

Mississippi Mud Pie

This may come as a surprise to some, but according to Wikipedia, Mississippi Mud Pie was not created in Mississippi. It's actually from California.

Rumor is that the name came from the fact that the brown crust of the pie resembles the brown banks of the Mississippi River. Where ever it came from it is sinfully delicious.

There are many versions of Mississippi Mud Pie but this is my favorite. The chocolate goodness of this decadent treat with its crunchy crust is unbelievable.

Prep time: 30 min
Cook time: 1 hour
Total time: 1 hour 30 min
Yield: 6-8 servings

Ingredients:

* Graham cracker pie crust (use store bought or make your own using directions on side of graham cracker box).

* 8 ounces bittersweet chocolate, coarsely chopped

* 1 cup coarsely chopped toasted pecans

* 1/2 cup (1 stick) unsalted butter

* 4 large eggs

* 1 cup granulated sugar

* 3 tablespoons light corn syrup

* 1/2 teaspoon salt

* 1 cup heavy cream

* 1/4 cup confectioner's sugar

* Additional 1 ounce bittersweet chocolate, shaved (for garnish)

* vanilla ice cream, as needed (optional)

Instructions:

Preheat oven to 350 degrees F.

Melt 2 ounces of the chocolate by placing it in a medium size, heat proof bowl set over a pan of boiling water.

Brush the bottom of the pie shell with the melted chocolate and scatter pecans over entire surface.

Using the same bowl, set over simmering water, and melt butter with remaining 6 ounces of chocolate.

Using an electric mixer on high, beat eggs, granulated sugar, corn syrup, and salt until thick, about 3 minutes.

Slowly fold the melted butter-chocolate mixture into the egg mixture. Not too fast or you might get scrambled eggs!

Pour mixture into the pie shell and bake 35 to 40 minutes or until top forms a crust and filling is just set.

Transfer pie to a wire rack to cool completely, and then refrigerate 30 minutes.

SEE NOTE BELOW BEFORE PROCEEDING

Using an electric mixer on medium speed, beat heavy cream with confectioner's sugar until soft peaks form.

Spread the whipped cream over the top of the cooled pie. Sprinkle the top with chocolate shavings.

Serve immediately or store in the refrigerator.

Serve with scoops of vanilla ice cream on the side (optional).

NOTE: As you know, whipped cream tends to melt and droop after a short time. If you do not intend to serve the pie within a few hours do not prepare or use the whipped cream until ready to serve. As an alternative, some people prefer to substitute the whipped cream by melting additional chocolate and drizzling over the top of the pie (see image above). Your choice.

Sweet Potato Pie (or Pumpkin Pie)

Since sweet potatoes have been traditionally cheap to buy and easy to grow, they became a mainstay in the Southern diet back in the Civil War days. They are not as popular today but baked sweet potatoes are often served on holidays and sweet potato pie is still a favorite anytime.

Here's a tip about this recipe: if you like pumpkin pie, just substitute a 15 oz can of pumpkin pie filling for the sweet potatoes and you have a pumpkin pie. All the other ingredients and procedures are exactly the same.

If you prefer not to use prepared (canned) filling, you can cook your own sweet potatoes very easily. Just boil about 4-5 large sweet potatoes (enough for 1 3/4 cups of filling) in plain water until a fork pushed into the potatoes enters easily. Then scrape out the inside of the potatoes from the peeling and process in a food processor until you obtain a paste consistency. (You can do this with a fork if you do not have a processor).

Prep time: 20 min
Cook time: 1 hour 5 min
Total time: 1 hour 25 min
Yield: 2 nine inch pies 8 + servings

Ingredients:

1/2 cup sugar

1 and 1/2 tsp ground cinnamon

1/2 tsp ground ginger

2 large eggs

1 tsp vanilla

4 oz butter (softened)

1 and 3/4 cups cooked and mashed sweet potatoes (or use canned pie filling)

1 can (12 oz) evaporated milk (do not substitute regular milk-it will not set properly)

2 nine inch uncooked pie shells (not deep dish)

Instructions:

Mix sugar, cinnamon and ginger in a large bowl

Beat eggs in a separate bowl; add vanilla and butter, mix well.

Pour egg mixture into dry ingredients while stirring.

Add sweet potatoes to mix and stir.

Add evaporated milk. Mix well.

Pour mixture into pie shell(s).

Bake in pre-heated 425 degree oven for 15 minutes

Reduce heat to 350 degrees and bake 40-50 minutes or when a toothpick stuck into center of pie comes out dry.

Cool pie 1 hour before cutting. Top with whipped cream and cherries or pecans if desired. Refrigerate left-over but do not freeze.

Peach Praline Pie

Praline refers to the combination of pecans and brown sugar blended together as a topping or filling. This pie uses a yummy praline topping to compliment the peach filling.

This is a great summer favorite when fresh peaches are available. Canned peaches may be used but it takes on a totally different character so we recommend using only fresh peaches. You simply must add a scoop of ice cream on top of the crunchy praline crust.
Difficulty: Medium

Prep time: 30 min
Cook time: 45 min
Total time: 1 hour 15 min
Yield: 6-8 servings

Ingredients:

9 inch unbaked deep-dish pie shell

For The Filling:

Ingredients:

4 cups peeled, sliced peaches (about 4-5 medium peaches)

1/2 cup granulated (white) sugar

3 1/2 tablespoons tapioca (use quick cooking instant)

1/2 teaspoon cinnamon

1 teaspoon lemon juice

For The Praline Topping:

Ingredients:

1/2 teaspoon cinnamon

1/2 cup pecans, chopped

1/4 cup unsalted butter, at room temperature

6-8 whole pecans to garnish top of pie

Directions:

Preheat oven to 350 degrees

Prepare the filling by combining peaches, sugar, tapioca, cinnamon and lemon juice in a large bowl. Mix well and allow to sit while making the topping (at least 10-15 minutes).

Prepare the praline topping by combining the flour, brown sugar, cinnamon, chopped pecans and butter in a medium size bowl.

Use your fingers to mix until the topping is well combined and crumbly. There should be no lumps in the mix.

Assemble as follows:

Use a fork to pierce the bottom of the pie shell in several scattered places.

Sprinkle 1/4 of the praline topping mix over the bottom of unbaked pie shell.

Pour peach filling mixture into pie shell and sprinkle remaining praline topping over peaches.

Place pie on a baking sheet lined with foil and bake for 30 minutes.

Check outside (fluted) edge of pie crust. If starting to burn cover just the edge with foil.

Continue to bake until peaches are tender and topping is golden brown, about 10-15 additional minutes.

Remove from oven and garnish top of pie with whole pecans. Allow to cool completely before slicing.

Southern Pecan Pie

An old Southern favorite, Pecan Pie is always sure to please. Some serve it with ice cream although this may not be the traditional Southern way, they go together very well.

Even novice cooks can succeed with this easy recipe. The only caution in the recipe is to be sure to mix the ingredients well or the pie may not set. Our test pie came out perfect the first try.
Difficulty: Medium

Prep time: 20 min
Cook time: 45 min
Total time: 1 hour 5 min
Yield: 8 servings

Ingredients:

1/2 cup sugar

1/4 cup butter (softened)

1 cup corn syrup

1/4 tsp salt

1 tsp vanilla

3 eggs

1 to 1 1/2 cups pecans

9-inch deep-dish pie shell (unbaked) store bought or homemade Pie Crust Recipe

Directions:

Preheat oven to 350 degrees.

Cream (mix) the sugar and butter well in a medium sized mixing bowl.

Add syrup, salt, and vanilla. Mix again.

Add eggs one at a time and mix after each.

Stir in pecans (save a few to place on top of pie after cooking).

Pour mixture into unbaked pie crust.

Bake in preheated oven until top is brown and pie set (about 45 minutes). Toothpick stuck in center of pie should come out dry.

Tips: Be sure to mix ingredients well. Otherwise the pie may not set up.

You can use chopped or whole pecans for the filling but whole pecans on top of the pie are more eye appealing.

Store in the refrigerator.

May be reheated in microwave before serving (about 15 sec).

Sorghum Molasses Pecan Pie

Here's a twist on the traditional Southern Pecan Pie. The deep, nutty flavor of sorghum molasses makes this pie a little different.

My grandmother made this pie when I was young and it was my favorite. She lived way back in the country without paved roads or stores nearby. She did not have store bought sorghum molasses but she made molasses in her own kitchen. This may not be grandmother's actual recipe but it taste pretty close.

We found that we had a little left over batter using a 7" pie shell and did not have as much batter as we wanted using a 9" shell so we suggest using a 7" pie shell and having a little left over.

Prep time: 20 min
Cook time: 40 min
Total time: 1 hour
Yield: 6-8 servings

Ingredients:

uncooked 7-9 inch pie crust

5 eggs

1/3 cup sugar

1 and 1/4 cups sorghum molasses

1/2 cup chopped pecans

1 cup whole pecans

Instructions:

Preheat oven to 350 degrees F.

Place eggs in a large bowl and beat well.

Add sugar and sorghum molasses. Using a mixer, beat for three minutes.

Add 1/2 cup chopped nuts and mix well by hand using a large spoon.

Pour mixture into the pie shell and cover the outside edge of pie shell with a narrow strip of aluminum foil to prevent the rim from burning.

Place pie in preheated oven, on the middle rack.

Bake until the top of crust begins to brown (about 20-30 minutes) then remove the aluminum strip from the edge of pie shell.

Continue baking until crust is evenly browned and a toothpick stuck in the center of the pie comes out clean (about 35 to 40 minutes **total** bake time).

Remove from oven and cover top of pie with remaining 1 cup of whole pecans.

Be sure to mix very well in steps 3 and 4 or the pie may not set.

Ice Cream Sunday Pie

This is my favorite dessert recipe. It takes a long time to make but most of that time is just waiting for the pie to freeze. The actual making of the pie is not difficult.

Prep time: 20 min
Total time: 20 min plus 3 hours freezer time
Yield: 6-8 servings

Ingredients:

2 pints vanilla ice cream, softened

1 (9 inch) graham cracker crust

1/2 cup plus 2 tbsp. caramel sauce

1/2 cup plus 2 tbsp. fudge sauce

1/2 pint whipped cream or desert topping (Dream Whip)

Instructions:

Use a large spoon to scoop 1 pint ice cream into thin slices, and spread on bottom of pie crust. Smooth with back of spoon.

Spread 1/2 cup caramel sauce over ice cream.

Freeze pie until solid. (may take an hour or more)

Remove frozen pie from freezer and top with another 1/2 pint ice cream.

Spread 1/2 cup fudge sauce over ice cream.

Freeze pie again until solid.

Remove frozen pie and top with final 1/2 pint ice cream. Drizzle remaining 2 tbsp. each caramel and fudge sauce over pie.

Freeze pie until solid.

Prepare whipped cream or Dream Whip (beat to soft peaks) and spread around edge of pie. Freeze until ready to serve.

Bourbon Pecan Chocolate Pie

You need not be concerned about the bourbon in this pie making it unfit for children. The alcohol boils off during cooking so there is no significant alcohol in the pie. The bourbon only adds flavor.

If you are good working with pastry you can make your own pie shell for this recipe. Or a store bought pre-made pie crust works O.K. The filling resembles a pecan pie but with a delightful chocolate chip base. A very decadent desert.

Prep time: 20 min
Cook time: 50 min
Total time: 1 hour 10 min
Yield: 8 servings

Ingredients:

* 1 (9-inch) unbaked pie shell

* 1 cup semi-sweet chocolate chips

* 3 medium eggs or 2 extra large

* 1/2 cup sour cream

* 1/2 cup dark corn syrup

* 1 cup sugar

* 1/8 teaspoon Salt

* 1 teaspoon Vanilla

* 2 ounces bourbon (optional)

* 1 and 1/2 cups pecans, half chopped, half whole

Instructions:

Preheat oven to 350 degrees.

Cover bottom of pie shell with chocolate chips.

In a medium size mixing bowl combine eggs, sour cream, corn syrup, sugar, salt, vanilla, and bourbon. Mix well until smooth. It is important to mix well in this step or the pie may not set when baked (will not be firm).

Add the pecans to the mixture and mix. Pour batter into the pie shell on top of the chocolate chips (already on bottom of pie shell).

Place in preheated oven and bake for 50 minutes or until a toothpick comes out clean when inserted in the center.

Southern Chocolate Walnut Fudge

New cooks may find this recipe challenging but experienced cooks should have success. You can substitute your favorite nuts for the English Walnuts. As the recipe states, achieving a proper soft boil stage is critical. We strongly advise using a candy thermometer. We do not recommend attempting to double this recipe (it's difficult enough already).
Difficulty: Difficult

Prep time: 20 min
Cook time: 25 min
Total time: 45 min
Yield: 6-8 servings

Ingredients:

2 cups evaporated milk

1/4 cup cocoa powder

6 cups sugar

1 tsp salt

6 TBS butter (or margarine)

1 cup marshmallow cream

1 1/2 cups chopped English walnuts

Instructions:

Put the milk, cocoa powder, sugar and salt in a large sauce pan.

Stir the ingredients over medium high heat until the mixture comes to a hard boil.

Once mixture comes to a boil, STOP STIRRING and adjusts heat if necessary to maintain a hard rolling boil.

Cook until the mixture reaches the soft ball stage - 235 degrees F. on candy thermometer (see note below).

Remove from heat and let cool 10 minutes.

Stir in the butter, marshmallow cream and nuts. Beat vigorously until the real glossy look is gone.

Spread out in a 12 x 9 pan coated lightly with spray or butter

Wait until the fudge is set (hardened) to cut.

Note: Obtaining the proper temperature is critical to the fudge setting up. If temperature is too low or too high you will have a soupy chocolate mess or fudge that doesn't set properly. The best method is to use a candy thermometer, cook until temperature reaches 235 degrees F. If you do not have a candy thermometer you can cook until a drop of the fudge mixture in a glass of cold water immediately forms a soft ball (this can be tricky).

Holiday Fruitcake

This recipe may be a challenge for new cooks but should not be difficult for experienced cooks. It is flexible, in that additional ingredients may be added if desired. Specifically, additional dried, candied fruit, such as pineapple or lemon peel may be added.

The bourbon is used for flavor but if you object to using it you may substitute water. However, be aware that the alcohol boils off during baking and there is no significant alcohol in the cake.

Prep time: 20 min
Cook time: 2 hours
Total time: 2 hours 20 min
Yield: 12 servings

Ingredients:

4 cups of flour, sifted

1 teaspoon of baking powder

4 teaspoons of nutmeg

2 teaspoons of cinnamon

1 cup of butter or margarine (softened)

2 cups of sugar

1/2 teaspoon salt

1/2 Cup brown sugar

6 Whole Eggs

4 tablespoons vanilla extract

1/2 cup of bourbon (you may substitute water)

4 cups of pecans, coarsely chopped

1 pound of seeded Light Raisins

1/2 cup of candied Cherries; Green and red

Instructions:

Grease and flour two 9 x 5 x 3-inch loaf pans. Line the bottoms with waxed paper; grease and flour the paper. Set aside. Or you may use a well-greased 10" tube pan.

Sift flour, baking powder, cinnamon, salt and nutmeg together.

In a separate large bowl, combine butter and sugar, cream until fluffy. Add brown sugar and mix well.

Beat in eggs, one at a time. Stir in vanilla extract.

Add dry ingredients (from step 2) alternately with bourbon (or water). Stir in nuts, raisins and cherries.

Turn mixture into well-greased pan(s).

Bake at 300 degrees F. for 2 hours or until toothpick or knife inserted in center of cake comes out clean.

Remove from oven and let stand in pan for 20 minutes. Remove from pan and cool on rack.

Wrap in foil or put in an air tight container.

Beignets (French Donut)

Beignet is Cajun French for "French Doughnut". This recipe can be a challenge and we have had occasions when it was not to our liking but when it's good...it's really good. Well worth a try for the adventurous.

We found that rolling out the dough to 1/4 inch thickness did not make a beignet as full as we wanted so we rolled our dough closer to 1/2 inch. You might need to experiment with this.

This recipe makes about 40-50 beignets. You can half the recipe by using 1/2 the listed ingredients, except the yeast. Do not half the yeast.

Prep time: 20 min
Cook time: 15 min
Total time: 35 min
Yield: 40 beignets

Ingredients

1/2 cup shortening

1/2 cup sugar

1 tsp salt

1 cup boiling water

1 cup evaporated milk

2 packages yeast

1/4 cup warm water

2 eggs, well beaten

6 1/2 cups all-purpose flour

oil for frying, as needed (canola or peanut oil suggested)

powdered sugar as needed, optional

Instructions:

Cream together shortening, sugar, and salt.

Mix in one cup boiling water and one cup milk. Set aside.

Mix yeast well in 1/4 cup warm water. Add this and beaten eggs to the mixture and mix well.

Add 3 1/2 cups flour and stir in with a spoon. Add the remaining 3 cups of flour and mix. Put the dough in a greased covered container in the refrigerator for 30 minutes.

Place enough oil in a deep pot to provide about a 4 inch depth. Heat oil to 360 degrees F.

While oil heats, roll out dough 1/4 inch thick and cut into 3 inch squares with a knife. Use knife to cut 1/2 inch slit in the middle of each square.

Fry in deep oil until golden brown on both sides.

Powdered sugar may be sprinkled on top. Drain on paper towels.

Bayou Pecan Pie

This yummy pecan pie is fairly easy to make but be sure to mix well in step 2 below or the pie may not set up. The baking time can vary widely in various ovens so watch closely to avoid over cooking.

We're using a store bought pie shell here but if you are good at working with dough we encourage you to make your own. Home made just always seems to taste better.

Ingredients:

1 unbaked 9 inch pie shell

1-1/2 cups pecan halves

3 eggs

3/4 cup Sugar

1/4 cup brown sugar

1 cup corn syrup

2 tablespoons butter, melted and cooled

1-1/2 teaspoons vanilla extract

1/8 teaspoon salt

Instructions:

1. Preheat oven to 350 degrees.

2. Beat eggs in a large bowl until frothy. Add Sugar, brown sugar, corn syrup, butter, vanilla extract, salt and 1 cup of the pecans. Combine thoroughly.

3. Pour mixture into an unbaked pie shell, place on a baking sheet and bake at 350 degrees F for about 30 minutes.

4. Reduce oven heat to 325 degrees F and bake until filling is browned on top and crust is lightly browned; about 20-30 minutes. See note below.

5. Remove from oven and cover top with the remaining 1/2 cup of pecans. Allow to cool before cutting.

Note: Watch pie crust edges for burning. If burning, cover crust edge with aluminum foil and continue cooking.

Bread Pudding

Like many Cajun recipes, this bread pudding uses common, inexpensive ingredients (don't throw that 3 day old bread away).

Although this is an old recipe, it seems that bread pudding is seldom served now days. Many young people have never tasted it.

If there are young ones in your family that fall in this category, put on your apron and introduce them to this delightful dessert today.

Ingredients:

4 slices (3-4 day old) bread

4 tablespoons sugar

3 1/2 cups milk

4 eggs, separated

1 tablespoon vanilla

1 pinch salt

1/4 cup butter

1/4 cup raisins

Instructions:

1. Break bread into 1/2 inch pieces into a 1-1/2 quart **oven proof** dish. Set aside.

2. In a large mixing bowl, combine sugar, egg yolks, milk, vanilla and salt. Beat well.

3. Fold in raisins

4. Pour milk mixture over bread.

5. Cut butter into chunks and spread over top of bread.

6. Place the dish in a pan of water and bake at 300 degrees for 40-50 minutes, or until a knife inserted in the center comes out clean.

7. Make meringue topping by adding 2 tablespoons sugar to the 4 egg whites and beat until frothy.

8. Spread meringue topping on top of pudding and return to oven set on broiler position. Remove when meringue top is golden brown. You must watch continuously while meringue browns. Do not walk away, it will burn quickly.

Serve warm.

Easy Homemade Kahlua

If you are fond of Kahlua you are aware of how expensive it is. And did you ever want your Kahlua to be more potent? Less potent? More coffee flavor or less?

Well, make your own and you can adjust the ingredients to make it the way you want it. Make one batch using the recipe below and next time you can adjust to your taste if needed.

Ingredients:

4 cups Sugar

6 cups water

2 ounces instant coffee

1 bottle (1.75 liter) of vodka

1/2 pint dark rum

4 tablespoons vanilla extract

Instructions:

1. Mix Sugar and water and bring to a slow boil. Simmer on medium heat 15 minutes, stirring frequently.

2. Add 2 ounces instant coffee, stir and simmer 5 minutes longer. Stir constantly.

3. Remove from heat and cool to room temperature.

4. Add entire bottle of vodka, 1/2 pint rum and the 4 teaspoons vanilla extract. Mix well.

   Note: Make sure water/sugar mixture is cool. If it is still hot some of the alcohol will evaporate from the vodka and rum!

5. Rebottle and enjoy.

You may drink immediately but flavors will enhance if allowed to stand a few days.

Mix with coffee or drink straight mixed with 1/4 cup milk over ice. Be sure to use fresh milk. The Kahlua will curdle milk that is not fresh.

Pecan Pralines

Very simple recipe if you are familiar with the "soft boil stage" in making candy. If not, you should use a candy thermometer to assure obtaining the proper temperature.

Ingredients:

3/4 cup brown sugar

3/4 cup white sugar

1/2 cup (canned) evaporated milk

1/2 teaspoon pure vanilla extract

2 tablespoons butter (no margarine)

1 cup whole or large chunk pecans

Instructions:

1. Combine the brown sugar, white sugar and milk in a heavy pot and cook slowly over low heat until it reaches the soft ball stage (a drop of mixture in a cup of cold water forms a ball) or 238 degrees F. on a candy thermometer.

2. Remove from heat and add the butter, vanilla and pecans. Beat mixture with a wooden spoon until it is smooth and creamy.

3. Lightly spray a cookie sheet with cooking spray.

4. Drop spoonful of mix at a time onto sprayed surface.

4. Wait 10-15 minutes for praline to harden.

Note: If praline does not harden sufficiently, you probably did not get mix to proper temperature. You can put it back in a pot and cook again, making sure to obtain 238 degrees F.

Makes about 1 dozen pralines.

EXTRA
A Dozen Ways to Cook Gator

Alligator Cocktail Fritters

Yield: Approximately 12 Fritters

INGREDIENTS

    1 pound alligator tail meat, finely ground
    1 Florida sweet onion, chopped fine
    1 green bell pepper, chopped fine
    1 clove garlic, minced
    1/2 cup all-purpose flour
    2 teaspoons baking powder
    1/8 teaspoon mace
    1/2 teaspoon dry mustard
    1 teaspoon salt
    2 extra-large eggs, beaten
    2 tablespoons melted butter
    1 tablespoon Worcestershire sauce
    Optional: 1 teaspoon Florida hot sauce
    Canola or peanut oil, or a combination

DIRECTIONS

Grind the alligator or pulverize in a food processor. Add the chopped onion, pepper and minced garlic and pulverize with the alligator in the machine.

2. Sift the flour with the baking powder, mace, dry mustard and salt.

3. Beat the eggs. Add the flour mixture. Add the melted butter, Worcestershire and hot sauce, and combine with the alligator mixture.

4. Pour canola or peanut oil or a mixture of both into a skillet 1-inch deep. Heat to 380°F (the bubbling stage). Drop the batter 1 tablespoon at a time into the hot oil, turning the fritters over with a slotted spoon as they brown. Remove when browned on all sides.

Serve with Key Lime wedges and Tartar Sauce.

Alligator Sauce Piquante

As the name indicates, sauce Piquante has a peppery kick to it, although the pepper level can be raised or reduced to taste. A rustic dish with a long Cajun heritage, sauce Piquante is made with lots of extra seasonings and is traditionally served with rice. This recipe uses alligator tail meat, the cut sold by retailers. The sauce is versatile enough to be matched with any number of main ingredients—not only alligator but also turtle, pork, chicken, veal, conch, scallops and game. Many sauce Piquante fans keep a bottle of Tabasco handy when eating it.

This dish takes on added flavor when served the day after it is prepared.

For 6 servings

Special Equipment
- A very small, heavy skillet or 6½-inch crepe pan
- A long-handled whisk or wooden spoon
- A kitchen mallet
- A heavy 12-inch sauté pan

Ingredients

1 tablespoon vegetable oil
1 cup plus 1 tablespoon all-purpose flour, divided
2 pounds alligator tail meat, trimmed of all sinew, fat and silver skin
1/2 teaspoon coarse salt, preferably kosher salt, or to taste
1/2 teaspoon cayenne pepper
1/4 teaspoon freshly ground black pepper, or to taste
5 tablespoons clarified butter, divided
6 cloves garlic, cut crosswise into very thin slices
1 cup chopped yellow onions
1/2 cup chopped celery
1/2 cup chopped green sweet peppers
2 cups chopped Creole tomatoes*
1½ tablespoons minced fresh jalapeno peppers**
3 tablespoons minced Italian (flat-leaf) parsley leaves, divided
2 tablespoons minced fresh thyme leaves
1 cup good-quality dry white wine
2½ cups chicken stock
hot cooked white rice (preferably long-grain), stone-ground grits or couscous, for serving

**South Louisiana's Creole tomatoes are preferred for this recipe, although other good, peak-of-season regional varieties can be used.
**Jalapenos vary in heat level. The best way to reach the dish's desirable level is to begin with half of the amount the recipe calls for and adjust the amount of pepper to taste.

Directions

for the roux, in a very small, heavy skillet, heat the oil over medium heat until hot, about one minute. Add 1 tablespoon of flour and cook, constantly whisking or stirring with a long-handled metal whisk or wooden spoon, until the flour turns a dark-chocolate brown, three to four minutes. Be careful not to scorch the roux. Promptly remove the roux from heat and continue whisking thoroughly until it stops getting darker, two to three minutes. Set aside at room temperature.

2. Using a kitchen mallet, pound the pieces of alligator between two pieces of wax paper or parchment paper to tenderize the meat and make all pieces 1/4-inch thick, then cut the meat into rough bite-sized pieces, cutting across the sinews whenever possible to further tenderize the meat. Season the meat with kosher salt, cayenne and black pepper. Place 1 cup of flour in a small mixing bowl and dredge half the alligator pieces in it, shaking off any excess.

3. Heat 2½ tablespoons of clarified butter in a heavy 12-inch sauté pan over medium-high heat until hot, one to two minutes. Add the dredged alligator meat in a single layer and cook until dark golden brown, five to seven minutes on each side. Transfer the pieces to a plate or bowl as they brown.

4. Wipe the pan clean with paper towels and heat another 2½ tablespoons clarified butter until hot. Dredge the remaining alligator in the flour, and brown them as you did the first batch. Return the first batch of meat to the pan with the second batch.

5. Reduce the heat to medium-low and stir in the garlic. Cook the garlic until it begins to brown, one to two minutes, stirring and turning over the meat pieces almost constantly. Add the onions, celery and sweet peppers. Cook until the onions are translucent, about five minutes, stirring frequently and continuing to turn the meat over so the vegetables will cook evenly.

6. Stir in the tomatoes and jalapenos and increase the heat to medium. Cook for about three minutes, and then add 2 tablespoons of parsley and the thyme, wine and stock, stirring well. Scatter bits of the reserved roux over the mixture and whisk or stir until the roux is blended in.

7. Bring the mixture to a boil, then reduce the heat and simmer the sauce until the alligator is tender, about 30 minutes, stirring occasionally. Adjust the salt and pepper seasoning toward the end of cooking if needed.

Serving Suggestion: Serve immediately, or make the dish a day ahead and reheat it at serving time.

Serve over rice, grits or couscous, garnishing each portion with some of the remaining 1 tablespoon of parsley.

Crocked Alligator Recipe

INGREDIENTS

    10-14 Florida gator ribs (alligator)
    1 tbs. salt
    6 oz. barbecue sauce
    1 tbs. pepper
    1 tbs. garlic powder

DIRECTIONS

Season alligator ribs.

Fill crock pot with ribs.

Pour barbecue sauce over ribs.

Cover and cook until tender.

Fried Alligator Recipe

INGREDIENTS

    2 lb. Florida alligator meat, cut into bite-sized pieces
    Garlic, salt and pepper
    3 Florida eggs
    3/4 cup Florida milk
    3/4 cup flour

DIRECTIONS

Season alligator cubes with garlic, salt and pepper to your taste.

Combine eggs, milk and mix well.

Roll each piece of alligator in flour.

Deep fry at 325 until golden brown.

Cajun Alligator Tail Nuggets with Cheddar Grits

Cheddar grits are a popular breakfast side dish in the south. The cheddar grits add a nice mild complimentary flavor for the gator and Cajun sauce. Gator n' grits can be served for breakfast, lunch or dinner! This Louisiana Cajun alligator entree has no shortage of flavor!

Cheddar Grits:
Boil 2 cups of water over high heat in a sauce pot.
Add 3/4 cup of stone ground old fashioned hominy grits. (Instant grits are taboo! They become too pasty.)
Whisk the grits as they come to a boil.
When the grits just start to thicken, reduce the temperature to very low heat.
Whisk the grits often, to prevent lumps.
Add water, if the grits become too thick, before they become tender.
Gently simmer the grits, till they become tender. The grits should be almost as thick as polenta, but not stiff.
Add 2 pats of unsalted butter.
Add 1/3 cup of grated cheddar cheese.
Add sea salt and black pepper.
Stir the grits as the cheese melts.
Keep the cheddar cheese grits warm over very low heat.
Stir the grits occasionally and add water if they become too thick.

Chicken Fried Alligator Tail Nuggets:
It is best to pan fry the gator nuggets while the sauce is slowly simmering and reducing in the next step.
Cut 8 ounces of alligator tail meat into large bite size nuggets.
Season the alligator pieces with sea salt, black pepper.
Sprinkle 1 pinch of cayenne pepper over the gator nuggets.
Dredge the seasoned gator nuggets in flour.
Dip the gator nuggets in egg wash.
Dredge the egg washed gator nuggets in the flour a second time.
Heat a saute pan or cast iron skillet over medium heat.
Add enough vegetable oil, so the oil is about 1/4" deep.
Add 2 pats of unsalted butter.
Adjust the temperature, so the oil is 360°.
Pan fry the coated gator nuggets.
Cook the nuggets on all sides, till they become a golden brown color.
Remove the gator nuggets from the pan and place them on a wire screen roasting rack to drain off any excess oil.
Keep the chicken fried gator nuggets warm on a stove top.

Cajun Alligator Tail Nuggets:
This recipe makes 1 large serving!
Be sure to have all of the vegetables prepared ahead of time, before starting to cook the brown roux. Once you start making a brown roux, you cannot stop stirring, till the roux becomes a brown color. When the vegetables are added, the hot roux will stop cooking and the vegetables will be instantly cooked.
It is very easy to be burned by a brown roux spatter, so be careful when stirring the roux!
Heat a saute pan over medium/medium high heat.
Add 2 1/2 ounces of unsalted butter.
Add an equal amount of flour, while stirring with a whisk.
Stir the roux constantly, till it becomes a brown color.
Add 1 cup of small chopped onion.
Add 1/2 cup of small chopped mixed red bell pepper and green bell pepper.
Add 1/2 cup of small chopped celery.
Add 2 minced garlic cloves.
Add 1 chopped green onion.
Stir the vegetables with the hot brown roux.
Add 1 cup of dry white wine.
Add 1/2 tablespoon of lemon juice.
Add 2 cups of shrimp broth.
Stir the sauce as it comes to a boil.
Add 1 bay leaf.
Add 2 pinches of thyme.
Add 2 pinches of tarragon.
Add 1 pinch of oregano.
Add 1 pinch of basil.
Add 1 pinch of marjoram.
Add 1/4 teaspoon of Spanish paprika.
Add 3 or 4 pinches of cayenne pepper.
Add sea salt and black pepper.
Add 1/2 teaspoon of minced Italian parsley.
Reduce the temperature to low heat.
Gently simmer and reduce the sauce, till it becomes a thin sauce consistency.
Add the chicken fried gator nuggets to the sauce.
Stir the sauce and nuggets together.
Simmer the sauce, till it becomes a medium thin sauce consistency.

Gator Jambalaya Recipe

INGREDIENTS

    1½ pounds prime cut Florida alligator meat
    1 cup tomato sauce
    1/2 cup chili sauce
    1/2 cup chopped snow peas
    1/2 cup finely chopped red bell pepper
    1/2 cup chopped yellow squash
    2 teaspoons ground thyme
    1 teaspoon marjoram
    1 teaspoon salt
    1 teaspoon hot pepper sauce
    1/2 cup vinegar
    2 tablespoons all-purpose flour
    1/2 cup chopped green onions
    cooked rice

DIRECTIONS

Chop alligator meat into small pieces.

Combine alligator meat and next nine ingredients in a glass dish.

Cover and microwave on high for 6 minutes, stirring after 3 minutes.

Combine vinegar and flour; mix well.

Stir into alligator mixture.

Cover and microwave on high 4 additional minutes.

Remove dish from microwave, and stir in green onions. Serve with rice.

Gator Tater Salad Recipe

2 pounds Florida alligator meat
1 tablespoon vegetable oil
1/2 cup chopped Florida pecans
3/4 teaspoon minced garlic
2 cups chopped Florida potatoes, skin on, boiled
1 cup Caesar salad dressing
1 cup chopped Florida red bell pepper
3/4 cup crumbled Feta cheese
1/2 cup chopped Florida celery
1 teaspoon salt
1 teaspoon black pepper

Cut alligator meat into bite-sized pieces.

Heat oil in skillet over medium heat; add meat and cook for 5 minutes, turning once.

Add pecans and garlic and cook an additional minute.

Remove mixture from skillet and let cool.

Combine the cooled meat with remaining ingredients; mix well.

Chill overnight.

Marinated Gator Ribs

INGREDIENTS

    2 pounds Florida alligator ribs
    1/4 cup cider vinegar
    1/3 cup lemon juice
    2 tablespoons vegetable oil
    1 teaspoon season salt
    1/2 teaspoon season black pepper

DIRECTIONS

Place ribs in a shallow glass dish or large sealable plastic food storage bag.

Pour vinegar over ribs; toss to thoroughly coat all pieces well.

Cover dish or close bag; marinate in vinegar for 15 minutes in the refrigerator.

Combine juice, oil, salt, and pepper until well blended.
Reserve 1/8 cup marinade for basting.

Add remaining marinade to ribs.

Turn and coat well.

Marinate in the refrigerator for 45 minutes.

Remove ribs from marinade; discard marinade.

Grill over medium coals about 45 minutes or until ribs are tender, basting frequently with 1/8 cup marinade.

Pickled Gator

Ingredients

2 pounds alligator meat
- 2 teaspoons paprika
- 1 cup white vinegar
- 1 cup chopped red onions (large pieces)
- 1/2 cup vegetable oil
- 2 garlic cloves, minced
- 2 teaspoons minced garlic

Preparation

Cut meat into bite-sized pieces and sprinkle with paprika.

Coat skillet with cooking spray and cook meat on medium for 6 to 7 minutes.

Remove meat from skillet and let cool.

When meat is cool combine with vinegar, onions, oil and garlic.

Refrigerate overnight, stirring occasionally.

Remove meat and onions from marinade and serve with salad greens or pasta.

Sautéed Alligator Recipe

INGREDIENTS

1 lb. Florida alligator meat
4 extra-large Florida eggs, beaten
1½ cups all-purpose flour
1/2 cup drawn butter seasoned with salt and pepper

Dijon Mustard Sauce
1 cup mayonnaise
1 tbs. Dijon mustard
1 tsp. soy sauce
1 tsp. Florida lemon juice
Combine all ingredients and mix well.

DIRECTIONS

Make sure meat is free of fat.

Cut meat into small medallion like pieces and tenderize with a meat mallet until very thin.

Roll the medallions in seasoned flour making sure the meat is completely covered.

Dip each piece into beaten eggs.

Then quickly sauté in hot sauté pan with butter until golden brown on both sides.

Drain and serve with Dijon Mustard Sauce.

Garnish with lemon wedges and parsley.

Smothered Alligator Recipe

INGREDIENTS

2 lb. Florida alligator meat
1/4 cup cooking oil
1 Florida onion, chopped fine
1/2 cup Florida celery, chopped fine
1 Florida bell pepper
1/4 cup shallots, chopped fine
1 bay leaf
1/4 tsp. basil, chopped fine
salt and pepper
1/4 cup Florida parsley, chopped fine

DIRECTIONS

Sauté onions in oil until golden brown, and bell pepper, and celery.

Sauté until tender, add meat and seasonings simmer for 40 minutes.

Then add parsley and shallots about 5 minutes before serving.

Speared Gator

Ingredients

2 pounds alligator meat
1/2 cup water
3 tablespoons tomato paste
1 teaspoon ground coriander
1 teaspoon ground cumin seed
1 teaspoon paprika
12 wooden skewers

Preparation

Cut alligator meat into approximately 1 inch by 1 inch cubes.

Place four to five pieces of the meat on each wooden skewer until all the meat is used.

Put skewers in a flat bottom glass container and set aside.

Combine next five ingredients and mix well.

Brush mixture onto spears, making sure they are coated on all sides.

Marinate in refrigerator for 1 hour.

Cook 6 to 8 inches over medium hot coals for 6 to 7 minutes on each side.

Can be served hot or cold.

Stewed Gator

Ingredients

2 pounds alligator meat
2 tablespoons olive oil
1 cup chopped onions
1 teaspoon chopped garlic
1 28-ounce can diced tomatoes
6 ounces tomato paste
1/4 cup chopped fresh basil
2 teaspoons paprika
1/4 teaspoon black pepper
1 cup dry white wine
1/4 cup chopped fresh arugula

Preparation

Cut meat into 1 inch pieces.

Heat oil in large sauce pan over medium-high heat and sauté meat for 4 to 5 minutes.

Add onions and garlic; cook until onions are tender.

Add tomatoes, tomato paste, basil, paprika and pepper.

Cover and bring to boil; reduce heat and simmer for 10 minutes, stirring occasionally.

Add wine, cover and simmer on medium heat for 30 minutes.

Add arugula, mix thoroughly and serve.

Index

Contents... 2

Introduction.. 3

Section 1
TIPS

Southern Cooking Techniques.. 5

Cooking Tips.. 7

Baking Cooking Tips... 9

Barbecue Cooking Tips.. 10

Beef Cooking Tips... 12

Poultry Cooking Tips... 14

Seafood Cooking Tips.. 15

Vegetable Cooking Tips... 17

Seasoning Tips.. 19

Kitchen Gadget Tips.. 21

Care of Cast Iron Skillets... 22

Cooking Safety Tips.. 25

Southern Meals (What Goes Together)... 26

Section 2
Seasoning – Stock

Homemade Cajun Seasoning... 29

Beef Stock... 31

Chicken Stock... 33

Fish Stock... 35

Vegetable Stock.. 37

Seven Spice Dry Rub Recipes.. 39

Cajun Rub Recipe... 40

Section 3
Beverage Recipes

Refreshing Mint Julep.. 42

Southern Iced Tea... 43

Syllabub (holiday grown up's drink).. 44

Afton's Cold Peach Soup.. 45

Watermelon Ice... 46

Southern Holiday Punch... 47

Lime Sherbet Punch.. 48

Big Dave's Punch Recipe.. 49

Section 4
Bread and Biscuit Recipes

Help Fix My Biscuits.. 51

Biscuits for Dummies.. 53

Southern Biscuits.. 54

Perfect Biscuits... 56

Garlic Biscuits... 58

Red Lobster Biscuits (copycat).. 59

Southern Cornbread.. 60

Jalapeno Cornbread.. 62

Cracklin Cornbread... 64

Cornbread, Dressing (Stuffing).. 66

Southern Hushpuppies.. 68

Hoecakes Recipe.. 69

Dinner Rolls.. 71

Corn Fritters... 73

Sweet Walnut Zucchini Bread.. 74

No Zucchini...Zucchini Bread... 76

Walnut Zucchini Bread.. 78

Section 5
Breakfast Recipes

Breakfast Grits.. 81

Spicy Grits... 83

Sausage Gravy... 85

Potato Pancakes... 87

Best Waffle Recipes... 88

Biscuits, Southern.. 90

Grillades (gree-YHADS), brunch or breakfast Beef dish................ 92

Omelet Recipe Tips... 94

Cheater Omelet (for those that just can't make an omelet)............. 96

Classic Plain Omelet Recipe.. 98

Asparagus Omelet Recipe.. 99

Basic Cheese Omelet Recipe... 100

Cajun Omelet Recipe... 101

French Omelet Recipe... 103

Peach Omelet... 104

Ham Omelet Recipe... 106

Spanish omelet... 107

Section 6
Main Courses

Drunken (Beer Butt) Chicken.. 110

Turkey, Roasted.. 112

Southern Meatloaf Recipe.. 114

Stuffed Bell Peppers.. 116

Texas Style Chili Recipe.. 118

Beefy Cornbread Pie Recipe... 120

Southern Fried Chicken... 122

Buttermilk Baked Chicken... 124

Chicken with Potatoes and Peppers.. 125

Crockpot Chicken and Sweet Potato Stew.. 127

Jalapeno Lime Chicken.. 128

Corned Ham.. 130

Cajun Soup... 131

Cioppino - San Francisco Style.. 133

Crawfish Feast... 135

Eggplant Casserole.. 137

Fried Pork Chops………………………………………………………… 139

Hog's Breath Chili……………………………………………………… 140

Macaroni and Cheese…………………………………………………... 142

Hamburger Steak………………………………………………………. 143

Marinated Steak………………………………………………………... 145

Ketchup Glazed Meat Loaf……………………………………………. 147

Po Man's Ribs………………………………………………………..... 148

Tenderizing Grilled Pork Chops……………………………………… 149

Slow Cook Orange Sesame Ribs……………………………………… 150

Shrimp, Baked, Spicy………………………………………………….. 151

Tamale Pie……………………………………………………………... 153

Fish Fry - Fried Catfish………………………………………………… 155

Cajun Casserole………………………………………………………... 157

Seafood Casserole……………………………………………………… 159

Cajun Tomato Casserole……………………………………………….. 161

The Perfect Oven Roast Beef…………………………………………... 163

Classic Grilled Burgers………………………………………………… 165

Chicken Fried Steak……………………………………………………. 166

Chicken and Dumplings………………………………………………... 168

Sage Roasted Chicken Recipe…………………………………………. 170

Crockpot Chicken and Sweet Potato Stew... 171

Cajun Chicken over Rice.. 172

Cajun Pork Chops.. 173

Cajun Steak Rouille.. 174

Homemade Tasso (seasoned smoked pork)... 175

Chicken Andouille Gumbo Recipe... 176

New Orleans Chicken Etouffee.. 178

Pork and Pecan Stir Fry... 180

Pork Jambalaya... 182

Shrimp Jambalaya.. 184

Catfish Jambalaya Recipe... 185

Bayou Beef Stew.. 186

Crawfish Etouffee... 188

Cajun Seafood Gumbo... 189

Cajun Spicy Shrimp.. 191

Cajun BBQ Shrimp.. 193

Shrimp Creole.. 194

Cajun Bayoubaisse... 196

Irish stew.. 199

Section 7
Southern Barbecue and sauce Recipes

Simple Southern Barbecue Sauce Recipe.................................... 201

Sweet and Sticky BBQ Sauce... 202

Sauce for BBQ Chicken... 204

Old Tennessee Sweet BBQ Sauce.. 205

Oven Barbecued Ribs... 206

Barbecue Beef Brisket Recipe... 207

Barbecue Beef Sandwiches (cooked indoors)........................... 210

Baby Back Ribs Recipe... 212

Barbecue Ka-Bobs Recipe... 216

Barbecue Pork Spare Ribs Recipe...................................... 218

Crock Pot BBQ Pulled Pork (cooked indoors)........................... 220

Classic BBQ Chicken Recipe.. 222

Barbecue Salmon Recipe.. 223

Barbecue Shrimp Recipe.. 224

Coal-Fired Pico De Gallo.. 226

Grilled Hawaiian Hot Sauce... 227

Memphis BBQ Sauce.. 228

East Carolina BBQ Sauce... 229

Southern Slaw Dressing.. 230

Mint Pesto sauce... 231

Pink Peppercorn Cream Sauce... 232

Cranberry Relish... 233

Creole Mustard Marinade.. 234

Green Apple Salsa... 235

Chimichurri Marinade... 236

Southern Style Salsa... 237

Cilantro Lime Hot Sauce.. 238

Gravy, Turkey.. 239

Gravy, Sausage.. 240

Homemade Mustard.. 242

Homemade Ketchup.. 244

Section 8
Vegetables

Stove Top BBQ Beans (cooked indoors)... 246

Southern Vegetable Soup.. 248

Black Eyed Peas.. 250

Bourbon Sweet Potatoes... 252

Candied Yams (Sweet Potatoes).. 254

Collards Turnip Greens……………………………………….... 256

Collards with Cajun Tasso…………………………………….. 258

Corn Fritters……………………………………………………. 260

Fried Summer Squash………………………………………….. 262

Fried Green Tomatoes………………………………………….. 264

Hoppin John's…………………………………………………... 265

Mashed Potatoes……………………………………………….. 267

Fancy Mashed Potatoes………………………………………… 269

Southern Potato Salad………………………………………….. 271

Pineapple Upside down Sweet Potatoes……………………….. 273

Rice and Okra………………………………………………….. 275

Southern Fried Okra……………………………………………. 276

Southern Green Beans………………………………………….. 278

Sorghum Baked Beans………………………………………….. 279

Kitchen Sink BBQ Beans……………………………………….. 280

Sage Roasted Potatoes…………………………………………... 282

Salt and Vinegar Potato Bites…………………………………... 283

Vidalia onion Pie……………………………………………….. 284

Southern Vegetable Succotash…………………………………. 286

Section 9
Salads/Soups/Side Dishes/Appetizers

What Are Chitlins and Cracklins.. 288

How to Make Cracklins... 289

Fried Chitlins... 290

Ambrosia.. 292

Southern Potato Salad.. 293

Asian Salad... 295

Grilled Cheese Sandwich.. 297

Shrimp, Baked, Spicy... 299

Mom's Cole Slaw.. 301

Old West Cole Slaw... 303

Cha Cha Relish... 304

Deviled (stuffed) Eggs.. 306

Crab Cakes.. 308

Apple/Walnut Salad... 310

Macaroni and Cheese... 311

Chicken Pot Pie Recipe.. 313

Cream of Chicken Soup.. 315

Chicken Corn Chowder... 316

Chicken Noodle Soup... 317

Chicken Tortellini Soup.. 318

Lemon Chicken Soup………………………………………………….. 319

Mexican Chicken Soup………………………………………………… 320

Mulligan Stew………………………………………………………….. 321

Buffalo wings………………………………………………………….. 322

Cajun Chicken Wings #1 (Baked)…………………………………….. 324

Cajun Spicy Hot Wings……………………………………………….. 325

Chicken Bacon Kabobs……………………………………………….. 327

Chicken Liver Pate'…………………………………………………….. 329

Chicken Quesadillas…………………………………………………... 330

Chicken Kabob's……………………………………………………….. 331

Mexican Chicken Strips……………………………………………….. 333

Slightly Spicy Chicken Bites………………………………………….. 334

Too Hot Chicken Bites………………………………………………… 336

Chicken Salad…………………………………………………………. 337

Cashew Chicken Salad………………………………………………… 338

Curry Chicken Salad…………………………………………………… 339

Asian Chicken Salad…………………………………………………… 340

Chicken Salad Stuffed Tomato………………………………………… 341

Chicken Taco Salad……………………………………………………. 342

Mediterranean Chicken Salad…………………………………………. 343

Crab Salad.. 344

Baked Crab Dip.. 346

Dirty Rice... 347

Acadiana Rice and Black-eyed Peas.. 349

Stewed Corn-n-Tomatoes with Okra.. 350

Cajun Green Beans... 351

Collard Greens Recipe.. 352

Okra Gumbo Recipe.. 353

Red Beans and Rice.. 354

Section 10
Dessert Recipes

Never-Fail Pie Crust... 357

Apple Brown Betty... 359

Classic Apple Pie.. 361

Bread Pudding.. 363

Brownie Walnut Pie.. 365

Caramel Candy... 366

Perfect Chocolate Cake... 368

Cheesecake (no cook).. 371

Peanut Butter Cookies.. 373

Peanut Butter Pie (Easy).. 375

Pineapple Upside down Sweet Potatoes................................ 377

Mississippi Mud Pie.. 379

Sweet Potato Pie (or Pumpkin Pie)....................................... 381

Peach Praline Pie.. 383

Southern Pecan Pie... 385

Sorghum Molasses Pecan Pie.. 387

Ice Cream Sunday Pie... 389

Bourbon Pecan Chocolate Pie.. 390

Southern Chocolate Walnut Fudge....................................... 392

Holiday Fruitcake.. 394

Beignets (French Donut)... 396

Bayou Pecan Pie... 398

Bread Pudding.. 400

Easy Homemade Kahlua... 402

Pecan Pralines.. 403

EXTRA
A Dozen Ways to Cook Gator

Alligator Cocktail Fritters.. 405

Alligator Sauce Piquante... 406

Crocked Alligator Recipe.. 408

Fried Alligator Recipe... 409

Cajun Alligator Tail Nuggets with
Cheddar Grits.. 410
Gator Jambalaya Recipe... 412

Gator Tater Salad Recipe.. 413

Marinated Gator Ribs... 414

Pickled Gator... 415

Sautéed Alligator Recipe.. 416

Smothered Alligator Recipe... 417

Speared Gator.. 418

Stewed Gator... 419

We hope that you enjoyed this here cookbook. We are working on a part 2 now so keep your eyes out for it!

Look for these and other great books By David Pietras

From "Mommy to Monster"

The "Daddy Dearest" Club

The Manson Family "Then and Now"

When Love Kills

The Making of a Nightmare

THE INFAMOUS "FLORIDA 5"

Death, Murder, and Vampires Real Vampire Stories

The Life and Death of Richard Ramirez, The Night Stalker (History's Killers Unmasked Series)

Profiling The Killer of a Childhood Beauty Queen

No Justice For Caylee Anthony

A Texas Style Witch Hunt "Justice Denied" The Darlie Lynn Routier Story by

The Book of Revelations Explained The End Times

Murder of a Childhood

John Gotti: A True Mafia Don (History's Killers Unmasked Series)

MURDERED FOR HIS MILLIONS The Abraham Shakespeare Case

The Son of Sam "Then and Now" The David Berkowitz Story

A LOOK INSIDE THE FIVE MAFIA FAMILIES OF NEW YORK CITY

Unmasking The Real Hannibal Lecter

Top 10 Most Haunted Places in America

40 minutes in Abbottabad The Raid on Osama bin Laden

In The Footsteps of a Hero The Military Journey of General David H. Petraeus

BATTLEFIELD BENGHAZI

CASE CLOSED The State of Florida vs. George Zimmerman THE TRUTH REVEALED

CROSSING THE THIN BLUE LINE

THE GHOST FROM MY CHILDHOOD A TRUE GHOST STORY ABOUT THE GELSTON CASTLE AND THE GHOST OF "AUNT" HARRIET DOUGLAS...

Haunted United Kingdom

In Search of Jack the Ripper (History's Killers Unmasked Series)

The Last Ride of Bonnie and Clyde

The Meaning of a Tragedy Canada's Serial Killers Revealed

MOMSTER

Murder In The Kingdom

The Shroud of Turin and the Mystery Surrounding Its Authenticity

The Unexplained World That We Live In

The Good, The Bad and The Gunslingers

MOMSTERS Mothers Who Kill Their Children

KIDNAPPED A Parent's Worst Nightmare

Made in the USA
Middletown, DE
01 November 2015